GALLIC CHARTER

Foundations of Tomorrow's France

GALLIC CHARTER

Foundations of Tomorrow's France

BY

J. C. FERNAND–LAURENT

Little, Brown and Company · Boston

1944

DC
337
F4

28610

MAY ALL THE EFFORTS ANYONE MIGHT DARE TO MAKE TO SEPARATE
FRANCE AND AMERICA REMAIN FOREVER FRUITLESS

*—Inscription written by the Comte d'Estaing for a monument
in Boston to the Chevalier de Saint-Sauveur, who died in 1778
for the cause of the United States.*

Acknowledgments

This book is not a translation. With the exception of two chapters which first appeared (in somewhat different form) in *Harper's Magazine,* and of parts of three chapters which were published in French in a previous book, *Un Peuple Ressuscité,* it was written in English. I wish to thank *Harper's Magazine* and Brentano's (publishers of *Un Peuple Ressuscité*) for permission to reprint the material which they first presented, and also the editors of the *New York Times Magazine* for permission to reprint certain passages of Chapter XVIII which first appeared in their pages. And for her assistance in the preparation of the English text, I am deeply grateful to Mary Burnet.

Contents

GALLIC CHARTER

Foundations of Tomorrow's France

CHAPTER I

Personal and Otherwise

WHEN I reached this country in March 1943, having eluded the Gestapo and escaped from France, the official of the Fighting French who introduced me to my first American friends presented me as "the last man out." "Yes," said I, "who intends to be the first man in."

I mean to keep my word: as soon as a few square miles of French territory are freed, I must be there, because there is my duty.

I know what I left in France; I know what I shall find on my return, what is awaiting the liberators. This knowledge alone has given me courage to bear up under disappointments and to meet with calmness the most disconcerting misunderstandings. Vichy and Algiers are only incidents; it is France that counts. I know what she thinks, I know what she wants, and this certainly is enough.

But how can I begin to write a book about France without expressing in the first sentences my immense gratitude to the people of this country, whose tact and sympathy have done so much to make me forget the sorrows of a temporary exile? And how can I express my gratitude better than by trying to bring my modest contribution to the consolidation of that Franco-American friendship which, to all reasonable people, seems more than ever to be a solid base, a necessary condition of a pacific world?

I have had the very great satisfaction of finding that, in spite of individual prejudices and errors, the love of France remains deeply rooted in the mass of the American people, like a sure instinct. But the heart and the mind are not always in agreement, and I have also found that all too many Americans are unaware of the essential terms of the French problem. And why should this astonish us, when some of the French themselves, who have been away from home too long, display an equal ignorance and, instead of trying to explain the French situation to Americans, add to their confusion by indulging in the most painful quarrels, contradictions, and polemics?

And so, before leaving the United States to go back to France and again take up a share in my country's life, I should like to leave with my friends in America, as a gage of affection, these pages which I hope will serve as a report and an explanation.

Thumbing through a seventeenth-century travel book, you are likely to come across a map of the world where, beyond the known lands and seas, are large expanses marked *Terra Incognita*. "Unknown Territory"! Thus, on a map of the world at war, might France be designated in 1944. For she has changed so greatly during the past four years that even those of her own people who left her at the time of the Armistice of 1940, and who still think of her in terms of their memories, would hardly be able to recognize her now.

Even when the mind tries to forget, the senses remember. For a long time my ears will recall the double sound of footsteps in Paris under the occupation — the dull, heavy tread of the Germans' boots, and the light, brisk patter of the Parisiennes' wooden-soled sandals on the sidewalks. I shall always feel a pang of grief when, shutting my eyes, I see the Place de la Concorde in the grip of the German claw, with three Swastika flags floating above the Ministry of the Navy, the Hotel Crillon and the Palais-Bourbon. It will be hard to walk along the Champs-Elysées without feeling the presence of the gray-green columns which every day at noon parade down the stately avenue, keeping time to the rhythm of their goose step with their eternal — and infernal — singing. And never shall I forget the sight of the white German posters on subway walls, bearing, as a warning and a threat, the list of the hostages shot the day before.

Never before had I realized how great was the human capacity for suffering; there have been times, indeed, during the past four years when it has seemed impossible to endure such misery any longer. Yet millions of French men and women, with as much or more reason to complain, are continuing to share their country's long martyrdom. They are deep in my thoughts as I write.

I have known the leading actors in the tragedy through which my country is passing: Pétain, Daladier, Reynaud, Weygand, Herriot. I talked with Laval at the dawn of his fiendish power, I saw the rise of the traitors — of those who were ready to leap into the front ranks the day after the defeat and of those like Darnand and Henriot who are only now revealing themselves in their full stature as the Himmler and Goebbels of oppressed France.

I have had numerous conversations with many of them. Some of them I shall set down here, for the personalities of these men and the opinions they expressed should give to my interviews with them a certain amount of historical significance.

*   *   *

But of all the actors whom I saw struggling in that tragedy, the greatest and most pitiful was the French people. Quiet and dignified, drawn into itself, suffering starvation, deprived of its loved ones by death and separation, consumed with hate, for years it has waited and suffered and resisted, still believing, despite all, in the inherent justice of its cause and in ultimate victory. I am very much aware of my inability to describe forcibly enough its humble and daily heroism, to find words that will convey to the reader some of the spirit which animates it and which soon will hurl it flying to the side of the liberating armies in the final pitiless and terrible fight for freedom.

Ancient feuds have been melted away in the crucible of common grief, and the French people has become a single being with a tortured soul, burning with one flame, striving toward one goal. It is the central figure in the drama; it dominates the tragedy and gives it all its significance.

But reporting is not enough. It is also my duty to try to explain. I have no right to forget that I am not only a citizen of France, but an elected representative of the French people; and, as such, still have a responsibility toward them. The French Parliament cannot at this moment express the will of the people directly; those of its members who are in a position to do so are, therefore, all the more bound to try to speak for them to the outside world — to try to interpret the present situation as well as they can, and to draw from it lessons for the future.

I feel this obligation especially strongly because for the past twenty-five years I have, in one capacity or another, been a representative of my native city — either at the Hôtel de Ville, or in the General Council of the Department, or in the Chamber of Deputies; and, since 1932, in all three. For even longer, as a journalist contributing to a number of its newspapers, I have been perforce in close contact with its political life.

I was born in Paris; my parents, my grandparents, my great-grandparents too. Like Montaigne, I can say, "Paris has had my heart since my childhood. I am only French because of that great city."

They used to call me a Rightist — because, from the Speaker's desk, I sat on one of the right-hand benches of the Chamber of Deputies. There I belonged. But for twenty years, being of a very independent frame of mind, I refused to join any political group or party. No campaign committee, no organized supporters, ever backed me. I stood stubbornly alone. Pride? Bad temper? Both, maybe.

In March 1938, when the crisis reached a climax, when the sinister specter of war already loomed on a quickly darkening horizon, when it became obvious that it was no longer possible to play a useful role in Parliament as an independent (or *sauvage* as it was called in Parliamentary slang), I decided to join an organized party. In France a really organized party is not — as my readers will see later on — so easy to find. I joined the *Fédération Républicaine*. I do not regret it; in fact I am rather proud of it. Although a few of its members have become conspicuous henchmen of Laval, the *Fédération Républicaine* as a whole has behaved very well indeed through the trials of France, and I am sure that on the day of reckoning it will be shown to contain a very small percentage of collaborationists.

In September 1939 I took on as a wartime job, at the suggestion of my friend Georges Mandel, then Minister of the Colonies, the editorship of a large daily, *Le Jour*.

However, I was unable to get rid of its former staff. As a result, I had a constant indefinable feeling that there was a sort of fifth column in my own house that was sabotaging my work day after day and, when I was forced to be absent, betraying me. In the end, my suspicions turned out to be only too well founded. By the time I left France at the end of 1942 several former members of my staff were openly working for the Germans — one as a broadcaster on the Paris radio.

But after the Armistice there was, besides this secret enemy, the declared foe: the censorship. Whether it purported to come from Vichy or from Berlin, it was all the same thing. (In the Hotel du Parc in Vichy the offices of the French press control and those of the German press representatives are separated only by the width of a corridor.) We had to write anywhere from three to five articles a day if we wanted to get one into print — and that one was almost always extensively cut. And of course we had to resort to all sorts of tricks in order to fool the censors! For a while, beneath the official communiqué — always tendentious and garbled — I succeeded in printing in a box Pétain's famous sentence: "I hate the lies that have done us so much harm." But a series of "indiscretions" caused the paper's publication to be suspended time after time; and finally after one of these suspensions there was a public altercation before a plenary assembly of the press with Georges Marion — the ex-Communist and lieutenant of Doriot who had become head of the Vichy government's information service (and who was recently shot down by patriots just outside his office.) "I am perfectly willing to belong to the syndicate of the press," I said to him, "but I want no part of your syndicate of servants." And on May 21, 1941 — the same day, incidentally, that Professor Basdevant, legal adviser

to the Foreign Minister, wrote Pétain his famous letter
of resignation accusing him of betraying the Republic
he had been entrusted to preserve — I wrote my last article. The title, at least, the censors allowed me to print.
It was called "Choosing One's Duty."

From that time on began the part of my life of which
I feel I have the right to be proud. I joined the real
France, the one that is waiting and suffering and struggling, the France that lives for one aim only: liberation.
And I had the greatest source of consolation that any man
can have in a bitter struggle: I had as a confidant and
companion in arms my own son, who had been invalided
home from a German prison.

At that time the underground seemed to be a great
mystery to the outside world. Never shall I forget the
naïve question of a high American official at Vichy, in the
summer of 1942, upon hearing my report of our work and
plans in the underground and of the hopes we held for
aid from the United States to help us carry them out.

"How is it you have not been arrested yet?" he asked.

"Admiral, do I detect a note of regret in your voice?"
I countered.

He smiled, and I explained to him that from the viewpoint of the Pétain government (which kept repeating
as an essential item of its propaganda that the many
Frenchmen arrested every day were all Communists,
international Jews or Freemasons) the arrest of a man
so well known as a Catholic and moderate would be ill-
advised. As for the Germans, they wished to arrest me
all right and were soon to prove it.

As early as January 1942, my son had been arrested
and thrown into jail. He was placed on parole, but the
following October got another sentence: five years in

prison. This time he was forced to take to the woods. And it became obvious that I too, if I wished to stay out of the hands of the Germans, would have to leave. Still uncertain of my son's whereabouts, I escaped through Spain, crossed the Portuguese border on foot, and arrived in London in the first days of 1943. (Later I had news that my son was also safely out of France and had joined our army in the Middle East.)

All this was my own doing. I wanted to preserve my independence. Now more than ever I hold it as my most precious asset; more than ever — for the sake of my country — I am determined to make full use of it.

The day of victory and liberation is near. Then, in my own land, I shall be able to speak. In the meantime, I am here in a land where freedom of speech is held sacred. I repeat it to myself every morning: "This is the haven of democracy. Whatever happens anywhere else in the world, in the United States, at least, democracy will live forever." To be quite candid I must add that when I say this aloud in the presence of American friends some of them remark with a smile: "We hope so."

With these American friends the position of my country is, of course, often and freely discussed. Many of them fail to understand it. "Your French politics," they say, "are damned complicated!"

Of course they are. Do you think that American politics are so simple?

Two people who do not know each other may fall in love at first sight, but a lifetime affection can be built only on a mutual and complete understanding. I hope this book may help Americans to understand something about France — about her present position and the part she is bound to play in the postwar world.

But it is impossible to understand contemporary France without knowing something of her past — of the long conflict between tyranny and freedom, revolution and reaction, democracy and fascism, which makes up the whole of French modern history and which, on a worldwide scale, is the real cause of the convulsions of which we are the witnesses.

The fact that France is an old nation is at once her strength and her weakness. To climb to the daylight of liberty, she has had to extricate herself slowly, painfully, from layer upon layer of prejudices and servitude, deposited by thirteen centuries of absolutism. Where the American Republic was able to start from scratch, to build on fresh ground, the Third French Republic had to begin by liquidating the Monarchy and the Empire.

In 1791, France broke the bonds of the Monarchy and drank deep of the heady wine of liberty; she became intoxicated with it. Then, tired of the effort it had cost her, sated with military victories and horrified by the blood that had been spilled at home, she again accepted the domination of masters. Twice again she turned them out and twice again suffered their return. Why? Because the Past was watching her — ready, at the first sign of fatigue, the first slackening of attention, to rush from the shadows and fasten the shackles on again.

French political parties and groups are to be explained much less by economic or doctrinal considerations than by atavisms, traditions, inheritances. In the political history of France in our day, feelings have incontestably played a greater role than economic interests. And these sentiments are in the blood. The men who in our time have wanted — and in many cases still want — the end of the Third Republic are the authentic moral heirs of

those who strangled the First and the Second. The conflict of opposing forces which explains 1791, 1830, 1848
and 1851 likewise explains Pétain and his "New Order."
This struggle — sometimes hidden and sometimes openly
violent, but unceasing — between Revolution and Reaction, Progress and Prejudice, Democracy and Personal
Power — this struggle which anyone who knows how to
read history sees as the most classic and the most passionate of human dramas — this struggle continues today,
under our eyes. We are the spectators — but we are also
the actors.

To understand the conditions surrounding the present
phase of the conflict, and foresee what are likely to be its
results in the future, it is essential to know the circumstances under which, in the past, it was started, fought,
and — for a time — resolved.

The first Napoleon rose to power on the wave of reaction that followed the excesses of the Revolution. Nearly
half a century later, his nephew again exploited those
same excesses to impose his personal domination on the
country — and in his turn went down in defeat. Mac-
Mahon (whose resemblance to Pétain is astounding)
tried to oppose his authority to that of Parliament, and
Parliament won out; Boulanger, putting his personal
popularity at the service of reaction, became another candidate for "master" of the French people — and ended his
adventure in ridicule. These are reassuring precedents
which we must remember in the crisis of today.

Grandson of a Republican who was outlawed by the
Empire, I have always had a passionate love of liberty.
But it was only with my country's misfortune that I came
to realize to what extent it possessed me. France is as-
phyxiated; air is necessary to sustain life. We may argue

over ways of living, we cannot argue over life itself.

I have always tried to reconcile liberty with order — order obtained, of course, through the self-imposed discipline of individuals — and in the past have held demagogy as the worst enemy of democracy.

But just as exile makes one love one's country better, so the loss of liberty — or the threat of loss — makes one appreciate all its blessings. No price is too high to pay for it. The worst errors of the crowd are infinitely to be preferred to the tyranny of a single man. So I invite my American readers to come with me back to the sources of French liberty (which are also in part the sources of American liberty), sure of convincing them that, whatever assaults may be made against it, it will not perish. Pretenders to personal power will be swept away like straws before the great wind of democracy. The French Republic will live.

CHAPTER II

The Birth of the Third Republic

THE REPUBLIC! The same word, on French and American lips, undoubtedly expresses a common ideal, but symbolizes two very different realities.

The American Republic was born of liberation, the present French Republic of defeat. The United States never had a history other than her history as a republic. But in France, the tales of splendor and glory that school-children read in their first history books — stories of Jeanne d'Arc, Henri IV, Louis XIV, Napoleon — are souvenirs of the Monarchy and the Empire. In France, traditionalism does not mean respect for the "Founding Fathers" and their principles of religious as well as secular freedom, but respect for the Monarchy and the Church. The American Republic dates from the birth of the nation; the French Republic succeeded thirteen centuries of absolutism.

The American citizen has never known any other form of government than the Republic. In France, there are men alive today who remember the S-cond Empire. When it went down in defeat, the Republic was adopted by the majority of a single vote — almost by chance. Its first steps were faltering; in order to survive, it had to surmount one obstacle after another. The fact that in 1884 a special law was voted to protect it against overthrow is the most revealing evidence of its fragility. It was never really firmly established until 1889, and even after that date it continued to be discussed, attacked, threatened. It is still being threatened today.

Yet the republic founded on the ruins of Napoleon III's empire was not the first in France. The country had made its initial experiment with parliamentary government almost a century before.

Like the American Republic, the First French Republic of 1791 was the result of dissatisfaction with masters who, though physically close at hand, were figuratively just as far from the people as the English authorities against whom the American Colonies rebelled. But the great French Revolution was not built only on the negative element of dissatisfaction; it was also the fruit of positive ideas, contributed by the country's greatest thinkers over a period of fifty years. And the ironic part of it is that these ideas, taking root in a group of English colonial settlements in North America, helped mold their democratic destinies there over a decade before they were put to the test in the land whence they had sprung.

When La Fayette arrived in America in 1777, he found himself, so to speak, among friends: Montesquieu, d'Alembert and Diderot, Voltaire and Rousseau, had preceded him. In later years, he was often to tell his friends of the tremendous enthusiasm that took hold of him when, on first reading the Declaration of Independence, he found expressed in a few clear, authoritative sentences, the same ideal — the right to liberty, the right to equality, and the hope of fraternity — that filled the soul of so much of the French youth of his time. And it was the Declaration of Independence, brought back victoriously by La Fayette, which in its turn, in 1789, was to guide the authors of the French Declaration of the Rights of Man and of the Citizen. Thus the seed of revolution, blown from France in the first place, nourished American liberty and then, swollen with new life, fell again on its native soil and flowered in the French Revolution.

But the Revolution was to prove unable to consolidate its gains.

France suffering the most acute internal convulsions under the double threat of foreign invasion and bankruptcy; the Revolution triumphant, overcoming all obstacles, then exhausting itself with its own excesses; the people, tired of violence and bloodshed, again dominated by its atavistic love of order, ready to accept any authority that appeared; reaction installing itself in the midst of the general lassitude, then broken by a new shock; the Revolution resuming its course — these are the scenes in the prodigious drama that began at the instant when the Parisian mob paraded on a pike the head of the unfortunate Launay, governor of the Bastille.

In the course of a century this drama was to be repeated three times. The bloody excesses of the Revolution prepared the way for Napoleon. When the ceaseless expansionist warfare that is the inevitable consequence of dictatorship brought defeat on the country, Napoleon was liquidated in his turn, and the participants in the Congress of Vienna, restoring monarchy in France, attempted to clamp the lid permanently on revolutionary tendencies all over Europe. In France their plan worked well during the reign of Louis XVIII. His brother and successor, Charles X, tried to tighten the bit and was overthrown for his pains in the "bloodless" revolution of 1830. But the people were still willing to give monarchy another chance, and accepted Louis-Philippe, Charles's cousin, on condition that he provide the country with a written constitution.

Louis-Philippe recognized the changing times by calling

himself not "King of France," but "King of the French." He was above all King of the Bourgeois — in a land where money made the bourgeoisie, and the bourgeoisie, who alone had the right to vote, made the policies of the nation. And he was a thorough bourgeois himself.

As such he was unable to understand the new revolutionary torrent that was to sweep him away and to shake the last remaining thrones of Europe.

A few days after the Revolution of 1848, which had cost Louis-Philippe his throne, de Tocqueville said: —

Can you not see that the passions of the working classes, instead of being political, have become social? Do you not see that there are gradually forming in their breasts opinions and ideas which are destined to upset not only this or that ministry, law, or form of government, but society itself, until it totters from the foundations upon which it rests today? . . . Do you not hear them repeating unceasingly . . . that the present distribution of goods throughout the world is unjust; that property rests upon a foundation that is not equitable? And do you not realize that when such opinions take root, and when they spread in an almost universal manner, when they sink deeply into the masses, they are bound to bring with them sooner or later . . . the most formidable revolution?

De Tocqueville was right. Against Adam Smith's doctrine of economic liberalism, adopted by the capitalists and bourgeoisie and expressed in the policy of *laissez faire,* Marx and Engels were already setting their battle cry: "Workers of the world, unite!"

The Second Republic, result of the Revolution of 1848, lasted but four years. Its story is a short one of bursting enthusiasm rapidly quenched and followed by a haunting fear. The enthusiasm was for political freedom — the universal suffrage which Louis-Philippe had refused the people, and which the new leaders of the Republic immediately established; the fear was that of social disorder, which broke out almost immediately.

The violent political crisis had brought on a general slowing-down of business; many firms closed and there was a heavy increase of unemployed. This seemed dangerous, as the unemployed (and with them the chronic discontented of the land) took it for granted that the creation of the Republic would make, out of whole cloth, a panacea for their troubles. An attempt was made to pacify the workers, and to relieve their condition, when the government opened national workshops in Paris and other cities — *ateliers nationaux,* a sort of WPA of the time. Whether because of the newness of the workmen's emancipation or their feeling that they had no personal responsibility as far as production of goods was concerned, these shops went bankrupt and the government had to foot the bill. The shops were therefore closed, and the dismissed workers became so many rioters. The continuous and often bloody agitation which followed on the heels of this situation caused the majority of the people, and above all the peasants, to demand that authority restore order.

The fear of a Communist revolution (the moderates could not forget that the Second Republic had come within an ace of adopting the red flag as its emblem) prepared the way for a new dictator. As Pétain was to build his undeserved rise to power on the sacrifices of the heroes of Verdun, so Louis-Napoleon Bonaparte — or Napoleon the Little, as Victor Hugo called him — capitalized on the glory of Napoleon the Great. At first elected President of the Republic, he assumed dictatorial powers in the *coup d'état* of December 1851. But, in order to succeed, he was forced to break a strong and courageous opposition; and he repressed it with the greatest severity. Paradoxically, though his home policy was one of extreme authority, in his foreign policy he prided himself upon being a liberal and affected to favor the various European national aspirations. From this viewpoint his government was undoubtedly one of the worst France has ever had.

The result was nothing less than catastrophic. By fighting, defeating, and finally humiliating Russia with the help of the British in the badly conceived Crimean campaign of 1855; by fighting against Austria to help Italy achieve her unity in the Italian campaign of 1859; by failing to interfere in the Prussian–Danish War in 1864, and in the Austro–Prussian War in 1866, he permitted Prussia to prepare the Greater Reich and undoubtedly paved the way for future Pan-Germanism. It can safely be said that Napoleon III waged all the wars that he ought not to have waged, and failed to declare, when the Prussians defeated the Austrians at Sadowa, the only war he ought to have launched without the slightest hesitation—a war against Prussia.

Desiring war with France, in spite of the peaceful inclinations of Wilhelm I of Prussia, Bismarck resorted to forgery. He abridged a telegram from his master in such a way as to make Wilhelm's refusal to see the French ambassador—which was natural enough owing to the special circumstances—appear as an unbearable insult to French prestige. The Count of Gramont, Napoleon's foreign minister, might have been induced to handle the matter with greater delicacy if Napoleon himself had shown firmness and foresight. He showed neither; and by publishing the falsified telegram in all the chancelleries of Europe simultaneously, Bismarck forced Napoleon to declare war on Prussia. It was the Iron Chancellor's final move of genius for the unification of Germany: a German people attacked by a belligerent France would draw together and pour across the border. This is exactly what happened.

Defeat and invasion overthrew Napoleon III, just as it had overthrown Napoleon I. Once more, on the ruins of absolutism, France was to construct a republic.

The news of the disaster of Sedan — that Napoleon III and one hundred thousand men had been made prisoners — was brought to Paris on the evening of September 3, 1870. At midnight the Council of Ministers of the Empire addressed a proclamation to the people, announcing the defeat and declaring Paris in a state of siege, for the enemy was advancing on the city. The next day, around noon, bands of citizens began to collect on the Quai d'Orsay and on the Place de la Concorde before the Palais Bourbon, where the legislative body of the Empire was in session. Their ranks swelled rapidly, and before long they were swarming into the public galleries of the legislative chamber itself, clamoring for the downfall of the Empire and the establishment of a republic. Meanwhile, at the Hôtel de Ville, a "Committee of National Defense" was already in formation, under the leadership of two Republican members of the legislature, Jules Favre and Léon Gambetta. The confusion in the legislative hall was now so great that voices could not be distinguished, but when a few of the mob learned what was happening across the Seine, they scratched "To the Hôtel de Ville" on sheets of paper which they held up in the air, and led the way. The rest followed suit.

At 4:15 on the afternoon of September 4, 1870, the Third French Republic was proclaimed in the office of the

Prefect of the Department of the Seine in the Hôtel de
Ville. It was a provisional government taking its authority
from the fact that the Empire had simply ceased to exist.
The Emperor was a prisoner and the Empress, whom he
had made regent in his absence, had fled the capital and
was on her way to England.

Paris was soon surrounded by the Prussian armies, and
the Government of National Defense committed the un-
pardonable strategic blunder of getting itself bottled up
in the city during the siege. Cut off from the rest of the
country, it was without the means of directing or organizing nationwide resistance.

Gambetta, the fiery Republican, the partisan of the
fight-to-the-finish, the Clemenceau of his time, offered to
represent the government in the provinces. In view of the
prolongation of the siege of Paris, it was indispensable
for him, as Minister of the Interior, to be in direct contact with the departments. He therefore left by balloon
on the morning of October 7 to join the delegation which
the new government had sent to Tours to direct the administration of the rest of the country. On October 10, a
homing pigeon brought the news to the Parisians of his
safe arrival in the Somme region. Thence he proceeded
to Tours, where he found that the provinces were rising
everywhere in the defense of the fatherland.

In spite of his efforts, in spite of two or three victories
in the provinces and the exploits of the National Guard
— hastily mobilized, and almost without ammunition —
in spite of the heroic defense put up by the Parisians amid
starvation, disease, and the terrific twenty-three-day bom-
bardment of Paris by the Krupp guns, the Government of
National Defense finally was forced to conclude that further resistance was useless, that the war was irretrievably
lost. Its representatives signed an armistice between

France and Prussia on the twenty-eighth day of January, 1871.

The Franco–Prussian War had been lost because, as in 1940, the military leaders, Bazaine at their head, had judged the continuation of the struggle impossible and had preferred a rapid capitulation to the risk of an internal revolution. After the capture of the Emperor, Bazaine had delivered the fortress of Metz to the enemy with his army intact — the fortress of which Napoleon I had said, "Who holds Metz, holds Europe!" After the armistice he was tried before the War Council, which condemned him unanimously for treason. The presiding general was the Duc d'Aumale, the most promising of the sons of Louis-Philippe and an ardent patriot. Bazaine, in defending himself, contended that the fall of the imperial regime and the establishing of an insurrectional government in Paris absolved him, in a certain measure, of his duties as defined by the military code.

"Monsieur," replied the Duc d'Aumale, "France still existed."

France still existed indeed, in 1871, as it still existed in 1940; and, as in 1940, popular sentiment rose up against the ugly word "capitulation." There was, however, an essential difference between the situations of 1871 and 1940: in 1940, the German General Staff had seen to it that France should be entirely under the German boot, so that any popular opposition to the armistice must be expressed from without. It was expressed, and magnificently, by de Gaulle, on June 18, 1940. In 1871, French territory was only partially occupied, and the opposition was thus able to manifest itself in the interior of the country. It did so with violence.

The first of its leaders was Gambetta. Still in the

provinces, he was ordered by the government in Paris to promulgate a decree drawn up the very day after the armistice, calling on the voters to name candidates to provide a permanent government for the country. But the terms of the decree displeased him, and the revised decree issued over his signature from Bordeaux on January 31 announced that no individual who under the Empire had accepted a post as Minister, Senator (an appointive office), State Councilor, or Prefect might become a candidate to the new assembly, and that all those who had ever been "official candidates" to any legislative assembly held during this period would likewise be ineligible.

It had been Gambetta's intention to stigmatize the servants of the Empire, the regime responsible for the debacle. But, in the opinion of the other members of the government, his indignation had overstepped the bounds. They refused to give their consent to such a measure, which they saw as "restricting the right of the electors, and creating a veritable official candidacy by exclusion"; in their opinion, it would have been political condemnation for a crime not recognized by the lawbooks. The government, therefore, in repudiating the decree as drafted by its representative in Bordeaux, reserved the right to protect, in its integrity, the liberty of the voters.

Gambetta, who was Minister of the Interior and also Minister of War, resigned both offices in protest but was later elected to the National Assembly by an overwhelming vote.

Another protest came when the National Assembly, duly elected and sitting at Bordeaux, ratified, after six hours of deliberation, the treaty which deprived France of Alsace and Lorraine. The Deputies of these two provinces accompanied their resignation from the Assembly with a heart-rending message, which read: —

Delivered, in defiance of all justice and by an odious abuse
of force, to the domination of the foreigner, we once again
declare null and void a treaty which disposes of us without
our consent. Your brothers of Alsace-Lorraine, separated at
this moment from the common family, will keep for France,
while she is absent from their homes, a faithful attachment
until a day when she will return to assume her place at their
firesides.

A final pathetic note was added by the death, the same
night, of one of the Alsatian Deputies, who was also
Mayor of Strasbourg; he had succumbed to his patriotic
grief.

(I had occasion to see my colleagues, the Deputies of
Alsace and Lorraine, at Vichy in August 1940, on the
night of the day we heard of the brutal expulsion of
30,000 inhabitants of Metz and Strasbourg, which had
temporarily reverted to the status of German cities. Their
grief, their rage, and likewise their hope of a not-too-
distant reunion, corresponded quite exactly to the sentiments expressed by their forerunners of 1871.)

But the protest which was really to make itself felt —
and, alas, violently felt — was that of the city of Paris.
More than all the rest of France it had suffered from the
war. It had seen the formation of the Government of National Defense, which had declared itself determined to
win the war, and now this government had capitulated.
Its Assembly, dominated by defeatist provincials and ob-
livious to the feelings of the Parisians, had ratified a treaty
which imposed on the capital the supreme humiliation of
seeing German troops enter its gates. In short, in the eyes
of many Parisians, the government had come to represent
the very things which they had wanted to destroy when
they had first given it their support.

In reality, the Government of National Defense had had little choice. When it had taken the reins on September 4, military defeat — prepared by the preceding regime — was already inevitable. And when defeat came Thiers had been forced to consent to a partial, temporary occupation of Paris as the lesser of two evils.

The Prussians — who had demanded outright the cession of Alsace-Lorraine, Sarrebourg, the city of Metz, and an indemnity of 5,000,000,000 francs in gold — had given him the choice between such an occupation of Paris and the cession of the fortress of Belfort. Thiers deemed Belfort of the utmost importance to the future defense of France. He therefore accepted the humiliation of seeing a part of the Prussian army enter Paris.

Later Thiers himself, in his testimony before the Commission of Inquiry, admitted the importance of this occupation in preparing the Commune. "The entry of the Prussians into Paris," he said, "had been one of the principal causes of insurrection. I do not say that, without this circumstance, the movement would not have occurred, but I do say that the entry of the Prussians gave it an extraordinary impulsion. . . . There were 200,000 men in Paris who had been fed on the sentiment that it was cowardice and treason to deal with the Prussians."

The Prussians were to enter Paris on Wednesday, March 1, at ten o'clock. They were to occupy the space between the Seine and the Rue du Faubourg Saint Honoré, north of the Place de la Concorde, and as far as the Ternes. Their forces were not to exceed 30,000 men. Evacuation would take place immediately after the ratification of the preliminaries of the treaty by the National Assembly. The German army was to provide its own sustenance, and would make no requisitions.

On March 1, the detachments of Prussians entered Paris

and marched down the Champs-Elysées, occupying the space assigned to them. They were flanked by cordons of French troops. Access to the streets held by the Prussians had not been denied the Parisians, but almost to a man the population refused to take advantage of this freedom of movement. Public buildings, commercial houses, the Stock Exchange, had closed their doors; the *quais,* the boulevards, the suburbs, were deserted. Paris had voluntarily suspended all animation, and here and there could be read placards bearing inscriptions: "Closed on account of national mourning," "Closed on account of public sorrow." Black flags had been hoisted over public buildings and floated from the balconies of private dwellings. The Prussians did not have the satisfaction of parading under the Arc de Triomphe — it had been carefully barricaded at the Etoile — and from the Champs-Elysées they could see the eight statues which adorn the Place de la Concorde veiled in crepe.

On March 10, the National Assembly decided to leave Bordeaux and go, not to the capital, but to Versailles. Such an arrangement was hardly calculated to assuage the wounded feelings of the Parisians, and added to their resentment and distrust of the Assembly. This was further aggravated by economic considerations. One of the Assembly's first acts had been to annul the moratorium on rents and debts declared by the Government of National Defense. There was of course a clamor for immediate payment, and many of those who were liable were men who, during the long, weary months of the siege, had been kept from the miseries of unemployment only by the franc-and-a-half a day they received as members of the National Guard. Within a few days after the Assembly's arrival in Versailles, open insurrection burst forth. The National Guard, which had never been disarmed, inevitably came into conflict with the regular army at the service of the Assembly. As always in such situations, the most extreme elements got the upper hand. When at the end of two months the Commune was finally crushed, much of the city had been pillaged and burned, countless lives had been lost, and the rift between Paris and the provinces was deeper than ever.

On the morrow of a civil war which followed without interruption upon a war of invasion, in the midst of material and moral ruin of an incalculable extent, France was in the condition of a man recovering from a deadly illness — but a man of sound constitution, who is taking a new lease on life and getting back his strength rapidly. And I am convinced that the same thing will be true of the France that we will rediscover on the day of liberation.

Logically, the first question the nation had to decide was that of the form of the next government. To judge by appearances, the result could not be in doubt. Paris, where the Government of National Defense had first been set up, was predominantly Republican; but in the National Assembly, whose election this government had demanded, about two thirds of the members were Monarchists. The Assembly was the expression of the will of the people of France, who had freely elected its delegates. It would seem, therefore, that they had only to draw the conclusion and restore the monarchy. And yet, by one of those paradoxes so characteristic of France, it was, in the end, a republic which emerged from the deliberations of the National Assembly.

The Constitution of the Third Republic, known as "the Constitution of 1875," has been the stake of all the political conflicts which have shaken France for the past half-century, including those which have arisen in connection with the present war. It is this Constitution which Pétain, in abuse of the powers which were entrusted to him at Vichy on July 10, 1940, attempted to destroy; but it is likewise this Constitution whose authority three years later (in November 1943) he recognized in a fit of doubtful remorse. Finally, it is this Constitution which General de Gaulle has spoken of replacing by a "Fourth Republic." It is, therefore, the key to many events which we are witnessing at the present moment, and to others which will happen tomorrow in redeemed France.

Two contradictions are inherent almost in its name. First, it is not, properly speaking, a constitution, but an assemblage of constitutional laws, voted at different dates and at intervals more or less far apart, the last in 1875. And second, this Constitution, under which the Third French Republic has lived for so long, was not meant for a republic.

It came into being under particularly trying circumstances, and was four years in the making — four years overshadowed by the very present memory of crushing military defeat and bloody civil strife; four years of close struggle between the forces of monarchy and those of republicanism. When at last a republican form of government was adopted, it was almost by accident.

The defeat of the monarchical restoration was a drama which dragged on for almost five years. It was complicated by the fact that in the beginning there was not one pretender to the throne, but two: the Comte de Chambord, direct descendant of Charles X and chief of the elder branch of the Bourbons; and the Comte de Paris, son of Louis-Philippe, representing the younger branch, that of Orléans. Both of these had their supporters in the

National Assembly; and besides, there was even a considerable number of delegates who favored the Prince Imperial, the young son of Napoleon III, who, with his mother, had taken refuge in England. Yet it was obvious that the Monarchists could never achieve their goal unless they united behind a single candidate.

By the summer of 1871, after endless difficulties, the fusion of the monarchical factions seemed achieved. The Princes of Orléans, whose attitude throughout the negotiations had been very generous, recognized the priority of the elder branch, and saluted in the Comte de Chambord their legitimate sovereign. Most of the Monarchists believed that they were now at the end of their troubles. Serene in the knowledge that there was a Monarchist majority in the Assembly, they went ahead with their plans — even ordering the state carriage in which the new King would make his triumphal entry into Paris, and arranging the details of his coronation ceremony.

But they had counted without their candidate. The Comte de Chambord had a noble and straightforward nature, but was incurably melancholy, and had no taste for struggle or action. He was, above all, an exile — and we have had plenty of occasion, since 1940, to see how difficult it is for an exile to keep a true perspective on national problems. Hesitant, with only a limited confidence in the solidity of the throne on which he was invited to sit, and with his natural pride and reserve heightened by his years of exclusion from the land of his fathers, he was convinced that his chief value to the country lay in the fact that he represented the old principle of monarchy by divine right. And so, with puerile obstinacy, he persisted in clothing that principle in one particular symbol: the white flag with the gold fleurs-de-lis of the old regime. No other flag was worthy of him. The Tricolor, which the Orleanists were willing to accept, remained for him the symbol of a revolution which he wanted to deny completely. He was resolved to take up the traditions of the monarchy existing in 1789. In his opinion, the States General had been nothing but the revolt of an insurgent minority against the will of the people, the starting point of a period of "demoralization by falsehood, of disorganization by violence." It was on this unexpected obstacle — absurd, on the surface — that the restoration really foundered. It remained now to reconstruct the Republic. The process was not without pain.

By coincidence, it was on the very day when the Count of Chambord made the formal declaration of his uncompromising attitude in regard to the flag that the first supplementary elections were held to fill vacancies in the National Assembly. There were more than a hundred of these. Some were the result of resignations or deaths, but most had arisen from the fact that in the beginning a number of candidates had been elected by more than one department, and had had to choose which constituency they would represent. The returns were overwhelmingly favorable to the Republicans. The administrative policy of Thiers, elected provisional "Chief of the Executive Power of the French Republic" by the Assembly the preceding February, had reassured the country, and the Republicans were reaping the benefit. Succeeding partial elections continued to show the same trend, while, amid bitter battles between Monarchists who refused to give up hope and Republicans of various hues, the Assembly voted the series of "constitutional laws" which were to form the basis for a permanent government.

These laws, known in their ensemble as "the Constitution of 1875," did not proceed — and with reason — from any general plan or doctrinal conception. The As-

sembly was obliged to proceed step by step, day by day —
forced at every moment to maneuver, to bargain, to take
into account extraordinary circumstances. It did not do
what it wished; it did what it could. The Constitution was
therefore, above all, a compromise.

Of the three authorities — the executive, the legislature,
the judiciary — which, in every civilized country, are the
machinery of political life, the one which in this case was
least the subject of dispute was the judiciary. Napoleon I's
famous "Civil Code" was still the law of the land, having survived all the changes of government since his
time and proved its value; and along with it still stood
firm the general organization of the courts for which
he had provided.

The compromise character of the Constitution is most
strongly shown in the relations which it established between the executive and legislative branches of the government. Working within the framework of a provisional
republic, but anticipating an early restoration of the
monarchy, many of the Monarchist majority in the Assembly joined in voting to the "chief executive" powers
which they hoped, later, to be able to hand over to a
constitutional king but which, for the moment, they had
to leave in the hands of an elected president. These powers included the supreme command of the army and
navy, the power to sign treaties, to promulgate laws
enacted by the legislature (the Parliament) and to ap-
point the Prime Minister and Cabinet. These Ministers
were directly responsible to Parliament. The "chief executive" himself could not be held responsible for the
acts of his government, and he could be impeached only
for high treason. He had power to dissolve the lower
House of Parliament, the Chamber of Deputies, with the
consent of the upper House, the Senate.

Of this Parliament, only the Chamber was elected directly by the people, its members being chosen by universal suffrage for a term of four years. Senators were chosen by the Deputies, officials of the departmental and municipal administrations, and a small number of delegates named by the latter in proportion to the population. The Senate was thus conceived (like the House of Peers under the Restoration and the "Conservative Senate" under the Empire) as a brake on the Chamber of Deputies. It would be chosen by balanced and prudent electors (mostly provincials) known to their neighbors, by local administrators who had already given pledges of their experience. To assure the continuity of the Assembly, and to protect it from too sudden shocks, the Senate would not be elected all at once, but would be renewable by thirds, every three years.

Laws might be drafted and proposed by either House of Parliament or by the Cabinet. A bill could not become law until adopted in the same text by both Houses. But the Chamber of Deputies must assume the initiative in the discussion and vote of the Budget. The Chamber was to control the Cabinet by means of interpellations giving rise to general debates on questions of policy.

Granted to a constitutional monarch, basing his claims to office on heredity and reigning for life, the powers given to the "chief executive" by this arrangement would have sufficed to establish his independence of the legislative. But they were destined never to be held by a monarch, for, on January 30, 1875, by a vote of 353 to 352, the Assembly passed the Wallon Amendment making the "chief executive" a "President of the Republic" elected for a term of seven years. By a margin of a single vote — almost by accident, it seemed! — the Monarchists, who had come to the Assembly's first sessions so full of confidence, were finally defeated, and for the third time in her history France was committed to a republican regime.

Under these new conditions, what was the status of the "chief executive"? He was to be elected, not directly by the people (the conservative Republicans in the Assembly, remembering the *coup d'état* of Napoleon III, were desperately afraid of that!), but by the two Houses of Parliament — Senate and Chamber of Deputies — united in joint session. So it came about that the President, although he had the power to dissolve a part of the Parliament, was himself beholden to this very Parliament for his office. The theoretically necessary separation of the executive and legislative branches of the government had not been achieved.

Where, in the new Republic, was the real executive power to lie? Experience alone would tell — and experience was soon forthcoming.

CHAPTER III

The First Pétain: MacMahon

HIS MAJESTY CHANCE — as Frederick the Great was wont to say — may play his part in history, but it can only be a minor one: the part of logic is far more important, the same causes always resulting in the same effects. This principle is especially striking when applied to France; the saying "History repeats itself" assumes full value when examined in the light of her experiences.

Pétain was not a novelty to the country. He had already appeared at least once in French history — in the person and name of MacMahon.

On May 21, 1871, the regular troops made their first attack on the insurgents of the Commune in Paris. They were called the "Army of Versailles," and Marshal Patrice Maurice de MacMahon, Duke of Magenta, was their Commander in Chief. Seven days later the Commune had been crushed. MacMahon posted on the walls of Paris the following proclamation: —

People of Paris, the army of France has come to save you. Paris has been delivered! At four o'clock, our soldiers captured the last stronghold held by the insurgents. The conflict has ended today, order is established, work and security will be restored.

France had been horrified by the bloody excesses of the Commune. The hecatomb had ended on May 27 in a fusillade in which one hundred and fifty *communards* or *fédérés* were shot before the old cemetery of Père-Lachaise, where the insurgents had made their last stand. (The pilgrimage to the *"Mur des Fédérés"* has remained an annual and traditional ceremony to this day for Socialists and Communists.) France had called for order. Order appeared with the features of MacMahon.

The Commune itself — by permitting the Monarchists to represent democracy as ending inevitably, by the logic of its development, in terrorist demagogy — had stimulated Royalist propaganda and reinforced the action of adherents of the Monarchy in the National Assembly. Thiers now seemed to them to be the real obstacle to the Restoration. They therefore overthrew him on May 23, 1873 — two years after the Commune — on the strength of an interpellation of the Duke de Broglie: "A government," the orator had said, "has not done all when it has assured material order; its attitude, the doctrine it professes, the spirit which it breathes into its administration, must assure moral order." MacMahon, elected "Chief of the State" for seven years in place of the defeated Thiers — in the expectation of a forthcoming monarchical restoration — seemed to the Right in the Assembly the man best qualified to establish this "moral order."

MacMahon, as his name indicates, was of Irish origin. But the family had been established in France since the fall of the Stuarts, and the future Marshal studied at the seminary of Autun before entering St. Cyr. The first twenty years of his military career were spent in Algeria, where he took part in every important battle. During this period the famous General Bugeaud said of him: "I believe him to be an excellent officer, very soldierly, very firm; but I do not think he has the intellectual grasp necessary for governing Europeans and Arabs." He subsequently distinguished himself at Sebastopol during the

Crimean campaign and again in the Italian campaign of
1859, where he saved the day for Napoleon III at Magenta
and was rewarded by being created a duke on the battlefield.

But the Franco–Prussian War broke his sequence of
glorious successes. Commanding the First Army Corps,
he saw his advance guard defeated at Wissembourg and
was himself defeated (by greatly superior numbers) at
Reichshoffen. He ordered a retreat to Châlons to save
what he could of his disorganized army. He had decided,
as wisdom commanded, to withdraw to Paris, when he
received orders from the Emperor's government to march
on Sedan. Falling back on Paris would undoubtedly have
meant the collapse of the Empire, and MacMahon, under
the circumstances, showed more concern for the regime
than for the elementary rules of military prudence. To
abide by the government's commands he changed his
own, and wiser, decision, and ordered his army to make
that fatal march. Fortunately for MacMahon he was not
to witness the rout of his troops, for a shell splinter struck
him in the thigh, and the wound removed him from the
fight.

In his detailed study of the origins of the Third Republic, M. Gabriel Hanotaux describes MacMahon as
"without guile, a man of discipline and clannish loyalty,
and an excellent soldier," but adds that "the moment he
was immersed in politics, the Marshal was no longer
himself. His simple mind became entangled, his clear
sense clouded." Thus uncertain of his way politically, he
allowed himself to be guided by his overpowering native
instinct for order, and, in the interests of order, always
ultimately "bowed before the accomplished fact."

As I write, I have before my eyes, side by side, two
portraits: one of MacMahon and one of Pétain, both made

when their subjects were around seventy years old. The physical resemblance of the two men is striking.

M. Hanotaux gives us a portrait of MacMahon in these words: —

He was above middle height, slender and of soldierly appearance; his moustache was white, his hair also white, scanty and short, and his complexion ruddy; his deep-set blue eyes were at the same time stern and gentle, and his countenance open. His horsemanlike figure, from being continually submitted to the demands of deportment, the training of the profession, and a strong will, betrayed something spontaneous and jerky in his movements . . .

There would be very little to change to make the entire portrayal apply to Pétain.

MacMahon's administration saw the open struggle between the executive and the Parliament which was bound to result from the paradoxical provisions of the Constitution of 1875.

When MacMahon entered office in 1873 much of the administrative machinery of France's new government had already been set up: the essential powers of the "chief of state" had been defined — and defined, as we have seen, by a Monarchist majority which expected soon to make the chief of state a hereditary king. These men had put MacMahon into office to effect the transition from the administration of Thiers, whom they detested, to that of the monarch they hoped to install. But in 1875 the Wallon amendment destroyed all their hopes and perpetuated the paradox by which the "chief of the Executive" had the theoretical power to dissolve a part of the very body that had elected him. Clearly, the first serious disagreement between the President and the Chamber of Deputies would provide the test case in the inevitable struggle for power.

The religious question had traditionally been of primary importance in French politics, and it was precisely on the occasion of a religious problem that the conflict burst forth.

A law having been voted in Italy against the activities of the Catholic clergy, the Pope, on March 12, 1877, invited his bishops to bring pressure on their governments "to set aside all obstacles to the full and real independence of the Head of the Catholic Church." This was the signal for a campaign of petitions demanding French intervention in favor of pontifical sovereignty. The newspaper of Monseigneur Dupanloup, Bishop of Orléans, distinguished itself by its violence. On May 2, it addressed a veritable summons to the government. Two days later the Chamber, by 304 votes to 113, demanded that the government restrain the clerical agitation, and use the legal means at its disposal.

This was the signal for an open break. MacMahon, in complete disagreement with the Chamber, decided to remove his Cabinet and replace it with one of firmer tendencies which he was sure would back him to the hilt. The Cabinet had not been voted into the minority, but he dismissed it nevertheless, writing to its premier, Jules Simon: "I may not be, as you are, responsible to the Parliament, but I still have a responsibility toward France to which, more than ever today, I must turn my attention." This was invoking a superior power — that of responsibility before the country — which was not inscribed in the Constitution.

In default of a king, the National Assembly had elected a "chief executive" to a seven-year term — an executive invested, however, with very considerable powers. Following this, a republican form of government had been voted under intricate and obscure conditions and with the feeblest of majorities. The "chief executive," now become President, judged that this latter decision did not affect the authority previously vested in his office, and that the majority of the Chamber was now entering upon a road which appeared dangerous to him. He had therefore resolved to use the arms furnished him by the Constitution: having obtained the consent of the Senate, he would dissolve the Chamber and call upon the country.

The Chamber of Deputies was frankly Republican and anticlerical (then, as always in France up to very recent times, the two tendencies went hand in hand); the Senate was almost evenly divided between Left and Right, but leaned slightly toward the Right; and MacMahon himself was, of course, an out-and-out conservative. To strengthen his hand he dismissed the Simon Cabinet and called in a new one, a "Ministry of Combat," headed by the same Duc de Broglie to whose attack on the Thiers administration, four years before, he owed his office. The whole of the de Broglie Cabinet — which was to go down in history as "the Ministry of May Sixteenth" — was made up of Legitimists, Orléanists, and Bonapartists. It was the supreme assault of Old France against the new Republic.

With the consent of the Senate, the new Ministry pronounced the dissolution of the Chamber of Deputies, and proceeded to call for new elections. It was a gigantic battle in which the whole country was engaged.

In a decisive ballot before the dissolution, 363 Republicans had voted against the newly constituted Cabinet. That number became the basis of Gambetta's slogan in opening the new election campaign. "The 363," he cried, "will return 400!"

Both adversaries were equally resolved, equally violent,

The government was staking its all, and adopted all the procedures which had been employed by the Empire: white posters recommending lists of official candidates; pressure on government employees; the closing of drinking places, which were all too convenient spots for popular Republican meetings; hindrance to the distribution of Republican newspapers; the suspension of municipal councils and the revoking of mayors who showed Republican tendencies. The Prefects, the direct administrative agents of the central government in each department, were ordered to undertake official electoral canvassing in their respective departments. Marshal MacMahon himself set the example in the West, the Center and the Southwest — all, incidentally, regions where conservative sentiment was already so strong that he could be sure of a favorable reception.

The fight rose to a diapason of bitter threats and accusations. "We will make such hash of the Republicans that not even the dogs would want it!" wrote Cunéo d'Ornano, a Rightist candidate, in the *Suffrage Universel des Charentes*. But the Republicans had decided not to be made into hash.

Gambetta personally assumed the direction of their operations. For the first time in France, modern methods of electoral propaganda were employed. First, Gambetta assured himself of the united co-operation of the Republican press by calling together the directors of all the Republican newspapers in Paris and forming a Committee of Resistance. Then he and his colleagues made two decisions which were to assure them victory. First, they forestalled possible attempts to split the Republican vote by ruling that no other Republican candidate should oppose himself to any one of the 363. They then had the foresight to establish a program for their party which was intentionally moderate. The government had held up to the people the scarecrow of a Republican demagogy; its opponents replied with the platform of a conservative republic.

All the 363 presented themselves on the same platform; each conservative opposed one Republican. This perfect discipline, and the union of their electoral troops, assured the Republicans the victory. While Gambetta's prediction was not entirely realized, they obtained 327 seats to the 208 of the conservatives.

"Submit or resign!" was the challenge Gambetta then hurled at MacMahon.

MacMahon thought first of escaping from the dilemma by using force. General de Rochebouët was holding in readiness an order for the army. It was indeed up to the Marshal to submit and decide to accept a Republican Ministry, or dismiss Parliament and call forth the bayonets. A *coup d'état?* It was certainly possible. But in favor of whom? And it was precisely because the Marshal was not able to answer that question that he hesitated at last on the edge of the abyss.

Having once decided not to use force he was left no choice but to submit. He resolved to do this, and called upon Dufaure, a member of the Republican majority in the Chamber, to form a Cabinet. He remained in office throughout the following year, chiefly in order to act as official host to visiting notables at the Exposition of 1878. But before the year was out he had another serious disagreement with Parliament; and in January, 1879, tired of playing the role of a powerless "executive" in the hands of a Parliament antagonistic to all his beliefs, he resigned his office. He was replaced by an austere old gentleman with side whiskers, Jules Grévy, who inaugurated the series of "figurehead Presidents" which has continued to the present time. The defeat which the Chamber served up to MacMahon completely discouraged all his successors from taking up the battle where he had left off.

The interpretation of the Constitution with regard to the powers of the President of the Republic was fixed from that time on. The President was deprived in advance of all executive power. He had the right, naturally, to choose the Prime Minister, but he could do this only in accordance with the desire of the majority of the Parliament.

It is sometimes said that the President of the French Republic has as much authority as a constitutional monarch, but that he lacks the will power to avail himself of it. This is not exact. The spirit, if not the letter of the Constitution, forbids him to use his power; and in the interpretation of that spirit the MacMahon case set a precedent that has proved binding.

The consequence of this interpretation is not only that the President himself is completely at the mercy of Parliament but that the whole executive branch of the government becomes a mere subsidiary of the legislature instead of keeping the full independence which it ought to have. The Cabinet, which in practice really serves as the executive, may be removed by a vote of no-confidence on the part of either House of Parliament, but has no means of checking the Parliament in its turn; it cannot, as can the English Cabinet, put its case directly before the people. Hence, French cabinets became extremely unstable affairs, which the slightest adverse breeze from an unsympathetic Parliament could — and did — overturn. The lack of continuity in national policy that resulted was to cost the Republic dear. Its disadvantages, moreover, were soon to be realized, and were, as we shall see later, to provide a ready-made platform for enemies of the parliamentary regime.

Another interesting consequence of MacMahon's abortive *coup d'état* was the modification of the Constitution in another sense. Remembering that MacMahon's real aim had been to overthrow the Republic, the Senate and Chamber voted, on August 14, 1884, an amendment to the Constitution declaring the Republican form of government "intangible" — in other words, denying to themselves and to their successors the power to change the form of the regime simply by amending the existing Constitution. Since this Constitution was merely a series of laws, of which the provision for a Republic was only one, it would, up to that time, have been possible (as the Monarchists hoped) to overthrow the Republic simply by changing that particular law. By the amendment of 1884, the Parliament limited its own power to amend the Constitution in the future, with the intent of interposing one more legal barrier to future attempts to destroy the Republic. And, mindful of the ultimate goal of MacMahon and his clique, as well as of the *coup d'état* of Napoleon III, it added to the amendment a provision declaring that in future no member of any family which had ever reigned over France should be eligible to the Presidency of the Republic.

As for the man who had precipitated all this, he left the Presidential Palace of the Elysée poorer than he had entered it, dropped all connection with public life except the presidency of the Wounded Veterans' Aid Association, and lived his last years far from the turmoil of politics in dignified retirement. His career had indeed been a curious one.

* * *

As a soldier, MacMahon had served his country for half a century with perfect fidelity; he had won his title of Duke of Magenta on the battlefield. But the end of his career had been a succession of errors which cost the country dearly. France owed him the crushing military defeat of August, 1870; France owed him likewise, in 1877, one of the gravest political and moral crises that the country had ever known.

At Châlons he had been at the head of an army of 120,000 men and he knew, beyond the shadow of a doubt, that the march on Sedan would be a disaster; he had already given the order to withdraw to cover Paris. He ceded in the end to considerations which were purely dynastic, and in the attempt to save the prestige of the sovereign, he moved forward to throw his army into the bottleneck of Sedan.

He executed exactly the same maneuver, committed the same error, as President of the Republic. Playing blindly into the hands of the Duc de Broglie (a strong-willed reactionary who was perfectly conscious of the risk of the operation he was undertaking and determined to use MacMahon as his tool), he brought all the forces of the country into play and threw them into the ridiculous adventure of the Sixteenth of May, 1877, which was as incoherent, as illogical, and as badly planned as the march on Sedan.

The historical, physical, and moral similarities between the MacMahon and Pétain adventures are so numerous and so striking that it is hardly necessary to emphasize them further. The same sign, the same fatality, seems to have marked the two Marshals. In this connection it is interesting, at the present time, to compare two judgments which have been made upon MacMahon by two very different types of man.

The first comes from the fiery controversial writer of the Right, Edouard Drumont: —

One is forced to recognize that the latter period of Marshal MacMahon's life was not very beautiful, and will not magnify his name before posterity. Nothing, in fact, obliged the Marshal to entangle himself in these controversies, and it should be added that he never gave proof of anything but a relative loyalty to the cause he espoused. No doubt he did not go as far as treachery, but on several occasions he displayed the instinctive trickery of a child who tells a lie to get himself out of a fix.

On the 24th day of May [in 1873, when MacMahon defeated Thiers as chief executive of the provisional government] the Marshal deceived Thiers up to the last moment. Poor Thiers entertained for military men a sort of nursemaid's love; he loved tall men, epaulettes, and cannons. He had raised MacMahon's prestige — somewhat diminished by the disaster of Sedan — and he had made him a quasi-legendary personality.

In reality, the Marshal confined himself to leading everybody on.

The second judgment is in the words of the Jacobin Clemenceau: —

He let himself be led to the very brink of violence. No one was ever able to make him cross the terrible boundaries. His best claim to the gratitude of his countrymen — his real glory — will be to have vanquished himself, and to have silenced within him that which he had of depth and secrecy, in order to obey the clearly expressed will of the land.

To these two judgments should be added a third — that of MacMahon himself. Toward the end of his life, he confided to his old comrade General Ducrot: "Look here, old man, soldiers ought never to mix with politics; they don't know anything about it."

CHAPTER IV

Two Crises

THE DESPERATE ASSAULT of Ancient France on the young Republic — led by MacMahon and the Ministry of May Sixteenth — had failed. Personal power had been forced to yield to parliamentary government. But that did not mean that all conflict between the two tendencies had ceased — far from it. The Republic, although victorious, was still vulnerable. Before the end of the century two violent crises, coming almost on top of each other, had again threatened its existence: the Boulanger movement and the Dreyfus case.

Vastly different as were the origins of these two affairs, their political significance was the same: both were deliberately used by the conservatives and Monarchists as means to try to overthrow the Republic and return the country to the authoritarian regime they preferred. Both became issues which split the whole nation — and split it along lines which were philosophical and religious as well as political. On one side was the Monarchist and Catholic tradition; on the other, the Revolution and the freethinkers.

The political parties of France, then as even now, corresponded a great deal less to precise doctrines or programs than to a manner of being, a cast of mind. In France one is born of the Right or of the Left, as one is born blond or dark. I think I am giving my readers the surest key to French politics when I say that they are founded much more on feelings, on traditions, than on ideas or doctrines. The free will can, of course, modify or change a Frenchman's opinion, and the son may contradict the father. But these are the exceptions which prove the rule. One generation follows another; the sons replace the fathers; the frock coat gives way to the sack suit; labels and appellations change; outward appearances become modernized; but deep-seated mentalities are transmitted with life itself. And each time that the course of events has furnished the occasion (some kind of shock in the country's political life), they have clashed.

As a general rule, if a Frenchman was Catholic, he was of the Right; if he was a freethinker, of the Left. With the establishment of the Republic, the traditional alliance "of the throne and the altar" gave way to the union between the Church and reaction — or, as the Left expressed it vulgarly, "the saber and the holy-water sprinkler." The rift between this camp and the other remained deep.

The first of the two crises which brought them into conflict amounted in the end to nothing more than a colorful and romantic tale. The second was a tragedy.

Without exaggerating the truth, the Boulanger affair might be entitled: "How a cabaret singer almost blew up the Republic." It has been said that in France everything ends with a song. The Boulanger affair actually began with a song.

The people of France have a strong sentimental attachment for the army — "their army" — because the army is really the people themselves. A Frenchman may have unpleasant memories of barracks life, but in nine cases out of ten he will nevertheless speak of it with a smile of reminiscence, because it is part of his youth. Even if he is Leftist or antimilitarist, he will probably fall into step at the sound of martial music, for he has the love of the army in his blood.

The military review of the Fourteenth of July on the racecourse of Longchamps was the occasion, each year, of a popular celebration, the great fête of the people of Paris. The War Minister, General Boulanger, was at the dawn of his growing popularity when, at the review of the Fourteenth of July, 1886, he presided over the parade of the troops. He made a romantic figure, with his splendid bearing, his blond pointed beard, and his prancing black horse, and was wildly acclaimed by the crowds.

A few days later a cabaret actor adored by the Parisian public, Paulus, launched a song about the General called "Coming Home from the Review." Within a few weeks it was all over France. It was taken up in the streets, in the workshops, in fashionable salons, and became the rallying song of Boulangists.

The new Minister of War owed his post to Freycinet, who, the preceding January, had formed a Cabinet for Jules Grévy upon his re-election to the presidency of the Republic. Boulanger, at that time Director of the Infantry, had been practically imposed on Freycinet by Clemenceau. He was still comparatively young (he was forty-nine) and had had a rather brilliant military career — a campaign in Cochinchina, another in Kabylia, the command of the Corps of Occupation in Tunisia.

From the moment he went into office, the General displayed an eager appetite for popularity. He never missed a chance to make a public appearance. He showed spectacular marks of solicitude for the troops, shared their mess in the barracks, allowed them (great and unheard-of privilege!) to wear beards. Above all, on every occasion which presented itself in Parliament he displayed a ticklish and vigilant form of nationalism. The nationalists, therefore, flocked to his side. Déroulède brought him the support of the Patriots' League which he had just founded, with its newspaper *Le Drapeau,* and its watchword: *"Qui vive? France quand même!"* ("Who goes there? France after all!")

The political situation in France was particularly confused at the moment. Strikes of the miners of Decazeville and the glassworkers of Vierzon were indications of acutely unsatisfactory social and economic conditions. Revolutionary socialism was on the march; the country was full of anarchist propaganda, and some of the anarchists did not stop at propaganda. In addition to all this, in the fall of 1887 a scandal burst forth which was to force the President of the Republic into retirement and — it goes without saying — to be seized upon by the reactionaries as so much grist for their mill. On the Avenue Wagram, in Paris, a woman named Limouzin was found to have established a veritable agency for bartering in military decorations, with the complicity of several officers of the General Staff and of a Deputy named Wilson, who was the son-in-law of President Grévy himself.

Grévy might have kept parliamentary sympathies if he had recognized from the beginning that the "Chief Executive" had no right to hesitate between personal considerations and civic duties and obligations. But he was deeply moved by the distress of his daughter and wounded in his pride; he therefore hesitated, argued, tried to brazen the matter out, and finally, incapable of finding a Premier who would undertake to form a new Ministry under the circumstances, he was abandoned by all and forced to cede to the inevitable. He resigned on December 2.

Nor was this all. The attitude of Germany was growing more and more menacing. French pride was still smarting from the defeat of 1870, and the population showed an irritable susceptibility toward anything that appeared to be a provocation from beyond the Rhine. Déroulède saluted in Boulanger "the General of the Revenge," a title which Bismarck likewise conceded him in calling him the greatest danger to good relations between France and Germany. He was indeed adored by the masses, and he appeared to many as the leader who might be capable, on some future day, of facing the swaggering defiance of the perennial enemy.

The "*Brav' Général*" had been invented by the radical elements and made famous by the populace. But the Monarchists and reactionary forces lost no time in perceiving the role which they might make him play, now that he was drunk with success and permitting himself to be carried along on the wave.

A group of Monarchists, including Comte Albert de Mun, the Baron de Mackau, the Comte de Breteuil, the Marquis de Beauvau, the Duchesse d'Uzès, and Arthur Meyer, director of the Extreme-Right newspaper *Le Gaulois,* decided to use him to further the cause of the Comte de Paris, the Pretender to the throne. The idea was to "make the monarchy" with Boulanger, instead of "permitting that great popular force to be snapped up by the Bonapartists and the plebiscitarians."

At this point the Boulangist Affair began to take on the appearance at once of an epic poem and a dime novel. The aristocrats, the social idlers, the gilded youth, all threw themselves with enthusiasm and delight into the fray, as into a new Fronde. An ill-advised great lady, the Duchesse d'Uzès, played the role of the Duchesse de Longueville; and with mad generosity she placed her entire fortune at the disposal of the Boulangists. The atmosphere of conspiracy was complete: clandestine meetings, passwords, secret missions to London to see the Pretender,

intrigues in the halls of Parliament, trysting-places in the
suburbs of Paris — all these comprised a living novel
which intrigued the entire country. The public followed
the developments of the plot with breathless interest.

The Boulangist wave swelled and swelled, rolling together pell-mell the pure waters and the mire. It was to
end by carrying off with it all those enemies of the Republic who had seen in the movement a certain means
of shipwrecking the Republican regime.

The Freycinet Cabinet had been defeated and overthrown late in 1886, and General Boulanger had left the
War Ministry; the Republican Deputies were already
sufficiently alarmed to let it be known that they would
fight to the finish any Cabinet in which he might take
part in the future. In order to draw him away from Paris,
where his popularity had become alarming, the new
Ministry named him commander of the Army Corps
stationed at Clermont-Ferrand. His supporters protested
emphatically what they termed an "exile"; they reproached the government with wishing to rid itself of a
man of whom it was afraid. On the night of his departure for Clermont-Ferrand, a mass demonstration (which
had been arranged some time before) took place in the
Gare de Lyon. A huge crowd besieged the station, and
General Boulanger was almost prevented by his thousands of sympathizers from taking the train. To disen-
tangle himself from the delirious adulation of the crowd
he was forced to jump on the engine-tender.

Meanwhile, a committee had been organized to promote
enthusiasm for the General, using the most modern, per-
fected methods of publicity — posters, tracts, picture biog-
raphies, all distributed in profusion to swell his popularity. It was the first time in France that commercial
advertising methods had been applied to politics — a pro-

cedure which has since been used in Vichy to attempt to popularize the National Revolution and the legend of Pétain, and which has also been employed in London to popularize with pictures and pamphlets the person and achievements of General de Gaulle.

It produced the most stupendous effects. The ranks of the Boulangists continued to swell. And their composition provided an illustration of that recurring phenomenon which is constantly noticeable in French contemporary history — the junction of the two extremes of Right and Left. Monarchists hobnobbed openly with radical Deputies.

The government began to be alarmed. It surveyed the movements of the General closely, and discovered proof that on several occasions he had left his post at Clermont-Ferrand without permission, and had gone up to Paris in disguise. Premier Tirard decided to act. He relieved Boulanger from active duty and summoned him before a military commission which pronounced his dishonorable discharge for grave faults committed in the service.

It was a mistake. Boulanger became, overnight, the master of his movements and was thus generously granted by his opponents the liberty he needed to organize his forces.

At that time the law permitted a man to be candidate to a political office in several constituencies at once. The Boulangist henchmen decided to announce the General's candidacy to every available vacant seat, thus provoking a sort of plebiscite in his favor.

He needed an electoral platform. It was easily found — the revision of the Constitution!

Boulanger was elected in one district after another, first in the Department of the Dordogne and then in the Nord; his majorities were enormous. He entered the

Chamber of Deputies in triumph, and proceeded to celebrate his successes and his parliamentary debut by in-
troducing a bill suppressing the Senate and in fact re-
ducing the Parliament to a meaningless body, abolishing
ministerial responsibility, and instituting the plebiscite —
that is, general elections by direct consultation of the
people. This monstrous proposal was interrupted by an
altercation that led to a duel between General Boulanger
and Floquet, one of the Republican leaders — a duel in
which the General was wounded.

The Republicans sensed the danger and began organizing. Clemenceau, the erstwhile protector of Boulanger, had now become his implacable enemy, and took
charge of the operations against him. On August 19, in
supplementary elections. Boulanger was elected again in
new districts in the Nord, and in the Somme and in the
Charente-Inférieure. The action of the drama was becoming more and more tense, was marching towards its
fatal climax.

The occasion for the showdown at last presented itself.
A seat had fallen vacant in Paris. Clemenceau challenged
Boulanger to face the capital's verdict, and Boulanger
took up the challenge. The opposing parties engaged in
the electoral battle with incredible fierceness; everything
was put into action — political mass meetings, tracts, posters, campaign songs. . . .

The Republican strategy had been to choose an ex-
tremely colorless radical candidate by the name of Jacques.
Of course, one did not vote for Jacques; one voted against
Boulanger.

When the great day of January 27, 1889, came, the
General obtained 244,149 votes to the 162,419 for Jacques.

The General and his political staff had their headquarters in a drawing room of the Durand restaurant on the

Place de la Madeleine; the General was dressed in elegant evening clothes with his favorite flower, a red carnation, in his buttonhole. As the returns were announced, delirious mobs of his sympathizers invaded the restaurant, and were pushed back with difficulty by the police. To tell the truth, the municipal guards, who felt a good deal of sympathy for the crowds, made only feeble efforts to restrain them. Then the band began to play "Coming Home from the Review," and the surging crowds took up the chorus.

The presidential Palace of the Elysée was only a few hundred yards away. The General's sympathizers begged him to march there with them, to eject the President (Carnot), and take over the power. All the evidence goes to prove that the coup would have succeeded if it had been attempted. However, Boulanger resisted, quietly but obstinately, for a reason that was to be revealed only a good deal later. (When it did come out, one of his henchmen declared scornfully but correctly: "Caesar was only a Romeo of the barracks.")

Boulanger let slip this unique moment, this moment which the gods of chance offer only once in a lifetime. From then on the Boulangist movement was doomed.

The Republicans began by changing the method of voting in such a way as to make practically impossible such overwhelming expressions of opinion as those which had endorsed Boulanger. Next they formed a new Cabinet of very energetic men, including notably the hard-fisted Constans, who was made Minister of the Interior.

Constans had more than one trick in his bag; he knew the weaknesses of the General, and he maneuvered accordingly. Boulanger was unmarried, but he had a mistress to whom he was passionately devoted, a divorcée by the name of Mme. de Bonnemains. Very skillfully, the

police alarmed Mme. de Bonnemains, giving her to understand that she was about to be arrested, and persuaded her
to leave for Brussels. Boulanger, distracted by her departure and fearing that he too was on the point of being
incarcerated, hastened to join her in Brussels. Love had
held a greater part in his heart than politics. But shortly
after, Mme. de Bonnemains died — like a true romantic
heroine, of consumption — and on September 30, 1891,
General Boulanger shot himself on her tomb in the cemetery of Ixelles, near Brussels.

The whole Boulangist adventure had proved to the
Republicans that in spite of its apparent solidity the regime remained terribly vulnerable. However, from the
moment that the General's mistakes had permitted the
Republicans to gather breath, recover, and organize the
defense of the Republic, the latter had seized the advantage and, through cohesion and quick action, won
the day. The lesson was not lost to them.

Like the MacMahon experience, the Boulanger Affair
had brought to light a glaring weakness of the Republican
regime as it was then administered. This time the weakness lay not in the Constitution itself but in one of the
laws which implemented it: that which governed the
method of voting. The Constitution provided that members of the Chamber of Deputies should be elected by
universal suffrage, but did not otherwise specify the mode
of election. Up to 1885, elections had been carried out by
what is known as the *scrutin d'arrondissement* — that is,
the electoral unit was the *arrondissement* (subdivision of
a department), whose voters each cast his ballot for a
single candidate. (A candidate could, however, at this
time, stand for election in more than one district.) In
1885, however, at the instigation of Gambetta, the method

of voting had been changed and the *scrutin de liste* adopted. Under this system, all the *arrondissements* of a department were taken together as one unit, and each voter selected, from a list of all the candidates, as many names as there were vacancies in the department, the seats being distributed among the candidates who had received the greatest total of votes. Gambetta's idea in recommending the change had been that the older method favored localism and sent to the Chamber men who, while well known in their home districts, were likely to have little grasp of national problems or general ideas.

But the Boulanger incident showed only too clearly that the newer method also had its disadvantage. It permitted a popular candidate to pile up a staggering total of votes and to acquire, especially in cases where special elections called the voters of an entire department to decide on only one or two vacancies (as in the case of Boulanger's Paris election), an overwhelming endorsement that amounted almost to a plebiscite in his favor. Such plebiscites had in times past been the signal for a *coup d'état;* the Republicans remembered the example of Napoleon III and knew perfectly well how nearly Boulanger's election in Paris had led to another. They considered that in a country where the Monarchist minority was so powerful, such risks were too great to run. They therefore returned to the *scrutin d'arrondissement* — but with the provision that a man might be a candidate in only one electoral district at a time. But the question of the method of voting remained a lively issue, and in later years there were several changes back and forth between the *scrutin de liste* and the *scrutin d'arrondissement*. The second of these systems remained, as Gambetta had foreseen, the favorite of parties and candidates whose interests were centered in local affairs and who, whatever doctrines they might profess, were usually conservative in practical matters; it became known as the system of the *mares stagnantes* (stagnant pools). On the other hand, as time went on and the Republic won more general support, the great danger originally inherent in the *scrutin de liste* lost its importance, and its proponents were more and more convinced that it permitted freer governmental action and consequently more clear-cut and determined policies on the part of the government.

Another issue which Boulanger raised for the first time was that of the revision of the Constitution. The Mac-Mahon experience had shown up the unsatisfactory relationship between the executive and the legislature, and when Boulanger announced his slogan of revision large numbers of his hearers were ready to agree with him immediately, in principle. But on closer inspection his plans turned out to be — as we have seen — not projects for making a more perfect Republic, but schemes for establishing a dictatorship. The result was that after the failure of the Boulangist movement the word "revision" became indissolubly associated, in the minds of the Republicans, with the idea of a reactionary *coup d'état*. This spectacular attempt to revise the Constitution in an undesirable direction contributed a great deal to prevent — right up to 1940 — the adoption of reforms that were not only desirable but, in the light of experience, almost indispensable. In the troubled times through which the Republic was destined to pass, an executive authority responsible directly to the people, and just as independent as Parliament instead of subservient to it, would have greatly strengthened her position.

But if the Boulangist wave had swept away with it large segments of Monarchist sympathizers, the reactionary and clerical opposition remained strong. Its last great upsurge before the World War was to be occasioned by the celebrated Dreyfus case.

I cannot embark upon the recital of this supremely dramatic episode in the life of the young Third Republic without first recalling one of my earliest memories as a boy. The family was spending the summer of 1899 on the banks of the Marne, just outside Paris, when one evening my father returned from his office in the city — it was on the ninth of September — and appeared at the garden gate waving his newspaper excitedly in the air. "Condemned!" he cried — "Condemned!" It was Captain Alfred Dreyfus who had been condemned, for the second time, by the Military Court of Rennes.

The repercussions of this affair had penetrated to the remotest corners of the land. The Dreyfus case had torn France from end to end, had shaken families to their foundation, had separated brother from brother. And yet France had brought honor to "the Affair." She had brought honor to it because the unveiling of this national tragedy and its investigation before the courts had been motivated by the finest human sentiments — those of a passionate, uncompromising, and disinterested love of equity and the principles of right. An entire land rose up in order that one man should escape injustice and unfair condemnation. Friendships, families, personal interests counted no longer — the Affair dominated everything.

The famous Calas trial in the eighteenth century had been nothing in comparison to the ramifications of the Dreyfus case. Intellectuals, savants, professors, who had hitherto kept to their studies and their laboratories in austere reserve, came out of their ivory towers to throw themselves fiercely into the combat. The great mathematician Paul Painlevé, who was destined to become one of France's Premiers, would never have dreamed of entering political life except for this.

The dramatic tale began when one day toward the end of September 1894 a charwoman of the German Embassy in Paris, who was actually a spy in the service of the French Intelligence Bureau, found a document in a wastebasket which, upon examination by military experts, led these latter to the conclusion that an officer in the War Ministry had been guilty of treason. Because of the similarity in the handwriting, suspicion fell upon Captain Alfred Dreyfus.

General Mercier, Minister of War, decided to pursue the case. Three handwriting experts out of five decided that the document could serve as a basis of accusation. It was a note, unsigned and undated, written on onionskin copy paper, and announcing the transmission of miscellaneous information, notably about the hydraulic brake of our 120-mm. cannon. It was subsequently termed, during the court proceedings, the *bordereau,* or "memorandum." It was actually, said these experts, in the handwriting of Captain Dreyfus.

On December 22 the Military Court of the Command of Paris, sitting behind closed doors, unanimously condemned Captain Dreyfus to deportation and confinement for life "in a fortified enclosure," and decreed his military disgrace and degradation. Dreyfus had never ceased to cry "I am innocent!" — but they inflicted upon him the most dreadful punishment which an officer can receive: he had his military decorations and insignia torn from his coat, one by one, in the presence of his troops.

Yet, twelve years later, after untold suffering, and on the same spot in the courtyard of the Ecole Militaire in

Paris, Major Dreyfus, honorably reinstated, was to receive the Cross of the Legion of Honor.

To achieve this point of justice it had been necessary for France to pass through twelve years of political convulsions and battles whose consequences were felt until the eve of World War I. The Dreyfus Affair had dominated the internal politics of France during this entire period. It had determined the resignation of one War Minister after another, and had even overturned Cabinets in its path.

Dreyfus had been condemned, chained up like a beast in the hold of a transport, and conducted to Devil's Island off the coast of French Guiana. There he counted the endless cycle of his days under a torrid sun and behind a few yards of palisades while his family in France set to work implacably to search for the truth in his case.

At the start, the Affair had passed almost unperceived, and characteristically enough, when it was brought up for the first time at the tribune of the Chamber, Jean Jaurès himself had defended "the authority of the decision rendered." Little by little, it was being relegated to silence when, suddenly, on September 16, 1896, the newspaper *L'Eclair* published a historical account of the case, affirming that the decision of the judges had been determined by the communication to them of secret documents which had not been known to the accused and to his lawyer, Maître Demange.

A year passed, and the scourging press campaign which had surrounded this revelation had died down, when suddenly the publicist Bernard Lazare contended in a pamphlet that he had established the innocence of Dreyfus. At the same time, M. Scheurer-Kestner, Vice President of the Senate, notified the War Ministry of his intention of seeing that the case was revived, and displayed certain documents which, according to him, were conclusive proof that the famous "memorandum" had not been written by Dreyfus. Finally on November 15, 1897, the brother of the condemned man, Mathieu Dreyfus (actually on the advice of Scheurer-Kestner) denounced an officer of Hungarian origin, Count Walsin-Esterhazy, Major of Infantry on the retired list, as the real author of the memorandum.

Lieutenant-Colonel Picquart, an Alsatian, had become the head of the Bureau of Information of the General Staff. It was he who had reason to believe in the possible guilt of Esterhazy and had communicated his suspicions to his compatriot Scheurer-Kestner. The General Staff, in order to shut his mouth, had sent him to the far end of Tunisia.

Upon the revelations and intervention of Mathieu Dreyfus, Picquart was recalled to Paris to appear before the military tribunal. His testimony proved definitive, but the War Council, frozen in unbelievable stubbornness, refused to reverse its judgment, declared Esterhazy not guilty, and (incredible paradox!) ordered Picquart's arrest and imprisonment in a fortress.

From this day on the Dreyfus case ceased to be a legal drama, and became a political affair of extraordinary scope.

It was unfortunate for France that on the one hand the officer whose imprudent inculpation was at the bottom of "the Affair" was a Jew; that on the other hand the officers of the General Staff who directed the inquiry and brought proceedings against Dreyfus were named de Boisdeffre, de Pellieux, and the Comte du Paty de Clam — all notorious reactionaries, and all former pupils of the famous Jesuit School of the Rue des Postes. These two facts could not fail to rekindle the old religious passions in France that had almost been put to sleep.

It was done! France was divided from then on into two camps, into two camps which never ceased repeating, with equal passion and with equal frenzy, their respective leitmotifs.

"*Vive l'Armée! Vive l'Armée!*" cried the one. The army — that is to say, the defense of the national territory, the defense of order, the barrier against Germany, the barrier against demagogic revolution. The army was heir to the noblest traditions, the army was sacred, the army could do no wrong.

"*Vive la Justice!*" chanted the other. "An innocent man is more sacred to us than the whole General Staff. Because justice alone guarantees the life and honor of the citizens, justice is above all else. Whether they are military men or civilians, all judges have the same duty. If you want us to respect the army, let the army begin by respecting justice."

In the two camps, in the two choruses, the masses were of good faith. But behind the masses the chiefs, who in the background made capital out of the affair for their political ends, were much less so.

"In seeking to discredit the military judges, in insulting the army," some said, "the country is shaken to its foundation; behind this antinational campaign are Freemasonry and international Jewry. Such a campaign is possible only under the regime of disorder in which we are living. Once again," they declared, "the Republic itself stems from revolutionary demagogy. Down with the Republic!"

"Once again," said the others, "the eternal alliance of the throne and the altar, the saber and the holy-water sprinkler! The army has become an instrument of the Jesuits in the service of Reaction. Down with the army!"

That was the tone.

The juridical vicissitudes, more and more complicated, became unintelligible to the great mass of the citizens; the very origin of the Affair lost itself in the fog; they ended up by completely forgetting the unfortunate Dreyfus. The appellations *"Dreyfusard"* or *"anti-Dreyfusard"* were no longer anything but nicknames for the Right and the Left. The camp of the anti-*Dreyfusards* comprised almost exclusively the army, the conservatives, the clergy, the anti-Semites and the nationalists. The camp of the *Dreyfusards* was composed of Republicans, intellectuals and liberals, and generally speaking, all the Leftists. While nationalists and Monarchists were attempting to use the Affair as a lever to destroy the parliamentary Republic, the Socialists, on the other hand, profited by it to begin a campaign against militarism.

One thing was certain: once again the assault was on against the parliamentary Republic. Once again, the Republic and Parliament carried off the struggle. This victory they owed to their discipline and to their cohesion, but above all to the fact that the Republic from then on represented the will of the people.

On January 13, 1898, the novelist Emile Zola, then at the height of his fame and the most popular writer in France, openly defied the War Council as well as the libel laws by publishing in the newspaper *L'Aurore,* under the title of *"J'accuse!,"* an open letter to the President of the Republic which said, in part: —

A military court has just dared, by order, to acquit an Esterhazy — supreme blow to all truth, to all justice. And it is ended. France bears on her cheek this defilement, and history will write that it is under your administration that such a crime against society has been committed. They [the judges of Major Esterhazy] have pronounced an iniquitous sentence which will hang forever over our military courts and which will make all their decisions open to suspicion. The first military court [that which condemned Dreyfus] may have been simply stupid; the second [the one which acquitted Esterhazy] is obviously criminal. . . . I accuse [it] . . . of having covered this illegality by order, and of having committed in its turn a crime against justice in consciously acquitting a guilty man.

Zola was condemned to prison for a year. But he had achieved his end. All France had read the letter, and it had become utterly impossible for the government to let the Affair drop again.

The Cabinet was questioned anew in the Chamber of Deputies. Cavaignac, the War Minister, in order to protect himself, produced a note purporting to come from the Italian military attaché and intended clearly to establish the latter's connection with Dreyfus. A short time after, his colleagues, upon examining the document closely, discovered without difficulty that it had been entirely forged by Colonel Henry, the new chief of the Bureau of Information. On the afternoon of August 30, 1898, Colonel Henry confessed to the War Minister that he was the author of the forgery; he was arrested and conducted to the prison of Mont-Valérien, and was found the following night with his throat slashed by two strokes of the razor.

This violent *coup de théâtre* renewed the uproar. For many people it had been a flash of lightning in darkness. If it was true that an officer of the General Staff had deemed it necessary to fabricate out of whole cloth one document against Dreyfus, might it not be that the other so-called incriminating documents were of slight — if not insignificant — importance? Wisdom, reason, common sense commanded this judgment. Colonel Henry's confession constituted new evidence which made a re-trial imperative. From then on, Truth was on the march, and nothing could stop it any longer.

The Court of Annulment sent the accused man up before a new military court. He was brought back from Devil's Island and appeared at Rennes on June 3, 1899. It was the exact moment when the Affair was reaching its climax and passions were bursting forth with the maximum of intensity. I can see, as if it were yesterday, the headlines of the newspapers announcing that shots had been fired at Maître Labori, Dreyfus' lawyer. Partisans and adversaries of the condemned man had been fighting at the doors of the military tribunal.

He was condemned anew, but with extenuating circumstances, by five votes to two, and was sentenced to prison for ten years. The sentence was, in truth, not a judgment but a compromise; and compromise was unacceptable. Dreyfus was guilty or he was not. Treason does not admit of extenuating circumstances. One does not bargain with the truth.

The Ministry, headed by Waldeck-Rousseau, decided to pardon the condemned man in an effort to end the agitation, which would have become fatal to France in the long run. A few years later the Court of Annulment, having completely re-examined the facts in the case, rescinded and declared null and void the judgment of Rennes. From the viewpoint of the law the Affair was ended. Since then the confession of Esterhazy — who died in England whither he had fled — and the revelations of the German military attaché have proved beyond the shadow of a doubt that Dreyfus was completely innocent.

Politically, the Dreyfus case was not ended by the rehabilitation of the condemned man. Its consequences were far-reaching. The old political-religious struggle had been unfortunately revived. The Republic had carried the day; it had been strong enough to permit itself the pardon of Dreyfus. Unfortunately it did not resist the temptation to retaliate with excessive severity against its enemies.

The direct consequence of the Dreyfus Affair was Combism (derived from the name of the Premier, Emile Combes, a former Jesuit seminarist who had gone over to the liberals, and was now a fierce adversary of the religious orders). The Combist period was a lamentable fight between Catholic and anticlerical forces, a conflict which darkened and saddened the years immediately preceding the war of 1914–1918.

The Church had imprudently embroiled itself in the Dreyfus Affair, had exposed itself to attacks. They were violent. Not only were all the religious orders, men's and women's, temporarily dissolved, but the Chamber forbade any of their members to engage in teaching under any conditions for three years. (At the end of that time, it was decreed that no religious order could function in France without a special authorization, and such authorizations were very few.) Emile Loubet, the new President of the Republic, went to Rome and failed to visit the Pope, thus causing a rupture of diplomatic relations between the French State and the Vatican. The reactionaries in France replied to this outbreak by the virulent denunciation of Freemasonry (which in France for a long time had had a strongly marked anticlerical character). The country had rarely been so divided. A new law to define the status of the Church in France became indispensable with the nullification of the Concordat and the rupture with the Pope.

The parliamentary commission charged with drafting the bill chose to present it a Socialist, a newcomer to the Chamber — Aristide Briand. He put an accomplished cleverness, suppleness and artistry into the defense of the proposal submitted on behalf of the committee, won his point after heated discussions, and made his reputation on the spot. He was destined to play a preponderant part in French politics for the twenty years to follow.

On December 9, 1905, the Chamber voted the law of separation of Church and State, guaranteeing freedom of worship but declaring that the Republic recognized no religious cults and subsidized none. This law put an end to the agitation, and the Church, in spite of its fears, was the gainer in independence and dignity. It seemed that the old religious conflict, the scourge of France throughout her long history, was over at last.

And so it might have been if the Germans, immediately after the armistice of 1940, had not found, thanks to Pétain, the means of attempting to conciliate, or at least to neutralize, that large portion of French public opinion which comprises the Catholics by tradition and conviction.

In opposing himself to the lay regime of the Third Republic, the Marshal presented himself as the inspired defender, the restorer, of religion, threatened by Free-masonry. Among the principal articles of his "National Revolution" were the return of the religious orders, the recognition of parochial schools by the State, and obligatory instruction in the Catechism in all schools; thus he was able to pose as the champion of the Christian renaissance.

Cardinal Gerlier reminded me of this in an interview which I had with him in his palace at Fourvières in Lyon, in the course of the summer of 1942.

"Did not the Marshal," said he to me, "give back to us all that had been taken away from us for so long, and which we had hoped to recover?"

I dissented, telling His Eminence quite frankly that I

could not share his opinion; that I strongly feared that on the contrary, by his clumsy extremism, the Marshal had in the long run done a cruel disservice to the Church — that I was afraid, in short, that he was preparing for the post-war period a new and cruel form of anticlericalism in our country, a land which had not known anticlerical agitation for twenty years.

Fortunately — and this consideration permits me to hope that we will avoid the danger — the attitude of the great mass of French Catholics has been above reproach in the present ordeal of France. They have been in the first ranks in the resistance to the invader, in their protests against the persecutions, and in aiding the Jews. In this domain, as in so many others, the most obscure militants have preceded the chiefs. The Jesuits and the Dominicans, with only a few rare defections, have been at the head of the movement. And it is particularly the lower clergy, the poor country priests, who have shown themselves admirable in courage, foresight, and dignity.

The same thing is true of the Catholic youth — of both the student and the working classes. They have joined their patriotic ardor with their religious faith and are setting the example of an active apostleship. In the army of resistance, they demand and assume the most dangerous posts, and they hold them to the point of sacrificing their lives if need be. They have appeared in numbers before the tribunals of Vichy; they are still numberless, alas, in the German jails.

This attitude of the French Catholic world is our best pledge against a return to anticlericalism, which would be a disaster to the country. This is one of our greatest consolations in the present, a cornerstone of our hope in the future.

CHAPTER V

The Face of France

EARLY IN THE present century, travelers in France could see in the railroad stations through which they passed a series of very beautiful posters, done by some of the best-known artists in the country, and forming a picturesque exhibition of our regional types and costumes. There were Bretons in beribboned round black velvet hats; peasants from Auvergne with puffed-out cheeks blowing on bagpipes; girls from Nice with immense flower-bedecked straw hats and many-colored dresses; Alsatian women in black coifs with a tricolor bow at the back; Picards, Normans; woodcutters from the Jura on their skis; shepherds from the Landes perched on high stilts.

The same epoch saw the great vogue of the picture postcard. One series published about 1910 represented in reduced facsimile the front page of the country's leading newspapers, and superimposed upon each was a sketch of one of its typical readers. *Le Temps* carried an austere financier in gold-rimmed spectacles and *Le Journal des Débats* a solemn-faced judge with white side-whiskers, while the face of a ferocious-looking army officer appeared under the headlines of *La Patrie*. A clerk and a midinette were reading *Le Journal* together; a concierge in a tasseled cap nodded over a copy of *Le Petit Parisien;* and a besmocked peasant pored over an article in *Le Petit Journal*. A clubman in a shiny top hat looked out of the front page of *Le Figaro* and a debonair abbé out of that of *La Croix,* while an automobile worker stepped

forth from the columns of the newest paper of all, Jean
Juarès's socialist *L'Humanité*. Thus, on the eve of the
modern "thirty years' war," France offered a rich picture
of varied regional and social groups.

Each of these provincials, each of these newspaper
readers, was also a voter,* and the great number of political parties in France under the Third Republic stems in
part from their regional and class differences. But these
differences alone do not suffice to explain the complexity
of the political picture — far from it. For one thing, although France is a country with a long democratic tradition, the Third Republic is young, compared with the
American Republic; and, unlike the latter, it came into
being as the latest in a series of governments which had
held sway over approximately the same territory. It is like
a business house which has not been built from the
ground up with new capital, new resources, and a new
board of directors, but is formed by a merger of existing
corporations whose traditions, prejudices, previous commitments, and even personnel must all be taken into consideration in shaping the policies of the new firm.

Similarly, as we have seen, the carry-overs from the old
regimes in France were religious as well as political, for
invariably Church and State have gone hand in hand.

The French Monarchy of Clovis and Saint Louis had
been a Catholic Monarchy from its inception. True, more
than one French king had been at odds with the Papacy,
but these disputes had involved questions of temporal
authority, and had usually been settled to the advantage
of the Monarchy without an open break. The Reforma-
tion had brought Protestantism and a series of civil wars,
but the Protestants had remained in the minority and the
Protestant prince who emerged from the wars of religion

* Except the women; France has never had woman suffrage.

as Henry IV, King of France, was forced to embrace Catholicism upon acceding to the throne. So firmly entrenched was the idea of religion's close connection with the State that one of the first cares of the men of the French Revolution, in finding means to fortify free Republican action, was to try not only to destroy Catholicism in France but to set up a new religion — that of the Supreme Being — to take its place.

Napoleon's Concordat with the Vatican re-established the old connection, though on somewhat more liberal terms, and at the dawn of the Third Republic it still held good. The Catholics were identified with Monarchy, and the freethinkers and Freemasons with Republicanism.

We have seen that the Monarchist, Catholic factions were so strong that after the defeat of 1870–1871, when the National Assembly (whose temper is shown by the fact that it vowed the country to the Sacred Heart of Jesus and ordered the decision to be commemorated by the building of the Basilica of Montmartre) met to formulate a new Constitution for France, it was almost by accident that the country became a Republic at all. Thiers told Lord Granville that "the Republic suited everybody because it realized the wish of nobody," and he added in a formula which became famous, "The Republic is the regime which divides us the least."

At the beginning, then, the Catholics were lined up as adversaries of the Republic. A very important first step toward the upsetting of this purely negative position, which was as dangerous for the Catholics as for the country itself, was made by Pope Leo XIII. Judging that it was only fitting and proper to place religion over and above political parties, he made his ideas known in the Encyclical of January 10, 1890, "On the Principal Duties of Christians." As a direct consequence of this, one of the more liberal-minded among the Catholics in the Chamber, Jacques Piou, detached himself from the purely conservative groups and founded the party known as the *Droite Indépendante,* or *Droite Constitutionnelle.* The new party recognized as a "definite fact" the "great democratic movement of the century." It declared that henceforth, instead of being in open and systematic opposition, it would make every effort to "prevent evil," and would always "co-operate in good."

A little later, Cardinal Lavigerie, a prelate evangelist known as an apostle of antislavery, who had now become Bishop of Carthage, pronounced a celebrated toast on the occasion of a reception given in honor of the High Command of the Mediterranean Fleet. He formally invited the Catholics to accept the Republican form of government: "the policy of rallying" had been founded. Obedient to the Holy Father's directives, many Catholics became Republicans from then on; but they remained, with very few exceptions, strongly aligned to the Right — conservatives, traditionalists, reactionaries. It was taken for granted that a Catholic should vote Rightist: the mere idea that he could be on the Left was scandalous in itself and the position of a man like the Abbé Lemire, Deputy of the Nord, who sat on the Left, was incomprehensible to most Catholics.

The first elections held under the new Constitution returned a large Monarchist minority to Parliament. This took its place as a Rightist opposition, while the convinced Republicans founded the Center and Left. From that time forward the history of the Third Republic was to be, like the history of the nation since the Revolution, a gradual, although sometimes interrupted, swing to the left, the progressives of yesterday becoming the conservatives of tomorrow. Clemenceau furnishes an interesting example of this tendency. When he first entered Parliament he was labeled an Extreme-Left Republican; towards the end of his career he became the champion of the Right, and at the time of his candidacy for the Presidency in 1921 he was beaten by the Left. But it was not Clemenceau who had changed, it was the nation. The same tendency is also evident in the curious effort made by all Cabinets since 1902 to "fall to the left." This means that every Premier, no matter what his party, tries, when he sees himself doomed to defeat, to arrange things so that in the parliamentary vote which removes him from office he will be supported by the Left and opposed by the Right and Center. He knows that his future political prospects demand such a vote in the record.

Along with the Monarchists, the young Republic inherited another political party left over from bygone days: the Bonapartists or *plébiscitaires*. This second appellation was derived from the fact that one of the essential characteristics of the Empire as built by Napoleon was the direct appeal to the people on major questions (of which the most important was the election of the chief executive) by direct consultation or plebiscite. The Bonapartists lost all hope of an Imperial restoration upon the death of the young heir of the dynasty, the Prince Impérial, in 1879. But the fondness of certain of the French, and particularly of the Corsicans, for the Napoleonic legend served to keep the Bonapartist Party alive after his death, even though many who voted the *plébiscitaire* ticket did not understand the meaning of the term. Conceivably they did so because their fathers had done so and because they retained a sort of retrospective hero worship for the first Napoleon. Their sentimental education had included, in their childhood, Berenger's song, *"Parlez-moi de Lui, Grandpère, parlez-moi de Lui.*" ("Speak to me of Him, Grandfather, speak to me of Him.") One electoral district on the outskirts of Paris, the XVIIth Arrondissement, kept returning to Parliament for twenty years a *plébiscitaire,* a Corsican named Pugliesi-Conti, for no more cogent reasons than these. It was the same in the Departments of the Charente and the Gers.

In 1886, Parliament passed a law banning from French soil all members of families who had ever reigned over the country. From that date on, the Monarchy and the Empire became hardly more than a sentimental and melancholy memory of the past, though periodically the incorrigible reactionaries were to try to capitalize on what remained of Monarchist and Imperialist sentiment. The following year, Premier Jules Ferry said in a famous speech at Le Havre, alluding to the deaths of the two Pretenders, the Comte de Chambord and the Prince Impérial: "The Monarchist peril is locked in two tombs upon which there will never again blossom a branch of hope in the future."

But if the Monarchy and the Empire were now specters of the past, the state of mind of their supporters had hardly changed, for the Republic remained stubbornly conservative until about 1880. The Republic was conservative because the country itself was conservative. The word "conservative" was constantly — and officially — pronounced without shocking anybody, because it corresponded to a reality. France was conservative because almost everyone had something to conserve; because the immense majority asked only that this satisfactory state of affairs be maintained.

After about 1880, however, following the slow but continuous shift to the left which we have already noted, the Republic ceased to be conservative to become — very timidly at first! — democratic.

The liberal Republicans won their first decisive victory in the election of 1889. Then, as gradually the Monarchists and Bonapartists declined in number in the Chamber, they were replaced by conservative Republicans, and later by Progressives, moving over from the Center, while groups hitherto regarded as Leftists became the Center or Moderates in the new scheme. Meanwhile the resulting vacancies at the left end of the spectrum were being filled by representatives of new groups, hitherto unrepresented in the Chamber; most of these latter based their political beliefs on the doctrines of Karl Marx.

The tendency of ideologies inherited from the past, and seemingly totally unrelated to current realities, to persist as a force in politics might have been offset more rapidly had France been completely industrialized, as were some of her neighbors, in the late nineteenth and early twentieth centuries. She was not. Practically self-contained as far as food and basic necessities were concerned, she was not greatly dependent upon the export of manufactured goods to obtain raw materials in return. She had only enough factories to supply the home market. Such goods as she did export were chiefly luxury items, craftsman's products which did not entail the great concentrations of workers required for heavy industry. Predominantly she remained an agricultural country. On the eve of the present war, 55.8 per cent of her population was rural; and out of 8,500,000 peasants, 5,000,000 worked their own land. In the provinces many of these "little people" never left their native town or village. The biographers of the peasant poet Charles Péguy, the Tharauds, write of his youth in Orléans: "He had known there an old humanity whose individual culture, formed by local traditions and the experiences of centuries, owed nothing, or almost nothing, to the world beyond, a population very near the earth, a people of peasant workers, a people of artisans, rustics only yesterday, who in the exercise of their profession carried on the oldest virtues of the soil, men unbelievable in their capacity for work, in their pious respect for the well-done job — in short, a very old world, a world of long ago, much nearer the France of yesterday than the France of today." There were many other parts of France where one could find this "world of long ago."

Moreover, in politics, the provinces led the country.

It is interesting to note that from a political standpoint the influence of Paris on the country declined very greatly after 1871. Throughout the history of France the capital had played a preponderant role: it was Paris which had fought the Revolutions of 1789, of 1830, and of the Commune. It was Paris, too, which had set the stage for a Boulangist coup in 1889. The provinces, slower-moving and more cautious, ended by being alarmed by the capital's violences in both directions. They remembered with horror the excesses of the Commune; but they also remembered, with an ironical feeling of defiance, the Rightist extravagances during the Boulangist surge. From that time on in Parliament, Paris was held in a sort of quarantine by the Deputies of the provinces, who constituted a crushing majority — there were only 52 Deputies from the Paris section in a total membership of 620. On the other hand, the provincial Deputies, showing exaggerated susceptibilities, reproached the capital with an insufferably patronizing attitude toward them. It was therefore extremely difficult for a Parisian Deputy to play a determining role in the direction of national affairs. The representatives of the capital were influential in Parliament, but it was almost impossible for them to obtain a Cabinet post. Until 1940, no Parisian had ever been Prime

Minister except André Tardieu, who, thoug.. a native
Parisian, always represented a provincial electoral district.
The first Deputy from Paris to become Prime Minister
was Paul Reynaud, in 1940; and although he represented
a Paris constituency, he was not himself a Parisian. In this
case, the experiment was unsuccessful; the circumstances,
it is true, were not exactly propitious.

With the complete industrialization of England the
voters of that country became divided chiefly on economic
lines. Had the proportion of industrial workers in France
been large enough, a similar political realignment might
have taken place there, the small groups either being ab-
sorbed into one of two large blocs, or else disappearing
under the shock. As it was, such a realignment did take
place in the industrial centers of France, but in these centers only. Most of the manufacturing of the country is
concentrated in a very few large cities. In these the Socialists soon became very strong; later on the Communists, too, were to depend upon them for their main support. But the total number of industrial workers was not
large enough to change fundamentally the political picture of France, even if all of them voted alike. The picture remained as varied as before except that new colors
had been added while some of the older ones continued to
fade. Thus, whereas the preoccupation of the English or
American voter was chiefly economic, that of his French
counterpart might be anything from economic to doc-
trinary, religious, or — in a few cases — even dynastic!

Added to these reasons for the multiplicity of political
parties in France is the important one of the Frenchman's
individualism. Without overemphasizing a national characteristic which has served so many writers (including
even some of the French themselves!) as a too convenient
explanation for anything French which they do not under-

stand, we must make allowances for its effect on politics. It has influenced them in several ways.

For one thing, the limited extent of industrialization in France which we have just noted was not the result of economic factors alone; the independent temperament of the average Frenchman was always a contributing cause. He had behind him a long tradition of patient, careful handwork over which he had complete control and for whose products he was solely responsible; he was loath to exchange this birthright for a place along an assembly line, both because the work in itself was less congenial and because it took away a measure of his precious independence. Even when he was forced to accept modern methods he preferred to be his own boss rather than to lose himself in the mass of employees of a large concern. The census of 1921 showed that 69 per cent of French industrial workers received wages from a regular employer; that 19 per cent were independent or "free-lance"; and that 11 per cent more were themselves employers. Let us recall by way of comparison that the industrial population of England, about the same time, was 90 per cent regular wage earners, 6.3 per cent independent workmen, and 3 per cent employers. In 1925 there were over 8,000,000 unionized workmen in England to less than 2,000,000 in France. Even allowing for the difference between the total working population of the two countries, these figures, too, serve to illustrate the fact that politically the British workers were a much more homogeneous group.

But the individualism of the French affected the country's political line-up in more direct ways too. Most of the political parties were not really rigidly organized, and voters were often inclined to vote for a man rather than for a party. From time to time ambitious politicians, not

finding themselves advancing rapidly enough in the party
of their allegiance, broke away and formed parties of
their own. This technique had interesting advantages.
By founding his own party, a politician could get a good
deal of publicity. By choosing its name with care, he could
sail with the prevailing wind much more easily than
members of the older parties whose names and records
spoke unequivocally. An "Independent Socialist" could,
for instance, in the days when the Left was in the ascen-
dant, stress the second half of his label; when the Right
came into power, he could answer embarrassing questions
by saying, "Socialist, yes — but *Independent!*" Furthermore, men in such a position were much better placed to
obtain ministerial portfolios — both because they were considered "safer" on account of their lack of real political
coloration, and because, once a portfolio was offered them,
they were free to accept it. Such considerations explain
largely the birth of divers small parties. For example, men
like Marcel Déat and Frossard got out from under the
ferule of Léon Blum because as members of the Unified
Socialist Party they could not accept a Cabinet post without the authorization of their group, whereas they could
satisfy their ambition in becoming "Independent Socialists."

Since the long-range tendency of the Republic was a
gradual move to the left, it was chiefly in the ranks of
the Leftists that the constant splitting-off of new parties
occurred. Perhaps it would be more exact to say that in
most cases the names of the new parties indicated (advisedly, of course) a relationship to the Leftist political
groupings.

The political diversity of the nation was reflected in the
composition of Parliament.

Not long ago, in discussing plans for the rebuilding of the English House of Commons, Winston Churchill expressed the hope that the new hall would be oblong like the old one, and not semicircular: "We shape our buildings, and afterward our buildings shape us," he declared, complaining that "the semicircular assembly which appeals to political theorists enables every individual or every group to move around the center, adopting various shades of pink according as the weather changes." Mr. Churchill would never have been happy in either of the Houses of the French Parliament; both sat in semicircular amphitheaters, and groups and individuals did profit by the opportunity to "move around the center." In fact, it was chiefly this movement, this fluidity, which made French politics what they were: never clean-cut struggles between two main parties, but compromises, coalitions, in which the side which gained the support of the floating Center won the day.

The Chamber of Deputies (as well as the Senate) formed a real political rainbow, but one that contained far more different colors than does the spectrum. On the eve of World War II, what were the principal sections of the rainbow?

The elections of May 1936, which brought the Popular Front to power, had given 381 seats to the Left as against 237 to the Center and Right. Seen from the President's desk, from left to right, the main groups of the Chamber were: the 73 Communists under the leadership of Maurice Thorez; the 156 Unified Socialists under the ferule of Léon Blum; the 117 Radical-Socialists led by Daladier; 42 members of the Democratic Alliance under the leadership of Pierre-Etienne Flandin; 14 Popular Democrats; 9 members of La Rocque's *Croix de Feu* (later known as the *Parti Social Français*); 11 members of the Agrarian

Group; the Republican Federation of Louis Marin, group-
ing 54 members; finally 11 members of the "Independent
Right," of whom the chief was M. de Grandmaison.

It is only necessary to compare numbers to observe that
there must have been also a smattering of intermediary
groups comprising nearly 150 other Deputies. These were
scattered through both the Left and Right, but most of
them were to be found in the Center, whose ranks had
been formed chiefly from the motives that have been explained above, and of which neither the labels nor the
leaders were worthy of note.

As for the principal parties — what of their electors?
From what strata of the population did they come — to
what social categories did they correspond?

A political map of France would show notably three
great "fortified regions," three great strongholds of the
Right: to the West, the Vendée (land of the Chouans),
Maine and Anjou, Lower Normandy, Lower Brittany
(traditional country of the "Whites," the King's men); to
the East, the three Lorraine Departments (the Meuse,
the Meurthe-et-Moselle, the Vosges) — frontier lands, Republican, Catholic, and nationalist; to the South,
the Cévennes, an isolated mountainous region, fanati-
cal, where the influence of the clergy has remained very
strong.

Although less oriented to the right, the Pas-de-Calais
and a part of the Department of the Nord (where there
were numerous well-to-do and very pious Catholic families)
were also a reservoir of "moderate" votes. In fact, the West,
the North and the East voted Right — which once caused
a noted conservative to remark: "What a beautiful land
France would be if it stopped at the Loire!"

Nevertheless the voters who openly declared themselves

Royalists were only a small minority. They grouped themselves around the party called *L'Action Française,* founded in 1899, and presided over until the eve of the present conflict by Léon Daudet; it compensated for its numerical insignificance by the violence of its campaigns. From a parliamentary point of view its importance was nil; it was never able to send more than one Deputy to the Chamber — Léon Daudet himself, who was elected in 1919 but failed to be returned in 1924.

The small group of Right Independents included several of the greatest names of France; it grouped men of the type and the traditional mentality of Ancient France — but who called themselves Republicans and refused to compromise themselves with the turbulent *Action Française.*

The chief party of the moderates or "Center" was the Republican Federation, led by the Lorrainer, Louis Marin. Forbidding any sliding either to the right or to the left, it defined its program as follows: national defense, social progress within order, neutrality on the religious question, anticollectivism, antistatism. Its supporters came mainly from the small country nobility which had rallied to the new regime, the conservative bourgeoisie of the provinces, magistrates, professors, people with small incomes, heads of small business firms (particularly in the towns and cities of the North, the Northwest, and the West). But the greater part of its constituents were small-time farmers scattered over the entire territory, eager above all for peace and order, and confining their political demands to freedom to work their lands unhampered, as well as assurance for their children of the religious education which they had received themselves. In everything which concerned national defense, the Republican Federation gave its vote to whatever government was in power. By a curious paradox, it voted the military appropriations demanded by the governments of the Left which the Leftists themselves refused to vote.

Close neighbors to the Republican Federation in the Chamber were the "Christian" or "Popular" Democrats, or *Démocrates Populaires*. This was one of the newest parliamentary groups — small in number but interesting in the tendencies it showed. It represented the most recent and thoroughgoing attempt of forward-looking Catholics to reconcile the new social forces unleashed by the Industrial Revolution with the traditional teachings of the Church. We have already noted the endorsement of the Republic by Cardinal Lavigerie, in 1890; since then, various other Catholics had tried to go further in the same direction. The founder of "Social Catholicism," Le Play, borrowed a convenient label to cover a paternalistic attitude which demanded the authority of the Church in the State, of the father in the family, and of the employer in the factory. After Le Play, the aim of Marc Sangnier's *Sillon* was "to put the social forces of Catholicism at the service of democracy." Later, just after World War I, the "Christian" or "Popular" Democrat movement put the same idea into more explicit terms and urged the exact application of the teachings of Christ in political and economic life — a program which, if carried out, would have accomplished many of the same reforms which the Extreme Left and traditionally antireligious parties in France had been advocating for many years. It is also worth noting that, out of 14 members which the group comprised in the last Chamber, about a third had been elected with the support of the Leftist votes against the Right; the rest by Rightist votes against the Left. The party recruited its supporters, above all, in Brittany, the land of the humble clergy, and in Alsace, in Lorraine, and in the Basque country.

To the left of the Popular Democrats sat the nine members of Colonel de La Rocque's *Croix de Feu*. Few as they were, these men deserve particular attention. They were the only Deputies elected as representatives of any of the "patriotic leagues" which had become so numerous during the preceding decade, and their only predecessor in this capacity had been Léon Daudet of the *Action Française*. A great deal has been said and written about their chief, Colonel François Casimir de La Rocque — much more than his rather pale personality justified. Ambitious, but lacking any broad grasp of politics, he had no real political doctrine or even definite program. In spite of these rather considerable disadvantages, he might have become a figure of real consequence, for chance had placed him at the head of the best of the veterans' associations. Its name, the *Croix de Feu,* derived from the fact that all its members were men who had won the *Croix de Guerre* for bravery on the firing line. Hardly had he become its president when La Rocque began to use it as a political tool. First he enlarged it by admitting, as "National Volunteers," men who had not fought in the war and also women and young people. Later on, when the *Cagoulard* scare led to the dissolution of all secret political societies, he made it a regularly organized party, the *Parti Social Français*. The original prestige of the *Croix de Feu* and the political circumstances of the movement had permitted La Rocque to gather around his banner nearly a million supporters. But once he got them, he was completely at a loss as to how to use them. Furthermore, in the course of an investigation made in 1938, André Tardieu insisted that he could not have used them even if he had tried, because politically he was not independent. The former Prime

Minister publicly accused him of having on several occasions received subsidies from the government — from
himself, and from Laval. The accusation was heatedly de-
bated throughout a sensational trial, and although no
definite proof was furnished by either side, the affair
greatly weakened La Rocque's position.

The Democratic Alliance, led by Pierre-Etienne Flandin,
a group to which Tardieu and Paul Reynaud belonged
for many years, sat more toward the left. It harbored
in its midst a number of Ministers and former Ministers,
and a still greater number of ministerial candidates. The
party's economic and social program hardly differed from
that of the Republican Federation, and their respective
tickets were often mixed, but the Democratic Alliance,
in order to justify its position closer to the Leftists, showed
on the religious question an attitude which, though tech-
nically neutral, had strong Voltairian overtones. The Democratic Alliance had a General Staff, but few troops, and
it was a haven for the representatives of Big Business.

The benches of the Radical-Socialists began just beyond those of the Democratic Alliance.

One can safely say that the Radical-Socialist Party has
identified itself with the Third Republic. The "Radical
and Radical-Socialist Party," whose formation had been
prepared by the adhesion to "nonrevolutionary socialism"
of a certain number of Radicals, was founded in 1901. It
governed France from 1902 until the present day with
only two short interruptions, those of 1919–1924, and 1928–
1932. Of late, it has been presided over successively by
Edouard Herriot and by Edouard Daladier, and the
rivalry of the two Edouards has occupied the internal
history of the party.

Disraeli gave the word "radical" a particularly lofty
definition when he said that he was a radical to uproot

what is bad, a conservative to conserve what is good. The French Radicals appeared to be much less concerned with uprooting than with conserving. But this very "moderation" permitted the Republic to resist threats from both extremes, to live and to gain in strength, and I certainly do not wish to minimize the real service which their party rendered the country.

It is none the less true that the Radical-Socialist Party was absolutely representative of the great mass of the French middle class which, profoundly attached to its worldly goods, lives a sedentary existence in a closed circuit, completely shut off from the great currents from the outside world. The Radical-Socialists could also be defined as conservative anticlericals, for anticlericals they were — furiously under Combes (at the time when every good Radical "gobbled up a priest"), more discreetly but no less surely after the first World War. A popular saying compared them to the radish: "red outside and white inside," and to a great extent they justified this appellation too, for they most often voted with the Right on economic questions, with the Left on questions purely political.

To tell the truth, the Radical-Socialist party was neither radical nor socialist, but its double appellation ("I am a bird — see my feathers; I am a mouse — see my fur") placed it in a strategic position to swing itself from one side to the other, according to circumstances. Edouard Herriot and Edouard Daladier were able to be both chiefs of government in cartels of the Left (1924 and 1932) and members of Cabinets which bore the label "National Union" but were really out-and-out Rightist (1926 and 1934). To boot, they were successively the allies and the enemies of Léon Blum.

The electoral clientele of the Radical-Socialist Party was

recruited from public officials, civil servants, schoolteachers, small-town merchants, and rural landholders. Its success was most evident in the Southwest, where Toulouse was its principal stronghold, and it overflowed into the South of France.

Passing over a dusting of tiny independent and dissident groups of all shades of Leftist opinion, formed solely to satisfy the ambitions of men like Frossard and Déat, we come to the benches of the real Leftists — a third of the last Chamber of Deputies.

First of all the Unified Socialists.

The old French Socialist Party, commonly called "the S.F.I.O." (*Section Française de l'Internationale Ouvrière*), was founded in 1879 at Marseilles at a congress of workers from the industrial centers. It was first represented in Parliament in 1885, and won its first Cabinet post when Alexandre Millerand became Minister of Public Works in the Waldeck-Rousseau government in 1899. In a speech made three years before, this same Millerand had given the definition of the party's program which has remained classic: socialization of the means of production and exchange, attainment of power, peaceably, by universal suffrage, co-operation with the working classes of other nations. It is interesting to note that in the same speech Millerand reminded his hearers that in calling itself "internationalist" the French Socialist Party did not forget that it was French: "patriotic and internationalist, two qualities which, before us, the heroes of the French Revolution so nobly combined."

In 1896, the year of this speech, the first nationwide labor union in France — the C.G.T. (*Confédération Générale du Travail*) — was organized under the auspices of the Socialist Party with the purpose of defending "the moral and material, economic and professional interests of wage-earners."

When, in 1920, after the formation of the Third International, the French Socialist Party divided into two groups, the labor union prepared to do the same. The political group which seceded from the Socialist Party became the French Communist Party; its corresponding labor group became, in 1921, the C.G.T.U. (*Confédération Générale du Travail Unitaire*).

The split of the Extreme Left which resulted in the formation of the Communist Party was made on one essential question. The old, "Unified," Socialist Party, while seeking the co-operation of the workers of the entire world and keeping in contact with the Socialist elements of other countries through the Second International (of Amsterdam), made it a point to state specifically its national autonomy. The Communists, on the other hand, declared that the war of 1914–1918 had proved the failure of the Second International; it was henceforth obvious, they said, that the emancipation of the workers of the world would come only from a world revolution — that of the Third International (of Moscow). They no longer recognized any fatherland except that of the Soviets.

Because of their common origin, Socialists and Communists had the same electoral clientele; the workmen and small wage-earners of the big industrial centers of the North: Lille, Roubaix, Tourcoing, Valenciennes; of the East: Troyes, Mulhouse, Pont-à-Mousson; and of the Center: Lyon, Roanne, Le Creusot, Limoges. They found only a few adherents in the country districts, except among the vine-growers of the South of France, in the Departments of the Aude, of the Hérault, of the Var. (It is amusing to note that the party leader of the Socialists, Léon Blum, a Parisian dilettante and a strict teetotaler, was the Deputy

from Narbonne, an important center of the wine trade.)
A sizable number of schoolteachers and government employees voted Socialist likewise, and the party gloried in
the support of many savants and intellectuals. Léon Blum
himself, of a strictly bourgeois family of Parisian businessmen, a university man, a jurist and a scholar, was their
prototype. In the beginning the Communists gathered
their voters from the least privileged classes. They attracted fewer intellectuals than did the Socialists; the
writer Henri Barbusse was one of the first and the most
celebrated.

I have said very little about the Senate; however, the
picture which I have attempted to present of the Chamber of Deputies applies as well to the upper House — with
the reservation that the Senate, elected, as we have seen,
not by universal suffrage but indirectly, is made up of
older and consequently far more conservative men than
the Chamber. The Senate acts with regard to the Chamber as a sort of brake, regulating its movements in one
direction or the other. At the time of the "horizon-blue
Chamber" (the Rightist Chamber of 1919–1924), the
Senate moved strongly to the left. On the other hand, at
the time of the Popular Front, the Senate, having become
predominantly Radical-Socialist, moved into a position
which was strictly Rightist in comparison to that of the
Chamber, which was then of course Extreme Left.

Such, in its broad lines, was the picture of the French
political parties, the political face of France, on the eve
of the catastrophe.

Everyone remembers how the elections of May 1936 carried to power, under the name of the Popular Front, a
coalition of three parties: Radical-Socialist, Socialist, and

Communist. Events have amply proved that the Popular Front was not, at its inception, an affirmative popular movement for a social revolution, but merely a negative defensive action, a coalition against fascism.

Immediately after the triumphant elections of 1936 — the triumph of the Popular Front — Léon Blum, in an address to the Socialist Congress, analyzed the paradoxical situation which confronted him: "We have all fought the same electoral battle; we have all condemned the present social system. . . . It is a chaotic society, full of contradictions, and we must substitute for it something different. Neither the Socialists alone nor the Socialists together with the proletarian parties have a majority. Our duty is simply to carry out the Popular Front program. We are going to act within the framework of the present regime whose vices we have denounced."

This paradox was not to last more than eighteen months. It will be remembered how, after three different Popular Front cabinets, Daladier came to power in April 1938. Once again the Radical-Socialist Party cut its ties with the Left, and bound itself up with the Right — losing the Socialist votes but gaining those of the Republican Federation.

The paradox which had been so clearly and frankly denounced by Léon Blum showed up in a new light, and under tragic circumstances, another infirmity which has beset the Third Republic since its birth: the practical impossibility of forming a great autonomous party, and the constant necessity of coalition and compromise.

CHAPTER VI

The Right to Live

I HAVE ATTEMPTED to trace the political portrait of France
at the eve of the present world conflict, as it had emerged
from the ebb and flow of Revolution and Reaction since
the great days of 1789. But this general picture must be
seen in its relations to the particular social, economic, and
international problems which preoccupied the country
in the years between 1919 and 1939.

"The right to live"! The whole social problem is
contained in those four words.

What does the right to live mean to the individual?
In a true democracy it means that every citizen has not
only the right to live free from want, but the right and
duty to improve his condition to the utmost — provided
that he does not encroach upon another, and supreme,
right (one before which all other considerations must
yield): the right of the nation to live. For, as the nation
is nothing more nor less than the sum of its citizens, to
defend the nation's life is the citizen's first and foremost
duty.

Ever since 1875 — and, during the twentieth century,
by almost unanimous consent — France has lived under
a republican regime. Obviously, as long as it is the form of
government desired by the majority, the Republic, too,
has the right to live.

The right to live for the individual; the right to live

for the nation; the right to live for the Republic. Conciliation between — and too often the opposition of — these rights make up the whole of my story.

The individual's right to live may be called his social interest. The nation's right to live — and the corresponding duty of every citizen to defend the nation's life — may be called the national interest. Whenever the social interest of the majority of the masses and the national interests have been in accord, France has been strong and almost invincible. When they have conflicted, France has been weakened and exposed to reverses.

Social interest, when held within legitimate and legal limits, is highly creditable. National interest is always sacred. But the exploiting of either by politicians is dangerous and hateful.

The exploiting of social interests when carried to the extreme becomes demagogy. The exploiting of the national interest when carried to the extreme becomes supernationalism. The struggle between nationalism and demagogy fills the whole social history of France in the period between the two world wars. The exploiting of social interests would not have been possible — or at any rate would not have been so harmful — without the permanent financial crisis bequeathed the French nation by the miserable peace treaty of Versailles; and the exploiting of the national spirit would not have been possible without the permanent threat of Germany with which France was saddled by the same miserable treaty.

To comprehend our social difficulties more easily, it should be remembered that from the time of Louis-Philippe through the comparatively calm period of the nineties, and right up to World War I, the value of the French franc had hardly varied. The large silver five-franc pieces with the laurel-crowned head of Napoleon III were still in circulation on the eve of the conflict of 1914–1918, a tangible symbol of stability.

And five francs was just about the sum that any man had to spend per day to live decently. A skilled workman was paid five francs a day; a Parisian clerk or a department-store salesman earned 150 francs a month at the start, and his salary rose very gradually to 200 francs during the next ten years if he was very good.

So that, for a period of more than half a century, the French people — the thriftiest race in the world — were able to square their yearly budget to a cent: so many francs for clothes, so much for food, so much for lodging, and a small surplus for the café-concert on Saturday night. Vacations, for the working classes, were out of the question; and many other things which ought to have been considered necessities were unobtainable luxuries. Yet the miracle was that, within these narrow limits, they managed to save, and to buy French and Russian bonds. Popular savings banks originated in France and were more prosperous there than in any other country.

Suddenly, in midsummer of 1919, just as the last bugles of Bastille Day were dying away, the Frenchman read in the headlines of his newspaper that the pound sterling, which had for generations been worth 25 francs, had unexpectedly risen to 32 francs. This did not mean much to him, but when, very soon after, he found that the price of his morning roll had doubled, and that he had to pay two sous instead of one for his newspaper, he began to realize the significance of the fact.

The needs of war had brought the government to encourage mechanization and cartelization of French industry. The same heavy-industry firms which had worked for the war were the natural heirs and beneficiaries of postwar rehabilitation programs. And 70 per cent of the coal, 80 per cent of steel, 60 per cent of cotton, 70 per cent of sugar, 90 per cent of linen thread, 90 per cent of wool, and 90 per cent of iron ore were concentrated in the devastated areas. The first consequence was inflation; the second was the consolidation of the financial and material positions of the capitalistic groups destined to be the beneficiaries of this inflation.

The expressions "ceilings" and "rollbacks" and "wage stabilization" are now familiar to every American. Corresponding expressions became familiar to the French at that time, when the fight against inflation began. We tried all those means of combating it. We even tried the ingenious process of siphoning off the excess purchasing power in the hands of the public by new taxation, or "forced saving." The trouble was that these plans of the financial experts were all slow of accomplishment, and bread must be bought every day. "Siphoning off" works very well on paper, but in the long run it may siphon off the confidence of the people in its leaders. This is what happened in France.

Thus, with the first devaluation of the franc, financial worries were added to the very legitimate social claims of the workers.

When World War I broke out, social legislation in France was very recent and the general condition of the working classes still backward: an average workman was employed in the factory from nine to ten hours a day, and night work was still permitted; there were no paid vacations, no old age pensions. After the Versailles Treaty French workmen pressed their claims, and we can only wonder at the inhuman stupidity of their employers in not granting them these at once, and spontaneously. Is it not shameful to recall that up to 1932 the owners of the huge Renault factories had not organized any kind of old age pension for their thousands of workers?

But on the top of these permanent and basic claims, which were a purely French concern, came the daily claim for an adjustment of wages, a consequence of the instability of the franc, which was the curse put upon us by the international blunders of 1919.

All these claims, however, were no longer in the hands of the individual, but in those of his elected representatives, both in the labor unions and in Parliament.

The counterpart of the A. F. of L. in France, the C.G.T. (*Confédération Générale du Travail*), was sponsored by the Socialist Party, and after the political split of the Extreme Left in 1920, it too separated, as we have seen, into two parts. One kept the old name and remained under Socialist influence; the other, which called itself the "C.G.T.U." (*Confédération Générale du Travail Unitaire*), followed the Communists.

To use the American expression, both Socialists and Communists, both C.G.T. and C.G.T.U., had to sell their ticket to the same voters. From that time, they were rivals in advertising and demagogy. Each of them — in public meetings, in the union councils, and in Parliament — tried to outbid the other.

Because the claims of the working classes were only too legitimate, and because promising is a simple job, they easily found their followers. But they did not find as many as they might have, for while flattering the social interests of the masses they were at the same time open to suspicion from the point of view of national interest. Socialists and Communists alike, at that time, were antimilitarists and pacifists, and both voted in the Chamber against appropriations for the army and armaments.

The majority of the French people felt that this did not

make sense. They realized instinctively a truth which we have all been compelled to recognize since — that, as Walter Lippmann puts it, "The pacifist nation can disarm itself, but it does not disarm its enemies."

Thus, though enthusiastically followed by many because they presented themselves as the advocates of the social interests of the masses, Socialists and Communists were distrusted by others — by many more — who reproached them with ignoring the national interest.

This national interest was exploited cynically, on the other hand, by the supernationalists and Extreme Rightists. The Royalist *Action Française* was their daily paper, the journal *Gringoire* their weekly, the polemist Charles Maurras their apostle, and the Deputy Philippe Henriot their usual spokesman on the rostrum of the Chamber. If one were to believe them, they alone held the secret of true national interest, and they alone were worthy and able to defend it. They sold super-patriotism as the others sold demagogy.

Behind both were capitalists and bankers.

To oppose the C.G.T. the main industrial bosses of the country had set up their own Union, the C.G.P.F. (*Confédération Générale du Patronat Français*). Appealing to the patriotism of the war veterans and the impulsiveness of youth, various political societies, with their secret executive committees, their passwords, their military organization, began to appear and parade in the streets. There were the *Camelots du Roi* — something like the "King's Own," who were sponsored by the *Action Française;* the *Jeunesses Patriotes;* later on the *Croix de Feu* of Colonel de La Rocque; later on still, the fascist *Cagoulards*. Facing these were the Extreme-Leftist organizations: *Faucons Rouges, Jeunesses Révolutionnaires*.

The two opposing forces, working in the background

of a sincere outburst of public indignation, clashed on the Place de la Concorde on the night of February 6, 1934, under circumstances which later on I shall describe in detail. Because, on that day, the Republican regime had been in danger, the right of the Republic to live was solemnly and violently proclaimed two days later by the Socialists, demonstrating on the Place de la République, and by the Communists, parading with raised fists on the Place de la Bastille. These were about the last separate demonstrations of their kind by the two parties: 1936 saw them united, with the Radicals, "against fascism," in the general elections in May and June which brought the Popular Front to power.

From that day on in the Chamber, the Communists (they were now 73, whereas they had been only 10 in 1932) held about two thirds as many seats as the Socialists. Their success is easy to explain: they shared the position of supporters of the social interests of the poorer classes with the Socialists, but they had the advantage of making better use of the national interest. In the summer of 1936, Stalin had published a declaration stating clearly that it was the duty of the French Communists to support the national defense of their country. From then on they voted military appropriations, and began singing the "Marseillaise." Maurice Thorez, the most prominent of their leaders, honored Joan of Arc; in short, they prided themselves on being the foremost and most ardent of patriots. Once more the old rule applied: the fact that social interest and national interest appeared to be in full accord in their platform gave them their unexpected and overwhelming success.

When Léon Blum, President of the Socialist Party, came into power as chief of the strongest party of the Popular

Front coalition, he, like several of his predecessors, was granted by Parliament emergency powers (known as "full powers") for a period of one year. During that time he had the right to issue decrees which — by virtue of Parliament's delegation of power to him — had to all purposes the same authority and effect as ordinary laws — hence their name of "decree-laws." (To safeguard its constitutional rights, Parliament kept the right to ratify the decree-laws *a posteriori,* though in practice it never called them directly into question.) Blum used these decree-laws to enforce the basic reforms he had promised to the voters.

He summoned to his office in the Hotel Matignon the representatives of the C.G.P.F. and of the main industries, and gave them short notice to deliver their "spontaneous" agreement to his reforms. And the same men whose selfishness had opposed or delayed these reforms, granted on an hour's notice all that they had stubbornly and stupidly refused for so many years — and much more.

As to the most important of the reforms — paid vacations of two weeks for all workers and limitation of working hours — there was no serious division in the country. Even a man like Albert de Mun, and after him the Catholic Rightists, had advocated these for many years, and the Chamber approved them almost unanimously.

The trouble did not come because of the reforms, but because of the manner in which they were accepted. Strikes spread all over the country like an epidemic. Using a new tactic, the strikers refused to quit the factories, took possession of the machines and offices, turned the halls into canteens and dance halls, hoisted the red flag on the roof. How many disguised Germans of the fifth column were among the strikers is a question that will doubtless be answered later on.

The leaders of the Popular Front made the unforgivable mistake of forgetting that a democracy cannot live without discipline. Precisely because it is, in this case, freely self-consented, discipline must be stronger in a democracy than in any other regime. The reforms of Léon Blum were meant for the good of the working classes, and the ill-advised extremist leaders of those classes ruined their chances by their excesses.

Another old rule proved to be true once more: the red flag floating over Paris recalled to many the nightmare of the Commune, awoke in the French the atavistic instinct for order, the traditional respect for private property. The Senate expressed the feelings of the huge majority of the middle class when, in April 1938, it refused to give Blum a vote of confidence, and broke the Popular Front. The inevitable reaction set in: Daladier, the next Premier, formed a "National Union" Cabinet which was supported by the Rightists.

The super-nationalists and the *Cagoulards* set to work to make the most of the circumstances. The German fifth column had not waited for them. The ghost of the Bolshevist Bogy was shaken again before the frightened bourgeois. The catchword of the *Cagoulards* and fascists was "Rather Hitler than Thorez." The result was Pétain.

To many, Pétain meant order; to almost every Frenchman — for almost every Frenchman trusted his legend — he meant Honor. But Pétain represented a class. He had been pushed to power to defend the social interest of that class and, to defend it, he betrayed the national interest.

Some years before, in a time of political and social crisis, Herriot, in a speech before the Chamber of Deputies, had said: "Sons must not fight at the bedside of their sick mother." His enemies made fun of the sentence. And yet, the thought was simple, generous, and true. When the homeland is in a sorry plight, all social interests must yield before the national interest. It is a lesson which, since 1940, the people of occupied France have learned only too well.

CHAPTER VII

Commitments and Means

THE ALLIED SOLDIERS who went to war in 1914 — the great war for the cause of civilization — were told that, thanks to their sacrifices, it would be the last to afflict humanity. At a price of 1,600,000 dead and more than 4,000,000 maimed and wounded among the French troops alone, victory was achieved, and the apotheosis of France and her allies. Yet, twenty-two years later, on the same spot as the first one, a second armistice was signed. Only the roles were reversed.

How could France have slipped so rapidly from the triumph of 1918 to the collapse of 1940?

France was insufficiently prepared to sustain the war which broke out in 1939. This is an incontestable fact. France herself was largely responsible for her unpreparedness. Or more exactly, a certain number of her military leaders and civil servants were answerable; these men will be held to account by their country in the near future. But if France's weakness in the face of the enemy was partly due to her own errors, it was also due, perhaps even more, to a cause beyond her control. France was weak because, in the twenty-year interval between the two wars, she had not been able to recover from the frightful loss of men and substance which had bled her white from 1914 to 1918.

In 1939, Poland, France and Great Britain had the courage to face Germany, knowing only too well that they were insufficiently prepared. After the collapse of

Poland, France, because of her geographical position, was to take the first heavy blow. She was the first on the firing line, and she was the first wounded; but this gave the other nations time to prepare and to resist. True enough, she lost the first battle of this second phase of the titanic conflict, but because, challenged by Germany, she had had the courage to enter it. If after weighing all the risks she had backed down in September 1939, as in September 1938, and had consented to another Munich, what would have happened? If Poland had surrendered, instead of defying Germany, and if Britain and France had not met their obligations under their treaty with Poland, the citadels of civilization might well have been lost without a battle.

Sir Robert Vansittart, chief diplomatic adviser to the British Foreign Secretary from 1938 to 1941, wrote recently in a courageous article: "But for twenty miles of sea we should have shared the fate of France. We also failed to learn the wise lesson that power is necessary in peace as in war. Moreover a percentage of the responsibility for the collapse of France rests on our own lack of resolute policy during these forty years."

The relative unpreparedness of France in the war is one factor in the situation, but there is another. To those who may be amazed that France did not sufficiently bear up her end of the war — as if her unique mission in life were to sustain each time, and alone, for the benefit of all the civilized nations, the first impact of the barbarian hordes — we simply ask: This war for which France was unprepared, for which all the democracies were unprepared — was it really inevitable, could it not have been, should it not have been . . . avoided?

France has the right to answer that the war was avoidable; and that it would have been prevented, if the peace which terminated the world conflict of 1914–1918 had not been, by the collective fault of the Allies, lamentably bungled.

France wounded, bleeding, having barely escaped annihilation — France haunted by the memory of her century-old misgivings; France eager, hungry for peace and security — cried out for a barrier, that eternal barrier of the Rhine that Foch, Commander in Chief of the Allied Armies, had so often and so solemnly demanded during the negotiations of Versailles . . . and her Allies gave her a contract!

Furthermore, this contract was never to be carried out. It was entirely based upon the hypothesis of an effective League of Nations; and the League was never effective — it had been the personal conception of Woodrow Wilson, President of the United States, and the United States had refused to join it.

A League of Nations in which neither the United States nor Russia had a seat — where nearly 500,000,000 men were not represented — ceased to be a League of Nations; it became nothing more than a political club; it was no longer a tribunal but a debating society, a mock court. France, victorious, but already suspected of militarism by friends and allies, did not obtain the guarantees of security which she had legitimately demanded against Germany. And Germany, by a paradox which was a real challenge, remained intact.

True, the Reich had lost some territory, but chiefly because of due restitutions to France, Denmark, and Poland (as well as the fateful Danzig Corridor) and while Austria was broken up, Germany retained, in its main lines, her geographic unity.

But — and this was far more important — no radical

change was forced on her political and social structure; the Kaiser had gone, but his clique remained; all the princes and nobility kept their privileges; the magnates of banking and industry remained, with their money and their plants; the leaders of military and capitalistic reaction — the future artificers of fascism — retained their newspapers and their influence. The sovereign of Germany had been dethroned, and Germany's armies disarmed. Nevertheless, the real masters of the country, and the means of building up a new army to create a new generation of military-minded men and to prepare a new war, remained. And Germany, having capitulated before the Allied invasion — never having known the enemy on her soil, and having suffered no destruction whatsoever — would not admit that she had been vanquished. Versailles, for her, was not a treaty but a *Diktät*.

The destruction and ruin in France at the end of 1918 were immense. For over four years, the ten most populous departments of the country had been occupied by the enemy; this was the part of the land where the industrial plants were most numerous, the mines highly important, the fields intensively cultivated. The invaders had destroyed or carried back across the Rhine immense quantities of machinery and rolling stock, farm animals and agricultural implements. Trenches and high-explosive mines had thrown up the subsoil to a disastrous degree; 4,355,915 acres of arable lands had been ruined among the 9,366,000 acres of French territory destroyed by battle in the ten Departments of the Nord, Pas-de-Calais, Somme, Oise, Aisne, Marne, Ardennes, Meuse, Meurthe-et-Moselle, and Vosges.

Trenches had to be filled in, battlefields cleared of wrecked war matériel, villages reconstructed amid the ruins. The reparation of these territories could not wait, for the peasants and townsmen were flocking back to their lands.

The crushing debt that France owed her citizens and her allies was to have been redeemed by reparations paid by the Reich — by the country responsible for the devastation.

Germany was prepared to make an enormous cash payment, and we know today that she would have been able to do it. But the trainload of gold which was ready to be sent to us was literally switched off on a siding.

In war, Germany had been an enemy; but in peace she again became a customer of the two greatest industrial and commercial powers of the world, and a customer who, in order to retain her buying power, must be treated with consideration. Through the ascendancy of the British and American delegations at Versailles, the settlement of reparations in the peace treaty was put under the twin symbols of long-term credit and of imprecision: both the total amount of the debt and the length of time within which it was to be paid were left to be determined later on according to Germany's capacity.

Credit is the private hunting-ground of the financier. Because of the payment of the reparations by installment plan, the future no longer belonged to the people, but to the financiers; and the future was lost.

Whether large or small, rich or poor, "any state must bring its ends and means into balance," writes Walter Lippmann. The equilibrium between commitments and power ought to be the absolute rule of statesmen.

From a financial point of view, the commitments of France, the compensation of war victims and reparations for ruined territories, were immediate and terribly precise. But the means by which France was to be repaid by the Germans remained to be fixed by an International

Commission, and were undetermined and distantly due.

Furthermore, Germany was preparing with a diabolical cleverness to go into national bankruptcy. She offered a spectacle of frightful national misery to the pity of all. Her financial wizard, Dr. Hjalmar Schacht, began to solicit loans for her financial "recovery." The masterly device succeeded only too well. Germany ceased to pay France, and began gathering considerable sums from international banking concerns — sums which, under clever camouflage, went into preparation for a new war.

Better still, Germany pushed her slyness to the point of making one of her former conquerors, the United States, declare her a bankrupt. In July 1931, President Hoover, wishing to protect the enormous credits granted Germany by America and other countries, suggested a moratorium on reparations, and he suggested it publicly without giving France any warning. His move came as a *coup de théâtre*.

Too far removed from Europe, American public opinion failed to apply the principle of "ability to pay" — as the law would put it — equally to Germany, former enemy but a proved "good customer," and to her former ally, France, who unfortunately was not such a good customer.

From that moment on France, shorn of all illusions, had to charge up to "Loss" everything which Germany owed her by way of reparations.

I am convinced that this lack of the necessary balance between commitments and means is one of the most obvious explanations of France's downfall — one of the certain causes of the present war.

From the standpoint of her foreign policy, what were the commitments of France? To keep the watch on the Rhine; to bar the route to a new German invasion.

The means? Either a firm alliance with her former comrades-in-arms — an alliance which the United States repudiated — or "collective security." But collective security was a cruel and empty mockery without an international police force, a force strong enough to insure action on the decisions of the community of civilized nations.

Clemenceau had voiced, on American soil itself, the disillusionment of France. Touring the United States in the latter part of 1922, he admonished the Americans in no uncertain terms. He spoke first at the Metropolitan Opera House on November 21: "If the French had known there were to be no reparations, no execution of the Treaty of Versailles, Foch and Pershing would probably have gone right through to Berlin without waiting to sign an armistice." And he added, "I tell you plainly, as I told Lloyd George before the war: they are preparing war again!" In subsequent speeches he told his hearers that "There can be no entente in Europe unless America is in it," and warned them against returning into European affairs too late: "You will be obliged to come one way or another!"

To this blunt warning, what was the answer of the government of President Harding? A few days later, on December 8, 1922, Harding in his message to Congress declared: "I bring you no apprehension of war. The world is abhorrent of it, and our own relations are not only free from every threatening cloud, but we have contributed our large influence toward making armed conflict unlikely. . . . Treaties of armed alliance can have no likelihood of American sanction."

And because the world at large was "abhorrent of war," Germany — who desired it, who craved it, who lived for it — was left free to prepare it.

Because, since the abortive peace of 1919, France had no longer an autonomous foreign policy but a policy forcibly conditioned by that of her former allies, and because also of the quick shift of her Ministers, her diplomacy never ceased to vacillate — swinging between a conciliatory attitude toward Germany (personified in Aristide Briand), and coercion (identified in the rigid Poincaré), without ever deciding definitely to go all the way in either direction. It started by playing the card of the League of Nations with Edouard Herriot, and bet to the extreme limit on collective security. Then, convinced of the uselessness of its efforts, it returned to the conception of a policy of group alliances, of "blocs": the bloc of Western Europe — Great Britain, France, Italy; the bloc of the Balkans; the bloc of Central Europe — Czechoslovakia, Poland. Louis Barthou was the warm protagonist and artisan of this policy of blocs. But wisely — and his tragic death in 1934 was in this regard a disaster for France — he conceived of Russia as a cornerstone in this system. His successors did not have the wisdom to continue his policy. They were tempted to see in the bloc alliances mere links in the chain of the now all too famous *cordon sanitaire,* which was to "isolate" the Soviets. Even the most farsighted among them, such as Weygand, convinced of the need of a military alliance with the Soviets, refused to admit that a military alliance would imply in even the smallest measure a political alliance. I confess that, depending with too much confidence on the oracles and the so-called "specialists and technicians" of foreign policy, I shared this error with many.

Fate was to furnish the former allies, and all peace-loving powers, with a last chance of salvation. On March 7, 1936, Hitler sent German troops into the demilitarized Rhineland — the last vestige of the guarantee of security provided by the Treaty of Versailles. The Allies had only to make a gesture and all could have still been saved. France at first seemed resolved to take the risk; but London, from the very first moment, gave the plainest negative answer to the French representations. This attitude of the British, when it became known, strengthened the hands of the defeatists hidden in the French Cabinet, and eventually turned the balance in their favor. Hitler, therefore, entered the Rhineland and installed himself permanently. It was officially established, soon after, that the appearance of the smallest contingent of the French Army would have made him draw back. The Allies, by their abstention, gave him a triumph which consolidated his power, and made him the absolute master of Germany.

The story of what went on in the French Cabinet meeting that day is enlightening, for it shows already the evidence of cleavage between patriots and appeasers which was later to evince itself so clearly in the crisis of 1940.

When the cabinet meeting began, Premier Albert Sarraut and Pierre-Etienne Flandin, Minister of Foreign Affairs, were decided upon resistance — an attitude which Georges Mandel supported with fierce energy. Facing them was a trio of defeatists: Georges Bonnet, then Minister of Commerce; François Pietri, Minister of Marine; and Marcel Déat, the present arch-collaborationist, then Minister of Aviation (all of whom already knew the British decision).

They questioned Flandin on the attitude of Great Britain, and he was forced to admit that the British Government advised against resistance to the German move and refused to associate itself with the affair. The defeatists of the French Cabinet at once made capital of the British attitude, and General Gamelin, then Commander in Chief of the French Army, declared that he could not act unless there was a general mobilization — a statement which was later proved to be absurd. The defeatists declared themselves against such a mobilization, and won the day. The last chance to crush Hitler had vanished.

From then on war was inevitable. It would have taken an entire and united France to prepare for it. At this juncture, when the life or death of the country was at stake, what was the picture inside France? The red flag was floating over the armament factories in the industrial districts of the capital. These factories had been emptied by the strikes, their interiors transformed into dance halls. The government of Léon Blum was forming a "Ministry of Leisure," at the very minute that I, as a member of the House Military Affairs Committee specially charged with the inspection of armament factories, was witness to the fact that *only six tanks in one week* had come off the assembly line in the recently "nationalized" factory of Issy-les-Moulineaux.

I in no way mean to imply that the working classes were responsible for this state of affairs. The French Employers' Association could have — should have — avoided it, by giving spontaneously to the workers a larger share of the profits from their enterprises, as justice had been demanding for some time. I therefore do not consider labor responsible for the situation in Paris in 1936; but I do consider responsible certain leaders who had never held a tool in their hands in their lives, and who knew the working classes only to exploit them for their own political ends. And I consider responsible in a large measure a selfish coterie of employers, a group stupidly attached to a feudal conception of economy, defying the march of progress, whose blindness was a veritable provocation to labor.

This was none the less the situation as I have described it: whereas, before the growing menace of Germany, national unity was more than ever imperative to the nation's existence, a hot wind of hatred swept France in 1936, and it had barely died down when the catastrophe of 1939 broke over the country.

But before 1939 there was 1938 — the year of Munich — and before that there was the summer of 1936 — which saw the outbreak of the Spanish War. Here again, as she had done for years — and especially since the fatal error of the preceding March — France played a role secondary to Britain's. The official attitude of the British government — and following its lead, of the French government as well — was that this war in Spain was simply a struggle of ideologies, a bloody and atrocious conflict between political factions: the Left against the Right, the Reds against the Whites, the anarchists against the army and the clergy. The assistance given to Franco by Hitler and Mussolini, and to the Loyalists by Russia, was perfectly well known; and yet somehow the mass of people of both nations, while sympathizing with one side or the other according to their personal inclinations, failed to see the close connection of the war with their own future — failed to realize its importance as a training-ground for Hitler. The isolationist mentality took refuge behind the Pyrenees and the Bay of Biscay.

Fulfillment of the Socialist program to which his party was committed would have moved Léon Blum to align himself immediately with the Spanish Loyalists. But Blum had come to power, as we have seen, not as the chief of one party but as the representative of a coalition. Therefore he felt — and this scruple does him honor — that henceforth he was obliged to act not as a party leader but as executor of the will of the whole country, weighing all problems in terms not of party policy, but of the general policy — and this meant a close French solidarity with Great Britain.

Alexander Werth, of the *Manchester Guardian,* wrote in
1937: —

There is, of course, not the slightest doubt that about August
1st, the British Government clearly intimated to the French
Government that if, as a result of her "competition" with Italy
and Germany in sending arms to Spain, France were attacked
by the fascist countries, Britain would not consider the attack
an unprovoked one and the Locarno guarantee would not
come into operation.

And yet, what a twist of conscience it must have given
Léon Blum, this decision! His personal tendencies, his
past record, his political doctrines, the interests of his
party, all pushed him to support the Reds in Spain, who
were revolting against an attempt to establish a military
dictatorship. But fate would have it that, by the strangest
of paradoxes, the most Extreme-Leftist Premier France
had ever had did not dare oppose the intervention of Hit-
lerism and Fascism in Spain.

And then came 1938, the most shameful and fateful
year of all. I found myself facing Munich in September
of 1938 as I found myself facing the Armistice of June
in 1940. I was confronted with the terrible, irrevocable,
and accomplished fact, with regard to which I had not
had the slightest possibility of formulating an advance
opinion, and which I had been able in no way to foresee.
Thank God, I cannot in any manner be included among
the "Munichers," nor among the men who not only accepted Munich but wished ardently for it. As a veteran
of 1914–1918, and a member of a family decimated by the
war, I have too great a defiance and hatred of the German
in my blood to have in that regard the slightest hesitation
of conscience.

I accepted Munich with sorrow. But I confess today that this was a grave mistake. It would have been necessary to raise against Munich the great voice of the national conscience. In so far as I am concerned, I failed in my duty, but if I go out of my way to confess it, it is because my state of mind at that moment is indicative of that of the immense majority of the French population. The French saw rising before them, exactly twenty years after the slaughter which had bled them white, the specter of war; then suddenly, within a few hours, the specter vanished. They felt a deeply human and natural sense of relief and deliverance — not immediately understanding that the danger had only been postponed and that delay made it still more mortal.

In my own case, another consideration added itself to this purely physical sense of relief — a sense of relief too natural, after all, for anyone who possessed a measure of sincerity to be ashamed of it: I knew the deficiencies in our armament program. Could not the delay which Providence was according us be put to profit in repairing these deficiencies and setting us on our feet again? As a matter of fact, from September 1938 to September 1939 real progress was realized in this direction, notably in the field of antitank defense armament.

I had hoped that the delay would finally allow Great Britain to establish compulsory military service — the necessity was evident and imperative. In this regard, I share fully the opinion of Daladier, whom I can still hear declaring to me in his office of the War Ministry, Rue Saint Dominique, in January of 1940: "I will not undertake any serious military action until there are a million Britishers in the front line."

And still my hopes were ill-founded. They were ill-founded because we thought — wrongly — that the ac-

cord realized at Munich with regard to the Sudetenland
had set all danger aside for a time. We could not believe
— and Daladier, acting in good faith, did not believe —
that Hitler would commit the new and incredible crime
of the rape of the whole of Czechoslovakia immediately
afterwards, in May of 1939. Others who refused to believe it were the British Government, President Roosevelt,
and the great mass of American public opinion. We had
not yet entirely realized what Hitler was; we realized it
after his entry into Prague.

It became clear at that moment that Munich had been
a colossal error; that it would have been far wiser
to have risked war in 1938, unprepared and without British compulsory military service, but with the possible aid
of Russia and the certainty of the co-operation of Czechoslovakia, than to have taken it on in 1939 without the
Czech divisions, without the Skoda factories, and, above
all, deprived of the assistance of Soviet Russia.

CHAPTER VIII

The Roots Were Very Deep

WHEN HE became Prime Minister in June 1940, Philippe Pétain had behind him the immense majority of the people of France. French sentiment toward him was similar to that expressed in Charles de Gaulle's dedication to the Marshal in his book, *Au Fil de L'Épée* — a dedication which was, perhaps, only the thanks due Pétain for the laudatory preface he had written for de Gaulle's first book.

Pétain was the glorious hero of Verdun. True, his qualities as a commander had not always been flatteringly discussed by other military chiefs who had served with him in the first World War, but as far as the general public was concerned his legend remained unchallenged. Indeed, it had been constantly amplified and rounded out and presented to the public in ecstatic terms by all the governments of the Right and Left. It was the Daladier government, which had developed out of the Popular Front, that named Marshal Pétain Ambassador to Madrid. It was the Reynaud government which, during the tragic hours of May 1940, recalled him from Madrid to share the responsibility of power.

The great mass of the people, crushed by the sledgehammer blow of the 1940 Armistice, haunted by the need to recover the 1,500,000 young Frenchmen who were prisoners in Germany, to collect their scattered families, to face bravely all the misery of occupation — these masses, ignorant of what lay beneath the surface of events, placed their confidence almost universally in the "grand old man." Only a small number of the initiated were at work measuring the error of the Armistice, sounding the depths of the abyss into which France had fallen.

The immense majority of the members of Parliament judged that to Pétain, and Pétain alone — since he was responsible for the Armistice — should be reserved also the grave responsibility of its application. They saw in Pétain the man who had admitted — who had confirmed — defeat; but nothing at that time led them to see in him the major personage of a gigantic plot against France herself.

For many of those who had trusted at least Pétain's intentions, the *coup de théatre* of Montoire, in October 1940, was the first warning. Dumbfounded at the news of the handshake between Pétain and Hitler, they asked themselves: "Have we been mistaken? Have they fooled us? Who is this man?" Such was my case. Along with so many others, I began to suspect that Pétain was nothing but an end, a result. We began to see in the far-off past the beginnings of a deep-rooted plot. The Armistice and Montoire — defeat and collaboration — suddenly highlighted the conspiracy, and it became all too evident that it had been pursuing its course for years in the shadows. Recalling memories, putting facts together, gathering documents, we followed the thread painfully through the labyrinth of the past, and thus arrived at the sixth of February, 1934.

Let us follow this same thread in the reverse direction — from the Place de la Concorde on the night of the sixth of February, 1934, to Vichy in July 1940.

The riots of early February in 1934, in Paris, culminated in the tragedy of the night of the sixth. Popular indignation, not without instigation, was carried to a peak by the airing of a financial scandal which, at another time, and in another place, would have been simply the object of routine investigation and punishment by the courts. It fell to the lot of the Stavisky scandal to become a burning political issue. The noise around it, heavily accentuated by the elements of the fifth column (already at work) and by a small group of professional agitators of the Extreme Right, within a few hours transformed the center of Paris into Bedlam, and some 200,000 law-abiding Parisians into a ferocious rabble. The encounter between the public and the police was bloody; the consequences of the night were far-reaching, almost incalculable.

Serge Alexandre Stavisky, alias Alexandre, an embezzler of Slav origin with a jail record whom everybody knew as Alexandre and very few as Stavisky, had found a way of unloading upon certain banks and insurance companies in Paris several million francs' worth of bonds from the Municipal Loan Shops of Bayonne in the Pyrenees. He made the mistake of marketing them in excess of their value, was found out, prosecuted, bought himself off through his lawyers with nineteen court delays, fled toward Switzerland when the scandal broke, was stopped at Chamonix in France, and blew out his brains at the moment the police were tracking him down in his lonely chalet in the snow. A capital story for newspapermen, and almost made to order for fifth column propaganda. . . .

For it happened that the Mayor of the town of Bayonne — the seat of the embezzlement — was a Radical-Socialist, and so were several of Stavisky's lawyers. And like the Dreyfus Affair, which, at its inception, had nothing to do with the Jewish question but became in second instance a huge political controversy in which anti-Semitism was used as a pretext and a weapon, the Stavisky case waxed into a colossal political brawl in which the embezzler's crime seemed almost to disappear under the accusations and recriminations of the political personages involved or dragged in unwittingly.

What lent gravity to the situation on the night of the sixth of February was the fact that the manifestation which was scheduled was presumably to be sponsored by the associations of ex-servicemen. This fact alone complicated the role of the municipal authorities in their efforts to keep order in the city. The associations themselves, constantly divided by internal quarrels and personal rivalries, had hitherto failed to play any considerable role in political affairs. Suddenly they loomed large in the foreground.

On February 5, the *Union Nationale des Combattants* had passed a resolution accusing Parliament "of betraying from without the honor and interests of France, of violating the guarantees of liberty . . . substituting for the free expression of public opinion the calculations of private interests . . . of ruining the finances of the state, thus compromising the nation's integrity." Their declaration, widely published in the newspapers, had a rousing effect on the Parisians. To emphasize their resolution, the ex-servicemen planned to appear 20,000 strong before the doors of Parliament in an orderly demonstration on the following night, when the new Daladier Cabinet was to be voted in. Permission was refused them. They therefore decided to carry their resolution at that time to President Lebrun in the Presidential Palace, the Elysée.

The Place de la Concorde had been in the throes of disorder since three o'clock in the afternoon of the sixth. Large forces of *Gardes Mobiles* were patrolling all over the city; a strong police barrage had been thrown up around the Chamber of Deputies in the Palais-Bourbon, where the House was in session. The bridge leading from there across the Seine to the Place de la Concorde was guarded on the Concorde side, and from this point the crowds were attacked by the police when, after several hours of enduring from the rioters almost unbearable pelting with iron missiles and pieces of asphalt, the police opened fire on the *Solidarité Française,* a "patriotic society" which had just arrived 1500 strong with the avowed intention of taking the bridge by storm. Below were the dark waters of the Seine. One hardly dares to think what a gigantic holocaust of human lives was averted by the determined stand of the Paris guards and police that night.

The Royalist rabble-rousers and other professional agitators had been heckling the police for hours. There had been a taxicab strike in Paris for the last six days; furthermore, practically every bus and subway station in the center of the city had ceased to function at 6 P.M. The crowds leaving the big stores and the smaller shops naturally gravitated toward the great center of attraction, the Place de la Concorde and the Chamber of Deputies, in the shadows on the opposite banks of the Seine. The Parisian crowd is easily aroused. A few cuffs from the police and they're off. Thousands upon thousands of the participants in the demonstration of the sixth of February were onlookers, who, from time to time, became enraged, worked off their steam, and eventually went home to bed. But there were also acts of professional vandalism, like the burning of the autobus on the Place de la Concorde and the assault on the near-by Ministry of the Marine.

Toward seven o'clock, marching in close formation and all wearing berets as a sort of uniform, appeared the troops of Colonel de La Rocque's *Croix de Feu.* But their strategy on that dramatic evening astonished the police at the time, as it was later to astonish — and with reason — political observers and commentators. For the Colonel succeeded in carrying out a very clever military maneuver, which consists of appearing on the battlefield without coming in contact with the enemy, then disappearing without attracting his attention. Marching down from the Champs-Elysées, the troops of the Colonel-Count crossed the Place de la Concorde diagonally, and with remarkable speed — taking care not to get mixed up with any other group — turned left and followed the Quai des Tuileries as far as the Pont des Sts-Pères, crossed the Seine, marched up the Boulevard St-Germain, and massed themselves silently *behind* the Palais-Bourbon, where the Chamber was in session, while the riot continued in front of it and the other groups, which had rejoiced at the appearance of these reinforcements, were left nonplussed. Later on, at the time of the Tardieu-La Rocque trial, this singular strategy was recalled by those who doubted the complete independence of the Colonel as far as the government was concerned.

At 8:45 P.M., the *Union Nationale des Combattants,* having convened at the statue of Clemenceau near the Petit Palais, marched down the Champs-Elysées to the Place de la Concorde, twelve abreast, their flags in mass formation, their breasts covered with medals. They were marching "that France might live in honor and cleanliness." In spite of their appellation of "national," they comprised almost exclusively elements of the Center and Extreme Right. They were to encounter a feeble barrage of police at the entrance of the Place de la Concorde, brush it aside, proceed to the center of the square near the Obelisk, mark time, view the riotous scene before them, turn left and proceed up the Rue Royale toward the Faubourg St-Honoré.

At the head of the *Combattants* marched their president,

Jean Goy, Deputy of the Seine, a somewhat shady personage, always elected under difficulty and playing no particular role at the Chamber. He had, however, profited to
the maximum from his position as president of the veterans' group.

Hitler had assumed power in 1933. By November 1934,
the *Fuehrer* was receiving Jean Goy in Berlin — theoretically because of a wish to recognize the "sacrifice made
by the war veterans of both sides of the frontier." Hardly
had this happened when, on the first day of December
1934, Deputy Franklin-Bouillon, incensed, had denounced
in the Chamber the danger of these private meetings between French citizens and Nazi leaders. What Franklin-
Bouillon did not know then — although his loyalty and
his instinct had guided him in his speech — was that the
night before Jean Goy had given a sumptuous dinner in
honor of Oberlindober, president of the Nazi association of war veterans; and that Georges Scapini, Ribbentrop, and Otto Abetz had likewise been his guests that
night. Scapini, Deputy of Paris, blinded in the war of
1914–1918, had at first been an ardent nationalist, later
endorsed the policies of Gaston Bergery, and had finally
become the passionate advocate of Franco–German reconciliation.

To hide behind the war veterans, to use to conceal their
evil intentions the indisputable patriotism of the ex-
servicemen, was to say the least a diabolical conception
on the part of the pro-Germans; but to use the *blind*
Scapini in their plot was a maneuver of superbly ironic
infamy. Naturally, Hitler had hastened to declare to the
French veterans that he had no intentions of conquest to
the west, and to underline the necessity of a Franco–
German reconciliation which would be imposed upon the

two nations by pressure from "the comrades of the Great War."

An authentic Leftist democrat, a sort of pacifist simpleton, Henri Pichot, of the Federation of the Wounded Veterans, before 1936 had also made, in his turn, the pilgrimage to Berlin. Upon his return from his visit to Hitler, he had said in an interview: "We spoke freely together, quite like veterans of the front. . . ."

I was sitting in the Chamber of Deputies on that unforgettable evening of the sixth of February — while the rioters on the opposite bank of the Seine were winning the Battle of the Autobus from the harassed Parisian police force, and the autobus was flaring up like a ghastly torch, lighting the otherwise darkened scene; while a delegation of Rightist city aldermen, with a crowd of hoodlum Patriotic Youth tagging on behind, were endeavoring to get through the police barrage on the Quai d'Orsay and enter the Chamber of Deputies; while in the Chamber itself, Daladier, from the rostrum, was trying amid indescribable confusion to deliver the ministerial declaration and call for a vote of confidence.

I can still see the blind Deputy, Scapini, at the foot of the rostrum, shaking his fist in the direction of Daladier, accusing him of having given the order to fire into the crowd, and being shouted down with cries of "Fascist!"

Today, in 1944, Scapini is Pétain's Ambassador to Berlin. But what incredible trickster has placed the *blind* Scapini at the head of the Commission which is investigating the conditions of the French war prisoners in Germany?

Where are they now? The Deputy Philippe Henriot, who made the most of the Stavisky Affair at the tribune of the Chamber, is, together with Henri Béraud, journalist of the Extreme Right, the fiercest propagandist in the Nazi so-called "French Press." As for the Deputy Jean Goy, who died recently, he was to the last one of the most conspicuous collaborationists in Paris.

Certain politicians did not hesitate to exploit in the most cynical manner their experiences in the riots of the night of February 6. I remember one case in particular, which seems almost unbelievable.

The municipal elections of May 1935, in Paris, had returned a brand-new alderman to the district of the Ternes in the XVIIth Arrondissement. This district had regularly elected (for at least fifty years back) Bonapartists and ultrareactionary representatives. The newly elected alderman did not belie the tradition. He called himself Darquier de Pellepoix, although his right to the particle was more than doubtful. To tell the truth, his name was simply Darquier, and he hailed from a modest family in the Department of the Lot, in the Southwest.

Physically he was a big fellow approaching forty, well-set-up, monocled, and with something of the aspect of the classic Prussian officer — on the whole, he was rather displeasing.

A short time after his election he telephoned me one morning to inform me that he would very much like to pay me a visit and get better acquainted. As I was by far his senior in the Assembly, I asked him to lunch with me.

The fellow attacked brutally: —

"Look here," he said, "I've just gotten into the Municipal Council, and I don't know a thing about it. Most of our colleagues don't seem to be very intelligent. I've listened to a few of their speeches and they don't interest me very much. You, my dear President,* I know you from your record of political battles; you please me. I thought that you would be good enough to explain to me just what the Assembly is all about."

In view of the fellow's smoothness I became extremely cautious.

"It's quite natural, *mon cher collègue,* that in my capacity as a senior member of the council I should make an effort to guide you. It's like this . . ." And I proceeded to amuse myself by showing him in detail the truly complicated mechanism of municipal administration, and the rules and usage of our Assembly. I concluded: —

"And now, *mon cher collègue,* it is up to you to choose the branch of municipal activity to which you wish to devote yourself particularly — budget, transportation, highways, police . . ."

Darquier interrupted me: —

"*Mon cher Président,* you're unkind, you're making fun of me. There's only one thing that interests me — politics. The Municipal Council, which I have entered quite by chance, is for me simply a means to play at politics." He went on bluntly: "Look here, if you're going to understand me, I'd better tell you my story from the beginning."

And he proceeded to tell me, with unabashed cynicism, the following story: —

Having broken with his family, Darquier, penniless and seeking his fortune, had embarked some ten years before for Australia. There he met and married a young Englishwoman. He bought a sheep ranch with his wife's money and went in for breeding. This was profitable at first and he made money — which he promptly lost. At the end

* A term of address used for past as well as incumbent presidents of the Municipal Council.

of 1933 he was once again penniless, but in addition he was homesick, and he decided to return to France.

"Coming up from Marseille," he told me, "I landed in Paris at the Gare de Lyon on the morning of the sixth of February. I no longer knew anybody in Paris. I knew nothing about the political situation, absolutely nothing, and I would have been at a loss to say who was Premier. I wandered into a hotel on the Rue de Rivoli, jobless and exhausted, and I lay down on the bed in my room and went to sleep. Toward four in the afternoon I was awakened by the noise of enormous crowds in the Rue de Rivoli, all going in the direction of the Place de la Concorde. Since my head was aching, I decided to go out and get some fresh air and I went down into the street and followed the crowds.

"Arriving on the Place de la Concorde, I heard the crowds heckling Daladier, and I gathered that he was Premier. I asked the man next to me what it was all about. He replied that the war veterans were having a demonstration.

" 'About what?'

" 'Why Stavisky, of course,' the man replied, apparently indignant over my ignorance. That name, which I heard for the first time that night, didn't mean a thing to me.

"For several minutes I watched the scene before me. Policemen and rioters were face to face. When the police succeeded in surrounding a rioter, they pummeled him energetically. When the rioters were three to one against a policeman, they knocked him out. It didn't seem very sportsmanlike. . . . It began to bore me and I started to leave. All of a sudden a splendid-looking column of marchers coming from the Rond-Point des Champs-Elysées turned into the Place de la Concorde. They were four abreast, marching in time together, well in line

with their flags flying. That interested me and I went up
to them. I'm rather a big fellow, as you may have noticed,
mon cher Président," continued Darquier, adjusting his
monocle. "They pushed me up to the head of the pro-
cession. 'Forward, comrade, forward,' they cried. I got
in line ahead. Suddenly, the police, who were massed at
the head of the bridge, charged us in closed ranks. Fisti-
cuffs, gunfire. . . . I felt myself dripping with blood, I
fell, I was trampled on. . . . I came back to life two days
later in the hospital. I then learned by the papers that there
had been fourteen deaths on the side of the rioters on the
Place de la Concorde alone, and I was now among the
gloriously wounded.

"I remained at the hospital for three weeks, feeling
thoroughly bored, when one day I conceived the idea of
founding the 'Association of the Wounded of the Sixth of
February.' You know the rest."

I knew the rest, indeed. No sooner was he on his feet
than Darquier de Pellepoix, in his capacity as "President
of the Association of the Wounded of the Sixth of February" — of which he was the unique member — sought
out the curé of the Church of the Madeleine to ask him
to celebrate a Mass in memory of those who had died on
the sixth of February. The Mass was a great event; the
Church of the Madeleine was black with crowds; Darquier de Pellepoix, at the exit, received condolences
solemnly, imperturbably. The next day the entire Extreme-
Right press sang his praises. The following year, the May
elections gave him the district of the Ternes on a platter.

After our lunch-table conversation, I had no desire to
pursue my acquaintance with Darquier. Besides, the ad-
venturer hardly ever came to the Council. Penniless, living by day-to-day expedients, changing his quarters
every fortnight, he soon launched into anti-Semitism in

order to survive. He was Commissioner for Jewish Affairs in the government of Pierre Laval until, very recently, he was replaced by Charles du Paty de Clam — bearer of a name made sadly famous in the Dreyfus case.

The results of the riots of the sixth of February were tragically ironic: twenty dead in the city of Paris, and more than a thousand wounded. On the Place de la Concorde alone, fourteen rioters and one guard killed. In all, 1326 persons injured, of which 770 were guards and police, and 555 were rioters and innocent bystanders. These people were killed and wounded in order that France might live "in honor and cleanliness." Their protest was against "political immorality" — and the first result of the bloody demonstration was the return to power of Pierre Laval — the most immoral of politicians.

Laval's strategy had been simple. He had kept himself in the background during the entire Stavisky scandal. Presumably, he had had nothing to do with the riots. The mask which he was wearing on his ugly face was one of virtue. Early on the afternoon of the seventh of February he walked into the office of President Lebrun, followed by several members of Parliament. Among them was Jean Goy, his head bandaged — apparently from an injury of the night before (although no one could tell for sure whether he had been wounded or not). Jean Goy proceeded to threaten President Lebrun with a new demonstration that night if Daladier, whom he held responsible for giving the order to shoot, did not resign immediately.

Lebrun, who looked tired and despondent, was silent for a while, then lifted up his head and remarked: —

"M. Daladier has just sent me his resignation."

Laval, who was sitting near the President's desk, then asked him: —

"Mr. President, will you permit me to make a phone call?"

President Lebrun nodded and told Laval that he would find a telephone in the next room. Laval took the receiver and asked Long Distance for Tournefeuille — the country retreat of the former President of the Republic, M. Gaston Doumergue. . . .

The following morning, Doumergue, old and tired, returned to Paris to assume the premiership which had been relinquished by Daladier. With a great benevolent grandfatherly smile he beamed on the crowds of Parisians, hysterical with joy, who met him at the station of the Quai d'Orsay — crowds which only two days before had been milling around in the streets of Paris, ill-tempered and the easy prey of professional agitators. But while Doumergue became Premier and the ostensible head of the new Cabinet, Laval, working behind the scenes, was its moving spirit.

I do not believe that sufficient emphasis has ever been placed on the fact that the Doumergue coup by Laval in 1934 was purely and simply a rehearsal of the Pétain coup by the same man in 1940.

Laval availed himself of the scandal in 1934, as he availed himself of the defeat of 1940, to push into office an old man enjoying a large popularity, and, behind that shield of honorable respectability, to march to power. Both cases show the same technique, the same hypocrisy, the same craft of the same man. But while Gaston Doumergue, loyally, hesitated before the *coup d'état,* Pétain, with Laval to back him and the German troops of occupation ready to prevent rebellion, accomplished it. The cup of shame which the tempting devil offered him, he, Philippe Pétain, Marshal of France, drank to the dregs.

*   *   *

The World War veterans were thus moved around on the complex checkerboard of Nazi propaganda like the most ordinary pawns, and with the most consummate dexterity. But their moves had been prepared by a certain Traitor No. 1.

I had known Fernand de Brinon some twenty years back, when he was hardly more than a country squire out of work and feeling his way. He was generally seen in the bars and at the race tracks, accompanied by Robert de Beauplan — same attributes, same profession. Brinon, nephew of the Comte de Nalèche, director of the antiquated and conservative *Journal des Débats,* was authentically of the small nobility of France; Beauplan, whose particle nobody had gone out of his way to examine, let it be whispered about that he was the illegitimate son of a prince of Holland. Physically and morally the two resembled each other. Physically: face like the prow of a ship, sly sidelong expression, hair lustrously smooth, the bearing and doubtful elegance of a gigolo. Morally: an immense appetite for money, and — not a scruple.

Beauplan, a mediocre individual, is today editor of *L'Illustration,* which has become the pro-Nazi weekly par excellence; Brinon is officially Pétain's representative in Paris, and actually Hitler's ambassador to Pétain.

Successively race-track reporter to the *Débats,* then editor-of-all-trades on the financial sheet *L'Information,* our Brinon, always in need of money, was still feeling his way along when his marriage to a wealthy Jewess brought a solution to his financial problems.

Practically at the same time he suddenly passed from obscurity into political notoriety by the publication, in the *Matin* of November 22, 1933, of a sensational interview with Hitler. Hitler, according to Brinon, denied that he had any designs on Alsace-Lorraine, rose up in wrath against the idea of a war between France

and Germany—which, he insisted, could only serve
the cause of Bolshevism—and terminated his interview
thus: "You face a Germany nine tenths of which fully
trusts its leader; and this leader says to you: 'Let us be
friends.'"

A few weeks after this Brinon published the book
France-Allemagne. Herein he launched for the first time
the formula of "the European mission of Hitler." "France-
Germany" was to become, the following year, the name of
the Committee which was to devote itself to reconciliation with the Reich; and the furtherance of the "European
mission" (the "New Order" being still unformulated) was
to be its program. The France–Germany Committee
functioned until the spring of 1939. Following the annexation of Czechoslovakia, several of its directors—
either through fear or through remorse—proposed its
dissolution; but this action was taken entirely against the
opinion of M. Henry-Haye, who declared himself in
favor of its maintenance. Henry-Haye was an old friend
of Pétain—he had tried hard to work up enthusiasm for
Pétain as a presidential candidate in the last elections—
and he was to become, in 1940, Vichy's Ambassador to
Washington. The list of the other directors of the Committee reads like a roster of Vichy's leading lights; most of
them have been suitably rewarded with embassies, ministerial portfolios, and other important posts.

Brinon, as head of the Committee, was the chief of
Nazi propaganda in France, but he had a German boss:
Otto Abetz.

In 1939, Otto Abetz was thirty-five. He came from a
good Catholic family of Hanover. He visited France for
the first time in 1931, when he took part in a Youth Congress. Here he met several French journalists of his own
generation, among them Jean Luchaire—today installed

by the Germans at the head of the Syndicate of the French Press in Paris.

Abetz loudly proclaimed his faith in National Socialism, and sought assiduously to convert his French associates. Suddenly seized with a passionate love of France, he decided to live there permanently, and married a young woman from the Department of the Nord, Suzanne de Brouckère. He then organized in Berlin, with the blessings and support of the Nazi authorities, the German twin to the France–Germany Committee. When, in February 1938, Ribbentrop became Germany's Minister of Foreign Affairs, Otto Abetz was appointed his personal representative at Paris.

It must be admitted that with that faculty of adaptation which is so characteristic of the Germans, Abetz soon became exceedingly Parisian — in the worst sense of the word. He was seen at Montmartre, in Montparnasse, at the Académie Française — in all the ill-famed places. He also became very rapidly the friend of Bergery, Déat, and Doriot.

By 1936 the Brinon–Abetz team — Brinon thenceforth became to patriots "M. von Brinontrop" — was solidly harnessed up and well in the hands of Ribbentrop and Goebbels, well-provided with funds, and ready to get to work.

It was Hitler himself who gave the signal for the opening of the great campaign, in his Frankfort speech of May 16, 1936: —

"We no longer have a hereditary enemy! People of Germany, is it your desire to oppress the people of France or to deprive them of their rights? The answer of the people of Germany is 'No! We do not wish such a thing!' "

The future collaborationists — the future participants in the Franco–German kiss — settled down to work.

*   *   *

Cleverly woven into the plot, the war veterans were only the advance guard. The ranks of the troops comprised five solid and principal elements: men of business and finance; denizens of French society; a large part of the press; some of the pacifists of the Left; and a group of parliamentarians. The Extreme-Right agitators played, in the background, the role of rabble-rousers and *agents provocateurs,* and were charged with whipping up the zeal of the lukewarm, exalting the excited, and exploiting the most insignificant occasions to cause confusion.

Hitler was enjoying only his second year of personal power in February 1934. A united France, entirely devoted to its rearmament, could have, with the minimum of aid from her former allies, held him in hand. The land must be divided at all costs, social troubles must spring up to compromise industrial output and, in consequence, retard war production. France must, above all, be made to fall out with her allies. An ambitious pro-fascist politician at the head of the government was the best guarantee of success, and Laval was the best man for the place.

Laval, a slacker in the first World War, totally lacking in physical courage, had failed, as we have seen, to show himself during the troubled period of the February riots as long as there were blows to receive and responsibilities to assume. He rushed forward, however, to reap the benefits of the disturbances. We have seen with what highhanded smoothness he arranged Doumergue's return to power.

But Doumergue, as later Pétain, was only a screen. His Ministry of "National Union" was there only for the purpose of preparing the way for Laval.

As early as November 8, 1934, Doumergue, well-intentioned but far too feeble, was on his way back to his country retreat at Tournefeuille. Laval, as Minister of Foreign Affairs in the Flandin Cabinet, and as Premier from June 7, 1935, until January 22, 1936, had ample time to flirt at leisure with Italy and do his utmost to compromise the situation between France and Great Britain. He was a stubborn Anglophobe by temperament and by ignorance, and he was never to pardon the British for checkmating him and forcing his retirement from the government at the time of the Ethiopian conflict.

At the height of the Ethiopian affair — in November 1935 — there occurred a small incident which to me was extremely revealing.

Léon Guerdan had been organizing for several years a series of lectures on politics in the Théâtre des Ambassadeurs. They had been extremely successful. This season Guerdan asked me to be the antagonist of Philippe Henriot in a debate on "British Friendship vs. Italian Friendship."

I made the mistake of accepting. I say "mistake" deliberately, because Henriot was the most sectarian, the most narrowminded, the most maliciously aggressive of adversaries. He served up all the old wornout formulas of exaggerated Anglophobia, dragged out the old Bolshevik Bogy, went into ecstatic praises of Mussolini and Laval. But the amazing part of the business was the extent to which he carried the audience with him. They swallowed all his arguments — which appealed to chauvinism and class prejudice rather than common sense — hook, line, and sinker; and I had the impression that I, although known as a moderate, had suddenly become suspect to my bourgeois audience simply because of the point of view I presented.

The defeat of the Hoare–Laval pact in the Parliaments of both London and Paris at the time of the Ethiopian affair forced Laval into retirement, but the clumsy and reactionary policy which he had had time to install had imposed new sacrifices upon all the lower-income groups. This policy was to bear fruit, for it paved the way for the Popular Front.

The May 1936 elections carried Léon Blum to power, ranged the Right elements of the country against the Left in new and violent conflicts, and fulfilled all the conditions favorable to the blossoming forth of the plot.

The most powerful argument of the conspirators was "the great fear" which haunted the French bourgeois: the imbecilic fear of losing everything which he possessed. The part of the bourgeoisie in the plot was mostly unconscious; it did not amount to open treason, of course, but it none the less brought the most effective help to those who held the threads of the conspiracy in their hands.

The *petite bourgeoisie,* the middle class, backbone of the country, had incontestably preserved all its traditional good qualities. The *haute bourgeoisie* was, of course, not corrupt as a whole; but there is no doubt that many of the most privileged, of those most in the public eye, failed gravely in their duty. They should have constituted themselves a veritable elite and, following a national tradition dating from Colbert, they should have given France a large portion of her best public servants. But while the famous governmental schools for engineers, financiers and diplomats, the Ecole Polytechnique and the Ecole des Sciences Politiques, continued to graduate brilliant students, these students, all too often, resigned from a career in governmental service as soon as they had made useful contacts and had acquired a reputation. Crossing to the other side of the fence, they used the acquaintances and relationships which they had acquired during their governmental careers for the profit of private interests, often to the detriment of the state. Thus, inspectors of public utilities became directors of private utility companies; governmental inspectors of finance became directors of private banks.

With a few rare and meritorious exceptions, the bankers had totally lost the sense of their social role. The fact that the innumerable governmental loans were subscribed to by the general public over bank counters insured the banks a virtual monopoly of public investments; it gave them at the same time a redoubtable influence over the politics of the country, and they drew from it tremendous profits. They scarcely bothered to exert their efforts in any other direction, and devoted the greater part of their activity to multiplying profits a hundredfold by investing them in the mighty international cartels.

A careful study of small business ventures ceased to interest them. It was not unusual to witness an honest small-businessman seeking justifiable financial aid in vain, while a shady financier would obtain without the slightest difficulty a loan of 50,000,000 francs from the Bank of France, which loan was destined to double his capital at a single stroke. The banking profession had become a profession for the lazy-minded.

This neglect of their social role by the big banks left the way open to adventurers and sharks. These individuals fell upon the public at large — the people of small means — and, far from being the helpful guides of the thrifty, became their despoilers.

Not only did many of the intellectuals of the *haute bourgeoisie* show a shocking lack of social conscience, but great numbers of the rank-and-file citizens who had no special claim to distinction other than money were fatally short-sighted even in their attempts to protect their own interests. False "conservatives" that they were, they remained blind to the real social revolution which was going on around them; apparently they lacked the elementary intelligence to ensure their own security by proposing, themselves, the necessary changes. They ignored the maxim of Disraeli which should have been the rule of their class: "To conserve is to maintain and to reform"; with blind and ferocious egotism they stuck only to the motto: "Maintain!"

Businessmen and bankers were satisfied with putting the motto into practice. But there were also the *gens du monde,* the society idlers — conceited, useless, the plague of every land. They were reckless enough to express themselves openly. The fearful Bogy, the "Man with the Knife between His Teeth," was on the march. Down with him by all means — "Better Hitler than Stalin!" Some even said, "Better Hitler than Blum!"

These blind conservatives were only a minority, but a minority waging a very harmful influence.

For one thing, they had full control of a very large portion of the press.

For powerful capitalists or industrialists, the purchase of a newspaper was an investment that paid twofold. They could put into the enterprise some of the excess profits which the government would otherwise have taken; and by controlling public opinion they were able to exercise pressure on the government which could be of direct benefit to their business. Such a conception of journalism produced some remarkable effects. There was the case of *L'Œuvre,* for instance. For years it was a liberal and republican Parisian daily read chiefly by Leftist intellectuals; then it was bought by a wealthy cognac king who hired Marcel Déat as his chief editorial writer. Gradually the paper went over to the most outrageous form of fascism; and it was there that Déat published, a few weeks before hostilities opened, his famous article called "Shall We Die for Danzig?"

In such a setting, German bribe-money was in clover.

Six weeks before the war Louis Aubin, one of the editors of *Le Temps,* and Jules Poirier, publicity director of *Le Figaro,* were arrested together with Jean-Gaston Amourette, an Extreme-Left Socialist, who was later convicted of having tried to obtain funds for the establishment of a "revolutionary" daily. Aubin and Poirier confessed to having been in contact with the German government through the intermediary of a man named Léon Hirsch, who had been arrested at the same time as they, together with a Baroness von Einem, a spy of the German aristocracy and relative of a German general who had commanded an army in France in 1914–1918. Unfortunately, the Baroness escaped.

Aubin and Poirier were indicted. They were also accused of having obtained control of a motion-picture concern, Pathé-Nathan, for purposes of propaganda. They admitted having received money — Aubin 1,000,000 francs and Poirier 3,500,000 — from the hands of the Germans.

It was obvious, with the arrest on the same day of two Rightist editors and a Socialist of the Extreme Left, that French justice was loyally on the march through the maze of fifth-column activity that Nazi money and propaganda had planted in France. The network of corruption and insinuation woven through the country by Hitler was complete. He had the needed accomplices in every corner of the land and above all among the two extremes, the Extreme Right and the Extreme Left. This design — the play of the one against the other, their alternate joining and severing — is the chief characteristic of the conspiracy and is seen all the way up to the *dénouement.*

To the Right, Hitler exploited "the great fear" entertained by the French bourgeois; to the Left he exploited
the gullible pacifism of the antimilitarists. Among the
latter was the trade-union leader Belin, Assistant Secretary General of the C.G.T., who was to receive as his
reward the post of Labor Minister in the Vichy government. And there were also Socialist henchmen of Paul
Faure, long-time rival of Léon Blum.

Again, one cannot say that these men were traitors,
but it is all too certain that the position which they had
taken, of appeasement at any price, and the propaganda
which they caused to exist under the circumstances, fitted
only too well into the scheme of others who were real
traitors.

Jacques Doriot, erstwhile Communist, was unquestion-
ably among the latter. A man with the physique of a Her-
cules, a broad face crowned by an abundant shock of black
hair, the hands of a butcher, a powerful voice, an incontestable gift for mass oratory — he was known as "Big
Jack" at the time when he shared the leadership of the
Communist Party in France with Maurice Thorez and
Jacques Duclos.

"Big Jack" obeyed the orders of the Comintern, inside
France and out. In 1926 he went to Morocco with the
avowed purpose of encouraging Abd-el-Krim's resistance
to France. He must still have on his conscience the
criminal responsibility of the lives of many of our young
soldiers killed in the Riff War.

As long as he was a Communist, Doriot would not permit any competition in the Party's leadership. He was
especially jealous of Thorez, his chief rival, a younger
man who nevertheless shared his gift for moving the
crowd. Doriot was greedy, however, for money and
power, and, in spite of the political doctrines he pro-

fessed, he was very sensitive to that sort of middle-class respectability which consists of being received in the "right" drawing-rooms and being seen by the "right" kind of people.

In 1936 he was re-elected as the Communist Deputy from St-Denis, a workmen's suburb of Paris which he had represented in Parliament for several years. Not long after, there was a senatorial election in the Department of the Seine and Laval was a candidate. His election seemed doubtful, and Doriot's influence with the St-Denis delegates was indispensable to him (for Doriot was not only Deputy of St-Denis but Mayor of the Township). Laval and Doriot lunched together in the luxurious Lapérouse restaurant. Doriot offered himself for sale and Laval bought him. From that day on the two men were intimately bound together; and from that day on Doriot led a gay life. In the salons of Paris, beautiful ladies fought together over this fashionable freak.

During the "phony" war Doriot, who had been called up as a private, was stationed at Senlis. He offered his services to Daladier for the purpose of informing him on the Communists in the army. Daladier refused to see him and turned down the renegade's proposition in contemptuous disgust. Not long after, however, the Germans accepted his services and he now rivals Laval in their favor. And the panic-stricken bourgeois, the despicable and pitiful victims of the Bogy, cluster around the two gangsters in Paris today.

All these appeasers threw down their masks during the Munich crisis.

In *Le Populaire* of September 18, 1938, Paul Faure denounced preventative wars, "of which we have always opposed the principle and the practice."

At the same time the Federation of the Socialist Party posted an antiwar and revolutionary placard on the walls of Paris and its suburbs.

On September 27 the Teachers' Union and the National Union of Postal, Telephone and Telegraph Employees placed huge posters all over France with the inscription, "We do not want war!"

They spoke exactly the same language as *L'Action Française,* which featured in a box at the top of the front page a parody of the "Internationale," including the admonition: "And if these cannibals insist on making heroes of us, our first bullets must strike Mandel, Blum and Reynaud!"

The camp of the appeasers naturally had its supporters in Parliament. It comprised a group of some thirty parliamentarians, in which there were Extreme Rightists, like Scapini and Tixier-Vignancourt; so-called Independents, like Bergery; Neo-Socialists, like Marquet, Frot, Gonin and Deschizeaux; and Socialists like René Brunet, Spinasse, and Paul Rives. This group, on September 2, 1939, dared lodge a protest in the hands of Daladier "against the French and British intransigeance," manifested by the governments' refusal to participate in an international conference (proposed by Italy) until German troops withdrew from Polish territory!

As early as 1936, the headquarters of the frightened fascists had renounced all attempts at straightening out the French political situation by the simple process of holding elections. Hope was gone unless a high-handed stroke — a new sixth of February, a new edition and a more happy one of the "Doumergue coup" — could be effected.

But they needed a man for that. Doumergue had been

a stuffed shirt; the next time it must be an authentic great man, one who had both prestige and popularity; but a great man, too, whose political acumen and experience would be sufficiently slight to render indispensable the tutelage of Laval — who (it was fully understood) would stand behind this august personage and be the real dictator.

It did not take long to choose. One man filled all these qualifications to perfection — Pétain.

Pétain, although of modest origin and something of a parvenu, embodied the spirit of the conservative to the maximum. To be convinced of this it was enough to hear him talk about his "estate" of Villeneuve-Loubet, and to witness the crabbedness with which he picked over his accounts with his farmer in the presence of his associates.

Pétain's career until the war of 1914-1918 had been totally commonplace. The pointed candor of his most important, and most recent, biographer, General Laure, Chief of his Military Cabinet, emphasizes the fact that at each stage of his career, Pétain owed his advancement to seniority. When World War I broke out, he was about to be retired with the rank of Colonel.

Pétain was never an aggressive type — he did not have the qualities of a Mangin or a Gouraud. Clemenceau wrote in his memoirs: "If I chose Foch it was because I was sure that, at least with him, we would die sword in hand!" And he traced in retrospect a striking picture of Pétain's pessimism. Poincaré and Foch both offered the same testimony as to Pétain's attitude in April 1918 — six months before victory, Pétain was talking about an armistice!

Pétain won his fame at Verdun, a long battle for position wherein the gains were reckoned in meters. It was above all an affair of organization and patience. These were Pétain's most characteristic qualities. He had the patience, the cunning prudence of the peasantry to which he belongs. He was much more an administrator, a handler of men, than a fighter. He was particular, attentive to the needs of the soldier, sparing of human lives, and paternal. These qualities served him admirably when the time came, after the wave of mutiny in 1917, to build up the morale of the French private. That was undoubtedly the greatest service he rendered in the war of 1914–1918, and it placed him henceforth in the foremost rank.

After victory Pétain, having been made Marshal, was covered with honors; but he himself added a very manifest vanity to his laurels. Contrary to the example of Foch and Joffre, he never retired into obscurity. He was delighted to hear his name on all sides, and he never missed an opportunity to show himself in public.

In 1926 he was given the relatively easy task of putting an end to the rebellion in Morocco, and his successful completion of the mission still further increased his fame.

About that time a curious development occurred in his character; his ambition assumed a new form — a literary form. He began signing articles in the *Revue des Deux Mondes* — articles which his friends prepared for him — and he allowed himself to be nominated for a seat in the Académie Française. The influence of the *Revue des Deux Mondes* and the Academy on Pétain was tremendous. During the same period, the Marshal, formerly a professed agnostic, began to cultivate certain prominent prelates. He accentuated his conscious orientation toward the Right.

His nomination to the War Ministry in the Doumergue Cabinet, in February 1934, was his first experience with politics. It was disastrous.

He began by showing an almost obsequious deference

to the members of Parliament, but in spite of all his efforts he was never able to get along with them. His War
Ministry was a failure from every point of view, and
the result was that it created in his mind a growing
resentment against the parliamentarians, which the
events of 1940 were to give him the opportunity of
avenging.

But his experience in the government did give him a
passion for politics. It was now that he began to conceive a
possible role for himself: he began discussing more and
more with his friends the need of reform, of setting morals
straight; he felt himself attracted to the young people
of the country, and he believed that his work would be
accomplished by means of these.

Some months after the Armistice of 1940 Fernand
Bouisson, former President of the Chamber of Deputies,
told me a story which showed how far this obsession had
gone, even in 1935. In May of that year, after the Flandin
Ministry fell, Bouisson was asked to form a new Cabinet
(a Cabinet which, as it turned out, did not survive its
initial presentation to Parliament). "That day," Bouisson
said to me, "I got one of the shocks of my life. I naturally
offered Pétain the War portfolio. He refused it; and do
you know what he asked me for? The Ministry of Public
Instruction!"

I hardly shared Bouisson's astonishment. Pétain's demand at that time was the logical development of Pétain's
mind. He had now conceived his "moral order." From
that moment on, the reactionary plotters began to plan
the role which they were to make him play, and the
manner in which they would capitalize on his prestige.

The vanity, the harsh peasantlike ambition, of the
parvenu Marshal served these plotters admirably. Pétain
was, of course, not a "dictator in spite of himself." For my

part I am convinced that he was at this point in a fair way to become a "dictator without knowing it."

Pétain was, in addition, an Anglophobe, which quality dovetailed admirably with Laval's policy. Pétain did not hide his Anglophobia — he published it far and wide. While War Minister in 1934, he made a speech at Meaux on Sunday afternoon, September 9, commemorating the battle of the Marne. On that occasion he referred successively to ". . . the British, whose solidarity with regard to us combines with a healthy realization of their personal interests . . ." and to ". . . our brothers the Italians, dreaming of a friendship which seems to be the perpetual sign of our relationship . . ."

The fascist plotters knew of Pétain's Anglophobia. They remembered too that in May 1935 the Marshal had represented the French government during the funeral ceremonies of Marshal Pilsudski at Warsaw, and that numerous witnesses of the scene had been struck by his excessive friendliness for Goering. As early as 1937, in well-informed salons, "Pétain Cabinets" were actually being formed, with anticipatory lists of Ministers duly drawn up. The year before this there had appeared a pamphlet by one Gustave Hervé, entitled *C'est Pétain Qu'il Nous Faut!* (*It's Pétain We Need!*) Its title could hardly fail to recall to the older generation of Frenchmen, at least, the refrain of the Boulangists' marching song, "*C'est Boulanger qu'il nous faut.*"

Hervé, a French journalist who had been a fierce anti-militarist before World War I, and who had succeeded in getting himself condemned to prison for shouting that the flag should be "buried in dung," later suffered a spectacular conversion. He became a super-patriot, and from 1914 to 1918 published a newspaper called *La Victoire*. When peace was signed after World War I,

La Victoire dwindled to a single sheet with very few readers.*

Undoubtedly various interesting documents will come to light with the freeing of France. Among these will be some that will establish that the pamphlet *It's Pétain We Need!* was edited in collaboration with the Prima press agency, and it will be confirmed incontestably that there is a close connection between the Prima agency and Ferdonnet, the "traitor of Stuttgart" — the French Lord Haw-Haw. Another mesh of the plot will appear.

The gratitude of the French toward the veterans who fought and won the war of 1914–1918 had crystallized around the name of Pétain, and legend had created his halo. To capitalize on Pétain, to the profit of defeatism — that was the crux of the plot.

From the birth of the Popular Front, Pétain, who had remained Vice President of the Superior War Council, received increasingly numerous visits and solicitations from all sides, sometimes at his office in the Invalides, often discreetly at the home of his friend Alibert. While the French people, driven to desperation by financial waste and perplexing social problems, were becoming more and more divided, the propertied classes, blind to everything but their own interests, clung to their patrimonies and turned more and more toward the man of Verdun as to a possible savior.

Prudent, incrusted in that cold dignity which is one of his great forces, Pétain listened to all propositions and reserved comment.

An extraordinary fatality — one of those errors which

* But it continued to exist — on money whose sources were never explained — and in 1935 it published the draft of a proposed new French Constitution which was obviously inspired by the regimes of Berlin and Rome.

history fails to explain — made of the unhappy Daladier (an unquestionable patriot) the tool which precipitated events. Daladier named Pétain Ambassador to Madrid in February 1939.

Perhaps in so doing he wished to draw Pétain away from Paris. For it was in 1938 that the famous affair of the *Cagoule* exploded. The *Cagoule,* the sinister black hood with which the conspirators of an earlier and more romantic day used to cover their heads, had given rise to the name "the *Cagoulards,*" which the conspirators in this instance pinned upon themselves. Their function and object, as a revolutionary organization of the Extreme Right, was to break by force the power of the Popular Front.

Full light has never been thrown on the *Cagoule.* But it was known at the time that it comprised a central group called the C.S.A.R. (*Comité Secret d'Action Révolutionnaire*), disposing of important armaments of suspicious origin, and that this group had ramifications among the staff officers of Pétain. One of them was Major Loustalot-Lacaud, leader of the numerous *Cagoulards* in the army, and formerly the Marshal's orderly during his term as Minister of War in the Doumergue Cabinet. With these facts in hand, Premier Daladier was forced to abandon the idea of dissolving the band publicly, because of the very immensity of the scandal, and perhaps preferred to withdraw Pétain from the scene.

Pétain thus left for Madrid in February 1939, but two months later he returned to Paris for mysterious consultations with his political associates. In May of the same year, the seven-year presidential term of M. Albert Lebrun drew to its close. Henry-Haye dreamed of making Pétain President of the Republic, and began a concentrated campaign in that direction, in the halls of Parliament. Lebrun, however, was supported by Daladier, and agreed to run for re-election. Pétain then declined to become a candidate. Nevertheless, among the 900 votes cast at the National Assembly, 14 ballots were found marked with his name.

The real Pétain emerged in the Embassy at Madrid, and blossomed in the dictatorial atmosphere of the Franco regime. The role of Ambassador gave the Marshal's vanity a puerile and intense satisfaction.

As for the defense of French interests, his ambassadorship proved a disaster. He was incapable of following affairs himself and he prevented his technical advisers from working freely. He intended to be neither advised nor controlled.

He made the acquaintance of the German military attaché at the table of the Spanish Minister of Foreign Affairs, Jordana, and he had a long conversation with the German *en tête-à-tête*.

The coming of war found him still in Madrid — or rather at San Sebastián, where, under pretext of his failing health, he had transported his Embassy and was receiving visits from numerous Frenchmen. By autumn, Pietri, former Minister of the Navy and a notorious Municher (today he is Pétain's successor at Madrid), had gone to see him. Returning to Paris, Pietri reported in conversations with his friends (other Munichers) that Pétain had a most pessimistic attitude toward the issue of the war. "Before long," it appears Pétain had said to him, "before long, they'll need me." Anatole de Monzie, in a book called *Les Ci-Devant* which he published in occupied France in 1941, reported an even more specific prophecy on Pétain's part: he says that Pétain called on him at the Ministry of Public Works on March 30, 1940, and told him: "They will need me in the second half of May."

On May 10, the Germans bore down on France through the breach of Sedan. Paul Reynaud, wishing to give the French some sort of reassurance in the immensity of the gulf that was opening, committed the final error: he called Weygand and Pétain to power on May 18. When he arrived in Paris, Pétain was already prepared for the Armistice!

CHAPTER IX

The Army of Yesterday

IMMEDIATELY after the Armistice of 1940, the Vichy government decided to hold the trial of the political and military figures on whom it wished to lay the responsibility of defeat. Not all the accused were then in France, but there remained, as defendants, former Premier Edouard Daladier, former Premier Léon Blum, former Commander in Chief Maurice Gamelin, former Controller General of the Army Pierre Jacomet, and former Minister of Aviation Guy La Chambre. They were to be judged by a court sitting at Riom, near Vichy. The trial finally began on February 19, 1942, but it had to be stopped in April, by order of the Germans, because it had ceased to be the trial of the political leaders of the French Republic to become — as was terrifyingly obvious — the trial of the military chiefs of the French army — above all, of Marshal Pétain.*

Fully conscious of their guilt, these military chiefs had found no better means to avoid being judged than to set themselves up as judges. The first care of the government they had formed and dominated was to discredit the politicians. They had instituted the Riom trial to try to prove that the war had been lost for lack of armaments, and they wished to pin the blame for this on the Ministers and on Parliament. (It is significant that the only military commander they indited was General

---

*Yet the accused, who had become the accusers, were not released; they are still in prison either in France or in Germany.

Gamelin, who had been relieved of his post before the Armistice.)

It is true that in 1939 France lacked modern armaments — particularly planes and tanks. But the causes of this deficiency were more complicated than the instigators of the Riom trial would have liked to pretend, and the evidence brought forward at the trial pointed firmly to the conclusion that it was the military chiefs themselves, and not the Ministers, who were principally responsible for it.

The politicians taken to task for the lack of armaments were those who had been in power in the years since 1936, when, after the reoccupation of the Rhineland, preparedness had been universally recognized as the most important issue in French politics. The prosecution cited the disappointing level of armament production during these years, attributed it to Blum's labor policies, represented Blum as a greater friend of union labor than of his country, condemned the Parliament which had kept him in power and, by implication, the democratic system it represented.

Blum, in his defense, reminded the court that whatever else might be said, production under the Popular Front had compared favorably with that of preceding years. To this the obvious — and justifiable — reply was of course that in such a time of emergency there was no excuse for not using every possible means to bring production up to a maximum. But on one point the defense presented unanswerable evidence — evidence that so embarrassed the prosecution as to make it necessary to suspend the trial: most of the modern arms we did have had been obtained at the instigation of the government and Parliament, *without the suggestion and sometimes against the wishes of the military chiefs.*

Take the question of tanks, for instance. It had been generally supposed that in tanks the French army was not only outnumbered, but overwhelmingly outnumbered, by the German army. Yet the debate at Riom on March 31, 1942, between M. Daladier and General Keller, former inspector of tanks, brought out the fact that, in May 1940, France had about 3250 tanks (and Great Britain 600) against Germany's 5250. To witnesses who criticized the inadequate number of our tanks M. Daladier pertinently pointed out that in 1934, when Marshal Pétain was Minister of War, the army had almost no modern matériel and that practically all the tanks in existence had been ordered by Daladier himself. General Keller was obliged to admit that in 1936 we did not have a single modern tank.

This situation was typical. It has been remarked with a good deal of justice that between 1918 and 1939 England and the United States prepared for no war, Germany and Japan prepared for the new World War, and France prepared for the old World War. Why? Because, along with her other difficulties, she had the added misfortune of having an antiquated General Staff, of which Marshal Pétain was the highest and most responsible representative. Pétain was Inspector General of the Army from 1922 to 1931, then Inspector of Aviation from 1931 to 1934, then Minister of War from February to November 1934; furthermore, ever since the last war, he had been Vice President of the War Council, the *Conseil Supérieur de la Guerre*. Thus, continuously, and with a prestige that gave him the highest authority, he presided over the destinies of our armies between the two wars.

On March 7, 1934, during the time when he was Minister of War, he told the Senate Military Committee: "Under present conditions, we cannot increase the length of military service, for Parliament will not consent to it. Perhaps the situation does not seem sufficiently serious, though in reality it is."

But he did not actually present the question to Parliament for a vote.

M. Daniel-Vincent, Vice President of the Committee, and several other members called the Marshal's attention to the necessity of protecting the coal mines of the Department of the Nord. Pétain replied: "We are not much interested in second lines of defense, for we are quite resolved to move forward. It is not our intention to fight on the frontier. We shall protect Lille, but not by fortifications in France. *Lille will be protected by fortifications in Belgium.*" (These fortifications existed already; the French army had used them in 1914.)

In June 1936 — three months after the German reoccupation of the Rhineland — I became a member of the Military Affairs Committee of the Chamber of Deputies. I felt it my duty to go immediately to see Pétain in his office at the Invalides. He seemed astonished at my visit; he turned his rather vague blue eyes on me and said, in a slow, tired voice: —

"*Monsieur le Député,* I know you by reputation and am happy to receive you, but to what do I owe the honor of your call?"

"*Monsieur le Maréchal,* the reason is a quite natural one. I have just been made a member of the Military Affairs Committee, and before getting down to work I wanted to pay my respects to you as the highest-ranking member of the army."

The Marshal was visibly astonished.

"I am deeply touched. . . . But this is the first such visit I have ever received."

"Really? I am sorry — both for the army and for Parliament."

"Parliament . . . Parliament . . ."

He did not finish his sentence; his tone expressed only too clearly his old bitterness against Parliament.

As I kept silent, he continued more brusquely: —

"Well, what do you want of me?"

"For myself, nothing; for my country and the army, a great deal."

I explained to him briefly how important I considered my job on the Committee to be. He was the highest-ranking officer in the army; his advice would be invaluable to me. Obviously he needed to be kept informed about the views of Parliament and the work of the Committee; I offered to call on him regularly and give him such information (a suggestion which he told me later — after the Armistice — he had been wrong not to accept).

First, I wanted to know what he thought about the law, passed just after the reoccupation of the Rhineland, increasing the length of military service to two years. Under the circumstances, did he think this term sufficient — or did he think the problem should be brought up again? My question obviously annoyed him.

"I do not know what the intentions of the government are. I have not been consulted."

"*Monsieur le Maréchal,* in your position, do you have to wait to be consulted?"

Then I asked the Marshal what he thought about fortifications: "Shall I consider, *Monsieur le Maréchal,* that the terms of the problem of fortifications are still the same?"

The answer was quick, almost sharp: —

"I have no reason to change my opinion."

Whatever else may be said against the French Parlia-

ment, as far as national defense was concerned it did not
fail in its double duty: on the one hand, to express the
fears of the public, denounce the lack of preparation and
warn the successive governments about it; and on the
other hand, to vote appropriations, all the appropriations
the military authorities demanded.

It is a fact that the Parliament denounced the danger
represented by the break in our defenses at Sedan, and
demanded the continuation of the Maginot Line as far as
the North Sea. It is a fact that the Parliament voted the
necessary appropriations for this undertaking, and that
part of these appropriations, which the General Staff did
not see fit to use, finally went to pay for the widening of
the gates of Paris! (They had to be very wide indeed to
permit the exodus of 1940.)

It is a fact that the annual budget voted by Parliament on February 28, 1934, included an appropriation of
603,000,000 francs for the manufacture of armaments;
but a decree of April 4, 1934, signed by Marshal Pétain,
reduced this appropriation to 476,000,000 — less than the
sum (500,000,000) paid every day to the Germans, now,
for occupation costs. A year of defense cost less than a
day of tribute!

It is a fact that the stenographic record of the Senate
Military Committee hearing of March 7, 1934, of which
I have already spoken, contains this astounding statement by Marshal Pétain: "Beyond Montmédy, we have
the Forest of the Ardennes. This forest is impenetrable, if
the necessary precautions are taken. . . . Naturally, the
edge of the forest on the enemy's side would be protected;
blockhouses would be constructed there. As this zone has
no depth, the enemy would be unable to entrench himself
there, but if he did make his way into the forest, all the
better, for we could then seize him as he came out."

It is a fact that, in spite of our lamentable lack of preparation — denounced many times in parliamentary committees — the General Staff and its most eminent spokesmen publicly proclaimed the most complete optimism.

In a speech made before a group of reserve officers at Lille, in July, 1939 — less than two months before hostilities began — General Weygand declared: "The French Army is stronger than ever. France does not want war. But if she were put under the necessity of winning a new victory, I can assure you that she would win it."

Between June 10 and June 20, 1940, the Germans captured a French railroad train at La Charité-sur-Loire, and found on this train, to their utter stupefaction, a large part of the archives of the Ministry of War. They made a selection of these documents, which the negligence of the General Staff had so conveniently abandoned to them — and published them in a White Paper, along with photographs of the originals. One of the most sensational of the documents reproduced was the minutes of the last meeting of the *Comité de Guerre,* held at Tours, at which General Weygand declared: "France was wrong to go to war without sufficient armaments and *without a military doctrine.*" The lack of "a military doctrine" was the fault of the higher officers and no one else. And by the admission of the most eminent among them, we had none!

In reality, Weygand was unjust. We had a military doctrine: that of Marshal Pétain.

We did not have enough tanks. But were those that we did have well used by the High Command?

The testimony of Generals Keller and Mittelhauser at Riom shows beyond a doubt that the *refusal of the General Staff* — following the lead of Pétain himself — *to oppose*

large formations of tanks to the Panzer divisions was at
the bottom of the collapse of the French army.

In his prophetic book of 1934, *Vers l'Armée de métier,*
published in English under the title *The Army of the
Future,* General de Gaulle, then a colonel, had emphasized what might be expected from the new machines, the
ruthless transformation of military tactics that they must
involve, the reactions they must have upon the structure
of armies. To the General Staff, enveloped in its usual
routine, this prophetic work seemed merely a slightly
shocking vagary on the part of a young colonel. Only the
nontechnicians, whose minds were not paralyzed as were
the professionally warped ones of the Superior War Council, understood its full significance.

The proposal laid before the Chamber by Paul Reynaud
to establish an armored corps, on March 31, 1935, was
wholly inspired by the new doctrine preached by Colonel
de Gaulle. But the military would alter nothing.

The Germans, on the other hand, had immediately
perceived all the advantage that could be derived from
these new and bold conceptions, which fell in perfectly
with the existing organization of their professional army.
They had immediately created the Panzer divisions.

Still the French High Command had failed to understand. The government was obliged, on its own initiative,
to increase the production of new tanks and to speed up
the manufacture of antitank and antiaircraft guns. Very
reluctantly and very languidly, the Command went into
the question of creating two new armored divisions.

In 1938, there appeared a book by a certain Colonel
Chauvineau, called *Une invasion est-elle encore possible?*
Just before the Riom trials, the police were ordered to
confiscate all copies of this book. For Marshal Pétain had
had the imprudence to write the preface, in which he

supported the author's theory of the continuous impregnable front: —

The continuous front is a reality which it is dangerous not to recognize. Colonel Chauvineau's particular merit is to have shown that the theory of the continuous front is based on the lessons of history and on the technical characteristics of modern weapons and fortifications.

In this extraordinary preface, Marshal Pétain conceded that . . .

Our country's capacity to bring to a certain halt any enemy who tries to penetrate inside our frontiers must not absolve us from attentively examining all new devices: tanks, submarines, and above all, aircraft. These last machines, still something of an enigma, have upset many of the old military ideas and contain secrets and mysteries still undreamed of.

This, we repeat, was written in 1938!

The next year, war actually broke out. And the High Command, having left the army in total inaction in purely defensive positions for eight months, threw it, in May 1940, into Belgium — the rashest possible sort of offensive at that date, and an offensive made on the spot selected by the Germans themselves!

At the sight of such incompetence more than one Frenchman was tempted to repeat Clemenceau's exclamation: "War in our time is too serious a matter to be entrusted to generals." Some of our generals — not all, thank God! — had not only proved their complete ineptitude in their chosen careers, but had also shown a lack of character and, in some cases, simply a lack of courage.

One of the clauses in our code of military justice provides for the court-martial of any commander in chief who surrenders in open country. I wonder if it is generally known that this clause was abrogated by a law of the Vichy government, duly announced in the *Journal Officiel de l'Etat Français?* It would be hard to find a more outstanding combination of cynicism and clumsiness than such an act at such a time. Its implication is evident: too many would have had to be court-martialed if the original law had remained in effect.

Thus, to protect themselves, the military chiefs seized the power, and by trying to keep it against the very evident and almost unanimous wish of the populace, they tried to make the country live under a regime of military paternalism. Pétain seemed to think that the French were children, incapable of making up their own minds; he treated them like children; and yet these same children were the sons of the men who had made Verdun and had made Pétain himself.

In their attempt to set up a dictatorship, these military chiefs showed their complete ignorance of psychology. They did not know the basic psychological law that any attempt to break a people's national spirit will end simply by making it stronger, nor did they realize the folly of trying to impose a backward-looking, feudal type of government on a people who found one of its greatest reasons for national pride in the very fact that, for centuries, it had been in the forefront of human progress.

It is, therefore, hardly surprising that these military chiefs, once they had become the masters of Vichy, faced a growing disaffection — a disaffection which at one point looked as if it might extend itself to the whole army they represented. This would have been a lamentable injustice, for if some of the chiefs were unequal to their task, the mass of the French troops had lost none of their traditional fighting qualities, and — had they been better led — would undoubtedly have shown the same courage, the same efficiency, as their predecessors of the first World War.

For there were, in 1940 as in 1914, isolated acts of daring heroism. There were the young cadets of the cavalry school of Saumur, who wrote a particularly touching page of military history with their own blood when they took it upon themselves to defend, against hopeless odds, the bridge guarding the entrance to the city. There were individual officers who were magnificent examples — like Colonel Marquis de Moustier, a Deputy who caused a sensation when he appeared as a witness at the Riom trial. He had been in command of the unit in which his son, a lieutenant, had asked for the privilege of serving. One day the father and son found themselves fighting side by side; and on that day the father carried back from the enemy lines the body of his son, killed in action.

Moustier was no political friend of Daladier; he was a Rightist and a bearer of one of the great names of France — and yet, in the Riom courtroom, he defended Daladier obstinately and courageously.

"You lacked armaments?" the presiding judge asked him.

"Perhaps I did not have enough," replied Moustier; "but was that a sufficient reason not to fight? We had been told that encirclement was inevitable. As far as I am concerned, I got myself and my men out of that encirclement all right; and the best proof of it is that I am here today. We fought our way out, and we killed as many Germans as we could. After all, wasn't that the main issue?"

His words produced a bewildered silence in the ranks

of the Vichy officials, who had long since ceased to consider that the main issue.

Despite all the misfortunes which Pétain's regime has inflicted on the French people, it has at least done them the immense good service of turning them forever against the idea of military dictatorship. Napoleon, whose authority on military matters is irrefutable and who himself had made a conclusive personal experiment with dictatorship, wrote: "The role of the military man is to insist despotically on what he wants — that of the civilian is to submit everything to discussion, to reason, to truth. It is to the civilian, rather than to the military man, that the leadership of society belongs."

CHAPTER X

The Convulsions of the Armistice

THE ARMISTICE of 1940 was not a rapid, clear-cut decision but a long and painful ordeal, a drama of conscience. It was not a brutal stab in the back of France, but a poisonous sore that festered slowly and painfully before the abscess burst.

To lift France out of the war, to tear her away from her allies, was a feat so contrary to tradition that the project could succeed only after terrible convulsions. These convulsions lasted more than a week. To be exact, it was between the Cabinet meeting of June 12, 1940 (in the presence of the President of the Republic at the Château of Cangé), in the course of which Weygand for the first time formally suggested the Armistice, to June 22 at 6:50 P.M., the exact moment when the signature of France was given in Foch's railroad car at Rethondes, that the irreparable was accomplished.

These convulsions had only a relatively small number of witnesses. This is a fact which it is necessary to emphasize. Parliament had absolutely no part in them whatsoever.

Paul Reynaud, as Premier, had been invested with extraordinary powers by the Chamber, and on June 10 his government had given the order to all the public services to leave Paris. Reynaud himself had left the same day. The offices of the President of the Republic had been installed in the Château of Cangé, near Tours. Reynaud was in the Château of Chissay; Georges Mandel, the Minister of the Interior, was at Tours. It was in this city that I saw him for the last time — on June 13, in the offices of the Prefect, where he had installed himself and was giving orders quite as calmly, and with just as much method and precision, as he had done in his usual office, Place Beauvau in Paris.

"It's hard," he said to me, "very hard . . . but we foresaw it. The important thing is to hold out . . . and we will hold out!"

The various Ministries had been dispersed in the surrounding châteaux — the Air Ministry was at Amboise, the General Staff was at Montrichard — and this dispersal of the great machinery of state seriously hampered the situation at a moment when rapid and united action was of capital importance.

By a cruel irony of fate, these châteaux of the Loire — calm, majestic, like so many jewels in the most smiling natural setting that could be imagined — these châteaux, guardians of so much history, heirs to so much glory, were to see unhappy men milling around in pettiness, cowardice, and confusion within the framework of their sumptuous architecture, and were to be silent witnesses to the greatest catastrophe that had ever come upon France.

It cannot be doubted that if, in the short interval between the government's arrival in Tours and its further move to Bordeaux, Herriot and Jeanneney (the presidents of the Chamber and Senate) had been able to call together the Assemblies — if Parliament had been able to make its voice heard — the course of events could have been changed. But the rapidity of events did not permit this. The members of Parliament were not able to regroup themselves until the government was in Bordeaux, after the abdication of Reynaud — and there, at Bordeaux, Laval was waiting for them.

The convulsions did not have, therefore, any direct witnesses except the twoscore Ministers and Assistant Secretaries of State who made up the Cabinet at the time. To my knowledge, beyond M. Chautemps (who has been in Washington since 1940), only one of these is safely out of France today: M. Queuille, Minister of Agriculture at the time, and at present in Algiers.

It is therefore very difficult to determine the exact proportion of truth in the numerous accounts which have since been published about these events, and I should be very guarded myself in broaching the subject if I did not have the direct testimony of one of the principal actors of the drama, my friend Louis Marin.

Louis Marin is one of the most striking, and also one of the most popular, members of the French Parliament, where he has sat for forty years as Deputy from Nancy. He is a Liberal of the Right, leader of the *Fédération Républicaine,* and has for parliamentary government an attachment that is almost religious.

With a face of a strongly marked type, crowned by pure white hair, a white mustache like a Gallic warrior, his inevitable blue polka-dotted bow tie, Marin makes a picturesque figure. He constantly punctuates his speech by shaking his right index finger in the direction of the Left. He always followed with the ardor of a young man all the debates of the Chamber, intervening in most of the discussions; but his unfailing honesty won him the esteem and the unanimous sympathy of his adversaries.

Paul Reynaud, when he was renovating his Cabinet just after the German onslaught of May 10, 1940, called him to the government as Minister without Portfolio.

In his attitude toward Germany, Louis Marin had the

clear and firm mentality of the patriotic Lorrainer. The war once begun, it must be carried on to the finish till victory, whatever the risks might be. He could not admit in this respect any sort of compromise, no matter how disguised. He was, with Mandel, of admirable firmness from one end of the tragedy to the other.

The publicity which — naturally enough — has fallen to the defeatists in the Reynaud Cabinet has not been shared by those who struggled with all their might to make the government determine to go on with the war. The most energetic of these was Georges Mandel, who was to pay for his patriotism with captivity and whose death was reported — falsely, we hope — a few months ago.

Mandel is political heir to Clemenceau. Through the miracle of patient and devoted imitation, many of the characteristic traits of the master were revived in the disciple. And yet, with regard to physical appearance, there were never two men so completely different.

Mandel is remarkable above all for his eyes of limpid blue, which contrast strangely with the gravity, the studied harshness, of the ensemble of his person. His hair, divided in the center by an immaculate part, his protruding lips falling in a contemptuous pout, his strong chin, are his other outstanding features.

Mandel is short in stature, and as a young man he was extremely slim. In 1903, when he made his first appearance in the offices of Clemenceau's newspaper, *L'Aurore,* clad entirely in black, with a stiff high collar (which he has never abandoned since) and a necktie like those worn at the time of the Restoration, he seemed so insignificant, so inconspicuous, that no one paid any attention to him. But Clemenceau used to say of him at that time: "Not much to look at, but very serviceable."

Rarely has anyone seen Mandel smile, even faintly, and no one in the world has ever seen him laugh. He says very little, and always talks in short, concise, hammering phrases. While he talks, his fingers join and twist in a curious gesture as if he were turning the globe between his hands. At the same time he curves his back like a cat trying to slide along a drain.

Mandel is as scornful of popularity as he is of criticism, and from the very beginning of his career he has made his way by sheer will power and sharp intelligence. He has always been noted for his clearness and logic, and his unfailing instinct for making himself useful to his master, as well as a love of complications for their own sake which has sometimes suggested the highest sense of diplomacy and sometimes a definite lack of scruple. He has the sense and the passion of authority to an exceptional degree. He knows how to command, and he knows how to make himself obeyed.

When Clemenceau took the leadership of France in November 1917 — in the tragic circumstances which we still recall, when the nation had been at war already for three terrible years — Mandel became his chief secretary and remained as such until the retirement of the Tiger. The mind of the hard-pressed statesman was left free for military and international questions, while Mandel virtually took over the domestic policy of France. His power became almost unlimited.

When Clemenceau fell, Mandel, who was by then a member of Parliament from the Gironde, began to play a role more important in the corridors of the Chamber than at the rostrum. He was not an orator, and made very few speeches during the entire span of his career. He knew, however, every important man in the country; he knew all the details of his record, his background, even

his private life. It was said that during his long rule in
the Ministry of the Interior under Clemenceau he had
collected a terrifying amount of information: bulging
dossiers and "little papers" with which he could "blow off
the lid" at any time and which made him the terror of
the politicians.

When Flandin became Premier in November 1934,
Mandel accepted the Ministry of Communications, and
continued in the same office in the Laval and Sarraut
Cabinets of 1935 and 1936. In April 1938, he became
Minister of Colonies in the Daladier Cabinet — a post
in which he showed, in a striking manner, his extraordinary capabilities.

When Reynaud came to power in March 1940, he made
Mandel his Minister of the Interior. At long last, the right
man was in the right place — the place where he should
have been years before. Mandel at once began hunt-
ing out the fifth column and the appeasers, and scores
of them had already been jailed when the collapse
came.

I saw Louis Marin very often at Vichy in the course
of the years 1941 and 1942. He arrived in the spa with
the government, to take his place in the National Assembly
— where, incidentally, he abstained from voting either
for or against Pétain; he had installed himself in the
very modest Hotel Aix-et-Chambéry, about two blocks
away from the sumptuous Hotel du Parc, where Pétain
resided; and in spite of numerous invitations and, later,
threats which were proffered him, he refused obstinately
to meet the Marshal. On the other hand, he was an assidu-
ous visitor to the American Embassy.

One day when I went to see him he said to me: —

"My good friend, our opinions are so well known that

we don't risk compromising each other! Come and take a walk with me in the park."

As we walked he said to me with a malicious wink: —

"Watch carefully the hats that will be tipped for us. It's the surest barometer. When the communiqués are favorable for the Germans, the opportunists here feign not to see me. When the British score points, I receive polite bows. Today the news is excellent; we will be bowed to quite often."

In the course of numerous conversations, Marin described to me many times the circumstances of the Armistice.

"Four meetings of the Council of Ministers were needed," he repeated to me, "four long and painful meetings, to strike down France. During the first we were not only a majority, we were unanimous against capitulation; Weygand alone proposed it; even Pétain was silent. In the second, the intervention of Chautemps, the desertion of Frossard (Minister of Public Works) and Jean Prouvost (Minister of Information and Director of *Paris-Soir*), began to upset the majority, but no decision had been reached as yet. In the third, we were in the minority. In the fourth, Pétain caved in completely, and we were beaten."

This was the frightful drama played for ten consecutive days in the château region of the Loire, between Tours and Bordeaux, without any other witnesses than its actors. The principal characters are well known: M. Albert Lebrun, President of the Republic, patriotic, honest, and well-intentioned, but totally ineffectual, and incredibly weak in purpose; Paul Reynaud; Pétain; Weygand; and, facing these two military men who were resolved to abdicate, the two political figures who embodied resistance, loyalty and firmness: Georges Mandel and Louis Marin.

The others had minor roles, but their roles nevertheless gave the defeatists a majority, and placed on their shoulders, in view of the circumstances, a terrible responsibility.

Basing my conclusions solely upon Marin's declarations, and upon such official documents as I have had in my possession, I have traced the record of that lengthy tragedy known as the Armistice of Bordeaux as follows: —

May 10, 1940: The Germans unleash their great offensive. The Nazi armored cars break through the gap at Sedan.

May 18: Pétain is called by Reynaud to the government and becomes Vice President of the Council.

May 19: Weygand is appointed Commander in Chief.

May 29: First note, extremely pessimistic, from Weygand to Reynaud, alluding to the possible necessity of a separate armistice.

May 31 and June 1: Meeting of the Higher Interallied Council. No reference is made to an armistice, or even to the possible discouragement of France. France and Great Britain are apparently agreed upon letting Weygand keep the general command of operations.

June 6: The Battle of the Somme is lost. The armies of the North are cut off. The British, under General Gort, evacuate Dunkerque. Churchill declares that Britain will resist to the last man.

June 7: It is clearly apparent that the war is lost on the soil of metropolitan France. A terrible dilemma is imposed upon the government! Either an armistice, or the continuation of the fight beyond France — that is, the immediate evacuation of the bulk of the French troops.

Perhaps most people do not realize the difference between a surrender, which is a purely military action and involves only the military command, and an armistice, which is both a military and a political action and involves the government. After June 7, 1940, it was evident that our armies had been crushed by the weight of superior numbers and superior weapons, and would no longer be able to fight on the Continent.

But our Empire, our fleet, a large part of our aviation, was intact. A surrender like that of Belgium and Holland — a purely military action — was inevitable, and everyone would have understood it. But Weygand would not hear of surrender; he, and Pétain too, wanted an armistice. Why? Because an armistice would involve the government, and Weygand and Pétain were already doing everything in their power to lay the blame on Parliament for mistakes which were really the fault of the High Command.

June 10: A new note from Weygand to Reynaud emphasizing the beliefs expressed in the first one, and insisting upon the very probable necessity of a surrender — with or without the consent of Great Britain — and of an armistice with Germany. Paul Reynaud leaves Paris.

June 11: Reynaud visits General Weygand at his headquarters at Briare. Here he meets Winston Churchill, Anthony Eden, and Sir John Dill. Reynaud asks for new and immediate aid from the British in the form of airplanes and matériel. Weygand now declares to Reynaud that the war is lost, and that only an armistice can stop the invasion. He succeeds in wresting from Reynaud the promise that his demand for an armistice will be submitted to the next meeting of the Cabinet; but Churchill knows nothing of this.

What a tragedy in itself, the psychology of these three protagonists — Winston Churchill, Paul Reynaud and Weygand — during these three crucial days! If these men had been able, if they had been willing, to exchange opinions, even frankly and brutally, from the first of June on, what evil things might have been avoided! But it seems that each hid himself from the other.

Winston Churchill loved France profoundly. As a matter of policy — and also out of delicacy — he did not wish to say anything that might give the impression that he suspected even the remotest possibility of a French desertion; and in addition, he wished to convey the idea that there was absolutely no question of his going back on his own word to the French.

Paul Reynaud, naturally much disturbed by the remembrance of the pledge he had given to England, and perhaps still resolved to hold to it, stiffened before Churchill and did not say a word to him about a possible armistice.

Weygand, soured and aggressive, ranked above Churchill on the military plane. He demanded from Great Britain immediate assistance, which he knew perfectly well she was incapable of giving; he pressed Reynaud to propose an armistice to the French government; he did not say a word to the British Prime Minister. That, said he, was Paul Reynaud's affair.

Reynaud finally sees Churchill alone; the members of the government are convened afterwards and must be content with his report of the encounter. They are able to get no direct impression of the British Prime Minister's state of mind.

June 12: Weygand gives the armies the order for a general retreat. Paris is declared an open city; the order is given again to evacuate what remains of Parliament, of the press, and of the public services.

June 12: Another Cabinet meeting, which has been preceded, the night before, by a general exchange of views between the principal members of the government. The Council meets at the Château of Cangé, under the presidency of M. Albert Lebrun.

Weygand reviews in a very pessimistic manner the extreme precariousness of the military situation, and concludes: "I do not want France to risk falling into the anarchy which will follow a military defeat. It costs my soldier's heart dearly to say that the Armistice can no longer be avoided."

Mandel bounds to the floor: —

"If you think you can't fight any longer, surrender your sword, General! There are precedents in our history — Napoleon III, Bazaine. Since you consider yourself beaten, cease firing. . . . But the war will continue. France will go on with the struggle at the side of her allies!"

Louis Marin adds his vehement protestations to those of Mandel. The Council of Ministers adjourns with the adoption of a proposal of Chautemps: they will ask Churchill to come to Tours the next day; they will inform him of Weygand's declaration, and will ask him under what conditions he will relieve France of her agreement with Britain not to conclude a separate peace.

June 13: Arrival of Winston Churchill at the airport of Tours. Reynaud meets him and informs him of the situation, assuring him that he will address a supreme appeal to Roosevelt to obtain American aid, notably in the form of immediate shipments of airplanes. Winston Churchill makes Reynaud promise not to make any definite decision before seeing him again. Reynaud returns to reconvene the Cabinet. A new attack from Weygand ensues. He declares that Communist unrest has broken out in Paris. Mandel hurls a formal denial of this, and picks up the phone in the room where the Ministers are in session, calling M. Langeron, Chief of Police of Paris. M. Langeron replies: "The Germans are at Aubervilliers and at Pantin; they will enter Paris tomorrow. The city is calm."

This denial ends the debate; no decision has been made; the adversaries of the Armistice are still in the majority; but Frossard and Prouvost are preparing to give in.

On the evening of the same day, June 13, Reynaud announces to the French by radio that he has made an appeal to President Roosevelt.

June 14: In the morning, in the Château of Chissay, Reynaud presents the American Ambassador, Mr. Biddle, with his appeal to the President of the United States. The government leaves for Bordeaux.

June 15: Installed at Bordeaux, Reynaud sees Sir Ronald Campbell, the British Ambassador, and informs him of his final intentions: he divides the government into two groups, one of which will leave for North Africa, to continue the war there, while the other will remain in France to face the Germans. Sir Ronald Campbell asks a formal guarantee that the French fleet will be sent to British ports. (This, of course, has been one of Churchill's chief preoccupations for some time.) New Cabinet meeting in the afternoon. New assault by Reynaud; new protests by Mandel and Louis Marin, supported by Campinchi, Navy Minister, and by Dautry, Armament Minister. Proposal of Chautemps: Why not

ascertain the Armistice conditions through the intermediary of a neutral country? If, as is probable, these
conditions are not acceptable, the government will then
be fortified for making the country understand its decision to continue the struggle.

Louis Marin rises vehemently against this proposal:
To demand to know the conditions of an Armistice is to
say that one is ready to conclude it; if one sticks his finger in the machinery to that extent, the whole body will
end up by being caught in it. Louis Marin, Mandel,
Campinchi, Dautry, now constitute the minority.

June 16: Paul Reynaud convenes the Council of Ministers, and communicates the message of the President of
the United States — in reply to Reynaud's appeal of
June 13. As might have been expected, Mr. Roosevelt
has given the assurance of as large a material aid as possible, but has said he could not promise military aid,
which only Congress could accord.

Pétain — who, it must be recalled, is still at this time
but Vice President of the War Council, under Premier
Reynaud — has remained silent behind Weygand, and
now breaks in clearly and brutally: Useless to discuss
the matter any longer; the Armistice is inevitable. If the
Council does not share his opinion on this point, he
will resign.

And now comes the most fantastic *coup de théâtre:*
Churchill's proposal, communicated by telephone, for
Franco-British fusion, for the total union of the two
Empires. The proposal is not even thoroughly examined by the Council, whose majority is lined up behind Pétain. The vote is put. The British proposal is
defeated: that means the Armistice is accepted. Paul Reynaud resigns.

*   *   *

Such is the summary of the tragedy in its general lines, with all the dryness of a diary.

I cannot assume for myself the right to judge men in France who are not in a position to defend themselves — least of all Paul Reynaud, who is today a prisoner of the Germans. Very moderately, I shall confine myself to declaring that, for my part, I shall never be able to understand why Paul Reynaud, chief of the Cabinet of a country at war and invested with extraordinary powers by the Chamber, did not believe himself authorized to make, or did not want to assume alone the responsibility for, the clear-cut and resolute decision which imposed itself, on June 13, after his interview with Churchill: to command Weygand to order a surrender of the armies in the field, and the immediate evacuation of our remaining armed forces; and at the same time to leave, with the government, to continue the struggle in North Africa and in the rest of the Empire.

For a man who has had a reputation for energy to have believed that, at a time when the fate of France hung in the balance, it was his duty to submit that decision to the fluctuating discussions of a series of Cabinet meetings, is beyond my comprehension.

I was not able to get in touch with Paul Reynaud after the Armistice, but I saw two of his intimate friends who had been permitted to visit him in his prison of Pourtalet in the Pyrenees. There they had found him engaged in writing with great regularity the heavy volume which was intended to be his justification. Both gave me the same explanation of the conduct of their friend.

Reynaud was persuaded that the harshness of the terms of the Armistice would shock the Cabinet and arouse public opinion to such an extent that Pétain would be compelled to resign immediately, and that he, Reynaud, could take up again with the decks cleared and could, with heightened authority, persuade the government to leave for North Africa.

It seems inconceivable that a man of Paul Reynaud's type could have entertained any such illusion. To have formed so fanciful a project was to have reckoned without the Germans, who continued to advance to the point of blocking the last available embarkation ports. It was to reckon, also, without the intrigues of Laval, who from then on was master of the situation.

And still, on the night of the sixteenth of June, after the resignation of Reynaud and the assumption of power by Pétain, all was not yet finished.

For three more days, France was to keep a chance of salvation.

How that supreme chance escaped her has not yet been entirely revealed. I believe I am in a position to make this revelation.

CHAPTER XI

A Lie and a Forgery

HUNDREDS OF ARTICLES and many books have been written about the pitiful Armistice of 1940. We have had various accounts by people who themselves took part in the drama — but who, even so, did not witness every scene — and various interpretations by others who have deduced from the final results the things that "must have happened" to bring them about; but to this day all the pieces of the puzzle have not been fitted together. In all the accounts there is a yawning gap which remains to be filled.

The fate of France and the course of the war were decided within a few hours, on the afternoon of Wednesday, June 19, 1940. While fate was pushing the hands around the clock between 3 and 4 P.M., much could still have been saved — and all was lost. In the morning, Pétain, frightened by the drastic German armistice terms — which he had been naïve enough to imagine his personal prestige would make more lenient — had made the decision to remain alone in France and let the French government, under Vice Premier Camille Chautemps, cross to North Africa at once. By night, everything was changed: all the Ministers had been ordered to remain in Bordeaux, and the opportunity to depart and carry on the war in the Empire — with the French fleet intact — had passed. The fate of France had been sealed.

What brought about this sudden reversal in the mind of the Marshal?

I have reason to believe that the historical decision to

transfer the French government to North Africa was changed not by Laval, as some have surmised, but through the personal initiative of a man who was and is a bitter enemy of Laval, and whose name is unknown to the average American and to many of the French themselves. He is Raphaël Alibert.

Before June 1940, Alibert had exerted a great deal of influence in the government, but always from behind the scenes. At one time he had fulfilled the functions of general secretary to a semipolitical organization of big industrialists known as the *Relèvement Français*. A convinced Monarchist, and a militant member of the *Action Française,* he had for many years been the friend and confidant and especially favored adviser of Pétain. At least once a week during the winter in Paris, Alibert, the Marshal, General Brécard (today Grand Chancellor of the Legion of Honor), and Henri Lémery (a senator who had formerly been Minister of Justice and of the Colonies) would meet at each other's homes. At these meetings, as in so many other Paris salons, the game of forming "Pétain Cabinets" was played — though here, of course, more seriously than anywhere else. The plans remained in a purely doctrinal and theoretical state; but they made valuable material for Laval to use when the time came for real business.

Alibert was legal adviser to the group. He was the author of all the legal and administrative documents which became the foundation of the new regime. To reward him, Pétain, after making him General Secretary to the Cabinet on July 12, 1940, appointed him Minister of Justice.

Alibert cordially detested Laval. While, as an intimate friend of Pétain, he himself had been the chief builder of the Marshal's political career, he had never had any connection with Laval until the last minute. Jealous of Laval, and disgusted and bewildered by his pro-German policies (for, though an ultrareactionary, he hated the Germans), he had contacted Peyrouton, and with this man, whose personal ambitions served his purpose so well, he worked out the whole scheme which resulted in Laval's arrest on December 13, 1940. We know that the arrest was of short duration. Detained for a few hours on his property in Chateldon under the custody of *Gardes Mobiles* and a detachment of Pétain's own bodyguard, Laval was soon set free by the intervention of Otto Abetz, who had come full speed from Paris with an imposing escort of armored vehicles.

One of Pétain's characteristics is the ease with which he can get rid of his most intimate and faithful collaborators after they have been compromised by serving him. René Gillouin, who wrote most of his speeches, Dumoulin de la Barthète, head of his staff, General Brécard, and Raphaël Alibert were all sacrificed one after another.

Laval, avenging himself through the Germans, brought about Alibert's dismissal as Minister of Justice. He was then relegated to the comparatively insignificant position of a member of the Council of State, whose headquarters had been set up in the town of Royat, near Clermont-Ferrand.

It was there that I met Alibert and heard his strange confession. Early in 1942, my son had been arrested for what I can only term "the crime of patriotism." Later he was placed on parole and assigned to Clermont-Ferrand as his enforced residence. I joined him there.

One gloomy Sunday afternoon we were walking toward Royat, the only direction in which we were permitted to go, chatting as we went. As we approached Number 57 Rue Blatin, where stood the flamboyant, arrogantly new building — or rather the numerous buildings — of Pierre Laval's *Moniteur,* we ran into Alibert, who was wandering along with bowed head, lost in his melancholy reflections.

"What are you doing here, M. Alibert?"

"This is where I live. They have made me a member of the Council of State, and the Council sits in Royat. Now they're talking about moving it back to Paris. Naturally, I am not going along. You can imagine the reception I'd get from the Germans!"

I was well aware of Alibert's bitterness and of the special reason for his being so unpopular with the Germans.

I turned to my son and said: "You see before you the man who made Pétain."

Alibert, who was obviously burning to give vent to his feelings, pounced on my words.

"You don't know how truthfully you have spoken, my dear Deputy!" And then, to my son, "Your father is right. It was I who made Pétain."

By this time we had all three stopped on the deserted sidewalk. And it was there, in that banal setting, that my son and I listened to his strange and tragic confession.

"Yes," said Alibert with the utmost gravity, "I made Pétain. You know what thanks I got! Now that I am free of all obligation toward him, I have nothing more to hide. I made Pétain — and I am not ashamed of it, for I did it to serve my country — I made Pétain *by means of a lie and a forgery.*"

With obvious relief at being able to unburden himself, Alibert went on, while I listened in a dazed silence.

"You must remember — for I know you were there — that during the night of Wednesday the nineteenth of June, Bordeaux was bombed. There were a number of casualties. That Thursday I received an urgent telephone call from President Lebrun, who insisted on speaking personally to me. His trunks were packed and he was ready to embark at Port-Vendres for Algiers. He was anxious to know the exact time of the sailing.

" 'I have been informed,' he quavered over the telephone, 'that the Germans have crossed the Loire between Nantes and Tours. I beg you to ask the Marshal what his decision is, and to let me know as soon as possible!' "

Indeed I did remember those hectic days. On Wednesday, June 19, the Cabinet — of which the Marshal had become Premier on the previous Sunday, succeeding Reynaud — had finally made up its mind. Both the Marshal and Paul Baudoin, his Foreign Minister, had informed Sir Ronald Campbell, the British Ambassador, by word of mouth, of the following decision: The President of the Republic and the Presidents of the Senate and Chamber were to leave immediately for North Africa. They would go to Port-Vendres by automobile and there embark on a cruiser. About forty Senators and Deputies were already on board the auxiliary cruiser *Massilia,* lying under steam at Le Verdon.

"I answered the President respectfully but avoided saying anything definite," continued Alibert, "and then went to see the Marshal. It was three o'clock in the afternoon. I found him alone in his office.

" 'Ah, so it's you, Alibert,' he said; 'you've come at the right moment. I must go to him; and you can accompany me.'

" 'Him' meant the President of the Republic. The Marshal has such an aversion to M. Albert Lebrun that he will never pronounce his name.

"We went out together and covered the few yards that separated us from M. Lebrun's office. When we entered he was deep in conversation with M. Camille Chautemps. The Marshal sat down without saying a word.

" 'Mr. President,' said Chautemps, 'I should like to repeat your instructions, just to be quite sure. We are in complete agreement, are we not? As Vice Premier, I am to leave at once for Algiers and there take over the leadership of the government. I shall convoke the Senators and Deputies, at least those who are able to follow us, and we shall take all possible measures to continue the war in the Empire. Marshal Pétain is to remain on French soil in order to insure by his prestige as far as possible the protection of life and property. You, Mr. President, are to leave immediately. Is that correct?'

" 'Quite correct,' replied M. Lebrun. 'My baggage is packed.'

"The Marshal confined himself to a nod as a sign of assent. The meeting was about to break up, and everything would be lost! It was then that I decided on the lie.

" 'Mr. President,' I said, taking the plunge, 'I must inform you of a very important piece of news, which I received just before coming here. I have not even had the time to inform Marshal Pétain. Yet I believe it to be of a nature to influence your decision. It is not true that the Germans have crossed the Loire. On the contrary, the High Command has informed us that our troops are offering stiff resistance, and that the river has not been crossed at any point.'

" 'That is indeed very important,' put in the Marshal.

"M. Lebrun was obviously disconcerted by this, and hesitated for a moment. I pressed my advantage: —

" 'Don't you think, Mr. President, since it is not quite so urgent now, that we can put off any final decision until tomorrow morning?'

" 'That would indeed be more prudent,' the Marshal seconded me.

" 'That means another delay,' said M. Lebrun with a sigh; 'but I shall remain prepared to leave. Let me have your dispatches as soon as you receive them. Remember, I am counting on you.'

"Chautemps said nothing. I exchanged a rapid glance with the Marshal as the meeting broke up. We had won out!

"That was my lie," concluded Alibert.

He was silent for a while, looked me straight in the face, then looked at my son and added: —

"But that was only the first round. The second was yet to be won. Here is my forgery.

"After I got back to the Prefecture, I was bombarded with telephone calls from Jeanneney, from Herriot, from Campinchi, all wanting to know whether the order for departure had finally been given. Something had to be done and I made my decision. Taking the Marshal's personal notepaper, I dictated to my typist an order for each of the Ministers to remain in his lodgings until eight o'clock the next morning, in readiness for instructions, and not to leave town for any reason before having received them. I took the Marshal's seal, stamped the orders, and signed them. That was my forgery. Without that forgery, Pétain would never have become Chief of State." *

Early the next morning — Friday — Pierre Laval, at the head of a delegation consisting of Georges Bonnet, Pietri, Marquet, Marcel Déat, Bergery, and Portmann, appeared before the President of the Republic and said to him threateningly: —

* Until 1940, this was the title of the President of the Republic; but, as assumed by Pétain after the Armistice, it indicated dictatorial powers.

"We have been told of your plan to leave. You must not do it. If you leave French soil, you will never set foot on it again. If you choose to leave in the hour of the country's worst misfortune, the people will raise the cry of desertion and perhaps, still worse, that of treason!"

The President yielded to the threat. It was the end! The vacillating character of M. Lebrun, and the lie and the forgery perpetrated by Raphaël Alibert, had prevented the departure of the government for North Africa and the continuation of the war, and thereby determined all the events that were to follow.

This was the confession Raphaël Alibert made me, by a strange coincidence, in front of Pierre Laval's own residence. That same evening, I recorded it as carefully and as exactly as I would make out an official report. I leave it to future historians.

CHAPTER XII

The Swindle

"The French Parliament abdicated!" Such is the brief
and caustic comment which has been made on the attitude and on the deeds of the representatives of the
French people on the day of their last session — July 10,
1940. It reflects the assurance of people who, far away and
long after the event, judge results without understanding circumstances.

The men who met in Vichy on July 10 knew that the
last chance of transferring the remains of French power
to North Africa had gone; by the will of Pétain and his
fellow defeatists the Armistice had been signed. They
themselves had had nothing to do with the signing of it.
They were confronted with the *fait accompli* and forced
almost on the spur of the moment — and under the threat
of German tanks massed at a distance of less than thirty
miles — to take the fearful responsibility of providing
some sort of machinery for the government of France in
the situation which it created.

The watering place of Vichy was a noisy, overcrowded
forum. Pétain and Laval had made their headquarters at
the Hotel du Parc, Laval on the first floor, the Marshal
on the second. Laval's ally Marquet, Minister of the Interior in the new Pétain Cabinet, ruled the baccarat room
of the Casino, and the Parliament was to hold its session
in the Hall of the *Grand Théâtre*. Senators and Deputies
had been summoned to convene on the shortest notice,

and most of them had had hardly forty-eight hours to deliberate before the meeting. I say "most of them" advisedly. Throughout the tragic days and weeks since the government had arrived in Bordeaux, a small clique — Laval's clique — had been constantly industrious, busily laying their plans to take the fullest advantage of the situation which Alibert, by his deception, had so diabolically arranged for the benefit of Pétain (and also, as it turned out, of Laval) and which was to culminate in the greatest political swindle of all times: the vote extorted from Parliament on July 10.

When he became Prime Minister, Pétain, however high his ambitions, had not yet begun to dream of a dictatorship. The most obvious proof of this is the composition of his first Cabinet. He had retained most of Reynaud's Ministers: Radical-Socialists like Chautemps and Chichery, Marxist socialists like Rivière and Février, Independent Socialists like Pomaret and Frossard. It was a classical Cabinet, designed to be acceptable to the Senate and the Chamber. It was, furthermore, a Cabinet in which Pierre Laval had no place. Pétain had offered him the Ministry of Justice, but Laval had refused to settle for anything less than Foreign Affairs; and Pétain (who disliked Laval then as I am convinced he has always disliked him) refused this post on the ground that it was reserved for Paul Baudoin. I myself happen to have further evidence of the state of Pétain's plans when he first became Premier, through an interview I had with him in Bordeaux just after he was offered the premiership. I was, at the time, editor of a Paris daily, *Le Jour,* which, in accordance with a government order to all newspapers, had left the capital on June 12. I got to Bordeaux in time for the Armistice and in time to hear Pétain denounce "the lies which have done us so much harm." In my next editorial I enlarged upon what I considered the most shameful of these lies.

At six in the evening, I learned that the censorship refused to permit the publication of my article. Astonished and indignant, I rushed to the Prefecture to demand an explanation of Alibert, then Pétain's chief secretary, who listened to my complaint and said: "Will you wait a minute?"

He left me alone and was back almost at once.

"The Marshal wants to see you."

Pétain, wearing a dark suit, was standing in front of the open door of his office. He had the proofs of my article in his hand.

"Monsieur," he said in his slow muffled voice, "I want to ask you to do two things. The first is to leave this article with me, for it is very good and I should like to keep it; the second is not to publish it."

I bowed without answering. There was a moment of embarrassed silence; then suddenly the Marshal motioned to me to come in.

"Come in, I have a little time and I want to talk to you."

In answer to his gesture of invitation I sat down beside him on a sofa.

"Sit near me; I'll hear you better. When I am talking with one other person I hear perfectly well, but when there are too many people I can't follow the discussion. In Paul Reynaud's Cabinet, there were more than twenty of us; I couldn't hear a thing. Today we are only a dozen, and I already hear better; tomorrow, when I cut the number down to five or six, everything will be quite all right."

This idea of how to form a Cabinet seemed to me remarkable, to say the least, but I really hadn't the heart to smile. The Marshal felt my surprise and, changing his tone, said: —

"Monsieur Fernand-Laurent, you came to see me four years ago at the Invalides." (This was when I had called on him in 1936 to discuss the armament situation.)

"*Monsieur le Maréchal,* you have a good memory."

He looked me straight in the eye and said in an even slower voice than usual: —

"*Monsieur Fernand-Laurent, I was wrong not to see you again.*"

I looked straight back at him.

"*Monsieur le Maréchal,* you were very wrong indeed."

The frankness of my answer didn't seem to displease him, but his face took on a graver expression. He doubtless understood all that I meant to imply.

"You have a right to know why I am asking you not to publish your article. Here are my reasons: —

"I denounced to the French people the lies which have done them so much harm, but I purposely refrained from saying exactly what those lies were. You have taken my statement and developed it. You have made a list of the most harmful of these lies. If the article were to be published, certain of your colleagues who have held Cabinet posts might think they were being attacked; they might think that your article, written with my approval, was the expression of my point of view. Well, just now I cannot afford to turn them against me: I may need them."

The Marshal waited a moment, turned away from me, and looked straight ahead as if he were facing the future.

"They have asked me to be Prime Minister [he had held the office for six days already] . . . it seems that they will soon ask me to take on other responsibilities. For the sake of the country I shall doubtless have to accept. But I shall need Parliament. Do you understand?"

Of course I understood. Pétain had always regarded Parliament with a strange mixture of scorn, hatred, and almost superstitious fear. But at that time he felt the need of conciliating it; he did not yet foresee its dissolution. In spite of his personal dislike for Laval, Pétain later listened to him only too complacently when the tempting devil presented his scheme for setting the Marshal up as a dictator.

"Well, go ahead," said he in effect, "but you will bear the whole responsibility. I am not going to appear until it is all over." The move was a shrewd one and quite in keeping with the Marshal's cautious character. This way he would have everything to gain and nothing to lose. Furthermore, he would be spared the ordeal of having to answer interpellations on the part of Parliament which might easily be fatal to his ambition. He shut himself up in his drawing room of the Hotel du Parc during the three fateful days of the eighth, ninth and tenth of July, and Laval was able to make full use of him as a hidden and powerful threat.

As the various members of Parliament arrived in Vichy, they found Laval and his coterie waiting for them. A meeting had been called for the purpose of presenting the Assembly with a bill giving full powers to Pétain. Laval, of course, wanted a bill passed in such terms that he could use it as a screen to set up the dictatorship he dreamed of, and he set out to convince the parliamentarians of the necessity of giving Pétain not only emergency powers (such as had been given to Daladier and Reynaud, and others before them) but, further, of giving him power to prepare a revised Constitution.

Here was the same old question that had never ceased to be an issue since the very birth of the Republic. In the first few years it had been the Leftists, the Republicans, who had wanted the Constitution revised because it was too adapted to the aims of the Monarchists. Then after Boulanger's attempted *coup d'état,* revision had come to be associated in the popular mind with reaction; for that reason, in spite of the obvious necessity for certain changes, no government had dared urge any. True, Doumergue, after the sixth of February scare in 1934, had made feeble efforts in that direction, but nothing had been done. Since the war, however, the question had again come to the fore. Most of the members of Parliament were at least of an open mind on the subject; its discussion did not shock them, or in itself serve as a warning of what was to come.

Laval had several trump cards in his hand: the respect, amounting almost to reverence, in which the overwhelming majority of the French people held Pétain; their deep concern over the prisoners of war; the uncertainty as to the terms Germany would demand to implement the Armistice; and the atmosphere of despair and confusion which reigned all over the country.

It must be remembered that, at that time, very few people had had the opportunity of hearing the proud call of General de Gaulle: "France has lost a battle; France has not lost the war — the fight goes on!" With the exception of a very small minority of men, who refused to despair but who drew their conviction much more from faith than from any sound reasoning, Vichy, as a whole, thought that Germany had won the war.

It must also be recalled that, two days before, there had come as a terrible blow to French morale the news of the British attack on the French fleet at Mers-el-Kebir. Vichy propaganda had, of course, presented the fact as a determined and cold-blooded act of aggression on the part of the British, and it was said that the latter had fired without warning. Nobody had any means of finding out the truth about this, but it was known that there had been about thirteen hundred killed and wounded, and the impression produced by such news at such a time was tremendous. Public anger rose to a climax and Vichy officials spoke openly of declaring war on Great Britain. Even to remain neutral toward our former ally under these circumstances was an act of courage.

The summons to members of Parliament to convene for an emergency session as a National Assembly had been broadcast by radio, and some attempt had been made to reach the Senators and Deputies by telegraph. But about two hundred of them did not get the message, or did not care to answer the call (desiring to avoid so grave a responsibility), or could not arrive because of transportation difficulties or because of the unwillingness of the German occupation authorities to permit them to cross the newly drawn line of demarcation between the occupied and unoccupied zones. The others had to travel under the most trying conditions in order to reach Vichy. For days and days they had witnessed on the roads the wretched trail of refugees — bombed or machine-gunned corpses; children separated from their parents, crying desperately by the wayside; old people gone raving mad in their terror. When the peasants and workmen heard that there was to be a meeting of Parliament, the unanimous outcry which followed Senator and Deputy in all the villages through which they had to pass was: "For God's sake, give us back our prisoners!"

The prisoners . . . There were 1,500,000 of them. Nothing can be understood of the political events of France in 1940 if this fact is not constantly borne in mind.

Pétain has often expressed (in words) his particular solicitude for them. It is the least he can do. For they are in a very real sense *his* prisoners.

Pétain became Prime Minister on June 16, 1940, at two o'clock in the afternoon. He had formed his Cabinet by 10 P.M. the same day. The next day at 12:30 he broadcast over the radio an order to the entire army to cease firing. At this moment the Germans had not yet crossed the Loire. Many French divisions could have fallen back across the river and saved their equipment and their men. They were prevented from doing so by the Marshal's order. To give this order — before delegates to the armistice conference had even been nominated — was to tell the Germans that they could advance without hindrance, that the victim would no longer even try to resist, that there was nothing left to do but seize her.

Thus, even before the beginning of the negotiations, the bugle of surrender had sounded. The consequence of this fact was tremendous: the cease-firing order was broadcast on the seventeenth; the Armistice was signed the evening of the twenty-second, and was not actually put into force until the night of the twenty-third — because the Germans refused to stop advancing until an armistice was arranged with the Italians as well. In this manner, for six days the Germans were enabled to take their time in surrounding and capturing hundreds of thousands of men who, *against their will but in obedience to orders,* had laid down their arms. On the nineteenth of June, the German Army crossed the Loire between Nantes and Tours. Bordeaux was bombed the same night. On the day of the Armistice there was fighting at the gates of Annecy, that is, practically on the Swiss border; the whole width of France had been spanned by the enemy armies.

Is it surprising that the Germans had been able to capture some 1,500,000 men — a number without precedent in history?

On this question I can furnish two pieces of evidence.

One comes from a general who, after the Armistice, commanded a group of divisions.

"I am proud," said he to me in his headquarters at Clermont-Ferrand, "that I am perhaps the only army commander who was able to bring all his equipment intact from Normandy to the neighborhood of Bayonne."

"Then, General, you must have had few of your men taken prisoner?"

"Alas," he answered, "I had as many as anyone else. How could it have been otherwise? My men were worn out with forced marches — completely exhausted. When they heard Pétain's voice over the radio telling them to stop firing, they were naïve enough to think that peace would come in a few days. How could I have gotten them to make the effort of another march? They preferred to be captured where they were, expecting that they would soon be able to go back home."

Another general who was in Rennes told me that on the morning of June 16, the city was prepared to defend itself. Barriers had been built across all the streets, and behind these barriers were men who, though exhausted, were resolved to fight to the end. The next day, after the Marshal's radio speech, they were ordered to abandon the barricades and go back to their garrisons — where, naturally, they were picked up by the Germans without any trouble.

Thus within a few weeks — and mostly within a few

days — France had had taken prisoner almost as many men as she had had killed in the whole four years of the first World War. For these prisoners, a prolonged captivity meant probable disease and death. And the blame for their plight rested chiefly on Pétain's shoulders. But this was not generally realized as yet. Most of Parliament, like most of the country, saw in him only the victor of Verdun.

By general consent it was decided that under the eyes of the enemy the public meeting of the National Assembly would only be a short formal ceremony and that all discussion would take place in a previous session behind closed doors, where Laval, spokesman for the invisible Marshal, would answer all questions and give all necessary explanations.

This meeting took place on the eighth. Here, Laval further developed the arguments he and his clique had already presented to many of the members individually. To reinforce them further, he produced a letter addressed to him and signed by Pétain, a letter whose text had certainly been inspired — and very probably dictated — by Laval himself. "As it is difficult for me to participate in the session," it read, "I beg you to represent my person. The vote on the project which the government is submitting to the National Assembly seems necessary for the salvation of our country." In effect, the project was that the Parliament give the Pétain government power to prepare a revised constitution.

Laval let it be understood that the powers the Assembly was asked to vote to the Pétain government would really be given to him, while at the same time he emphasized the idea that the Marshal's military prestige would help the country to obtain better terms from the Germans —

quick release of the prisoners, and economic conditions that would save the people from starvation. Here again he was clever. Pétain, in his first message to the French people after it had been decided to ask for an armistice, had said that he would negotiate "an honorable peace between soldiers," and many people (incredible as it may sound today!) actually believed that Pétain's prestige as a soldier would be an advantage in dealing with the Germans. On the other hand there were even then some people who, however much they respected Pétain as a soldier, distrusted him politically as a doddering clerical reactionary; these people preferred to leave the real power in the hands of a civilian even if they had no choice but a man with Laval's unsavory record.

Laval answered all interpellations from the floor with assurances of the purity of his own intentions, and reminders that if the Assembly showed itself too recalcitrant toward the man who had made the Armistice, the Germans might denounce it and continue to advance their tanks, which were on the demarcation line twenty-five miles away; the whole of France, then, would soon be occupied. The members of Parliament must think of their responsibility toward the country.

With most of the Assembly, the second of these arguments carried far greater weight than the first. Question after question was thrown at Laval by members who wanted to make sure that the text of the proposed law would contain guarantees against an overthrow of the republican regime.

Laval, while insisting that he, as much as anyone, wanted to defend the Republic, argued against making these guarantees too explicit, on the ground that a complicated text would displease the Germans. In the end, however, the text adopted did include the few words which at least preserved (as we shall see) the last chance of democracy.

Then the National Assembly met officially, on July 10, 1940, at 2 P.M. in the hall of the *Grand Théâtre*. Senators and Deputies sat together — roughly seven hundred of them out of a total membership of nine hundred. Léon Blum was there, alone, aloof, and very pale. Jeanneney presided. There was an opening speech by Herriot, in defense of Mandel and his companions who, at the time of the short-lived decision to move the government to North Africa, had embarked on the cruiser *Massilia,* had been accused as deserters, and had been arrested in Morocco. They had left, Herriot told the Assembly, with the full agreement of the government.

A long, careful, dreary report explaining laboriously the text which the Assembly would be asked to vote, and giving the most emphatic assurances with regard to the safeguarding of the Republic and the rights of Parliament, was read by Senator Boivin-Champeaux. There was nothing else — not one protest. Men whose republicanism, whose love of democracy, was above reproach — Herriot, Jeanneney, Blum, Louis Marin — had nothing to say.

Then came the vote. It was carried by 569 to 80, with some of those present abstaining (Edouard Herriot and Louis Marin among them). Those who did vote were divided into three very clear-cut groups.

First, the lucky 80. I say lucky because in the course of the events which followed their vote proved to be right, although at the time it really represented in most cases very little searching of conscience. What I mean is that these 80, with very few exceptions (I count Léon Blum as one of them), were mostly die-hards of the Extreme Left who had for years been trained to vote against everybody on everything. In fact, many of them had voted consistently against the extension of military service; against appropriations for armaments; against Daladier; against Reynaud. And even among the most Extreme Left party in the whole Parliament, the Socialists (the Communist Deputies had been arrested when war was declared), only 39 out of a total membership of 172 voted against Pétain.

As for the 569, they were divided into two groups.

One group saw in Pétain not only the maker of the Armistice but the man who would force upon France the new political and social order they had long wished for, and who would build such an order upon the Franco-German collaboration they had long advocated. The names of the men who composed this group are not generally known, but they may be found in an extraordinary document hitherto unpublished in the United States, and practically unknown in France itself: it is a "Declaration concerning the National Assembly," dated "July, 1940," and signed by 97 members of Parliament. It is a testament of faith setting forth at length the views and desires of the signatories; as a study of the collaborationist mentality, it would be hard to excel.

It lays the responsibility for the defeat of 1940 both on the Left, which it accuses of defending class interests exclusively, and on the Right, which it blames for defending the interests of "financial and economic coalitions" before the interests of the nation; then it attacks the regime for favoring both types of abuses. It laments the Republic's foreign policy between the two wars, and compares it to the immensely more efficient program of the Reich, concluding — in a passage that should be of particular interest to Americans — that France must follow in the path of Germany if she is to find ultimate salvation.

For the race toward a national form of socialism is universal, with the single exception of England among the great nations. Everywhere else, from the New Deal of the United States to the Stalinism of the U.S.S.R., and including the totalitarian states of Central Europe and the Iberian Peninsula, the peoples of the world have sought to attain, by spectacularly different means, identical ends.

It tries to reassure those who have qualms about the German attitude, and from this proceeds to a far franker declaration of the desires of the signatories than Laval ever made in Parliament: —

Certain people around the Fuehrer-Chancellor would no doubt like to profit from our defeat in order to crush us and thus avenge themselves for Jena, but others will understand, in virtue of the precedent of Jena itself, that it is impossible permanently to crush a real nation of 40 million inhabitants — above all when one is compelled to maintain order elsewhere among 40 million Slavs mixed with Germans in Central and Eastern Europe. . . .

We believe therefore that in the mind of the conqueror this or that tendency will prevail, according as to whether he finds before him in France men who will and can attempt the work of reconciliation and collaboration.

It is largely upon our choice — and an unequivocal choice — that our own destiny hangs.

The foreign policy which we have just outlined impels and even commands an internal policy. . . .

Such is, in our opinion, the road toward the future of France.

We must engage ourselves upon it without reticence, without reservations.

We do not propose to you a sullen France, brooding over her humiliation, because what has been defeated is only one aspect of France, and it deserved to be defeated.

We propose to reconstruct in ardor a France integrated into the New Europe. . . .

Among the 97 members of Parliament who founded thus, at one and the same time, collaboration and the authoritarian regime, was a sprinkling of men from various political groups, headed by Laval's henchmen, with the heaviest percentages coming from the same Extreme Right and Extreme Left whose influence on the country the document so indignantly flays,* and with a good many men who had never seriously pretended to be anything more than the opportunists they were. The collusion of the two extremes which I have already noted, and which I shall have occasion to bring up again, affirmed itself here in its most brutal and tragic aspect.

As for the second group — 472, a huge majority — they were of absolute good faith. They reasoned that since Pétain alone was responsible for the Armistice, Pétain alone should bear the responsibility of executing it. No one else could be charged with it.

What had they voted? I doubt very much that world opinion has ever fully known or understood.

They had voted three things, and no more: —

1. Considering the state of national emergency, they delegated full powers *"to the government of the Republic* under the authority and signature of Marshal Pétain."

2. And to what end? So that Pétain and his Cabinet might prepare a new Constitution, to be promulgated "after its ratification by the nation."

3. But they expressly provided that the Senate and Chamber of Deputies, as then constituted, should remain in function

* No Communists, of course, signed the document, since all the Communist members of Parliament (except those who had gone into hiding) had been arrested at the beginning of the war.

until the election of the two new Chambers to be provided for in the Constitution to be drafted.

Nothing could be clearer. The Parliament did not give Pétain any power of dictatorship. It delegated its power "to the government of the Republic, under the authority and signature of Marshal Pétain." And why Pétain? For an obvious reason: It is a constant political rule that he who has drafted a contract must be in charge of carrying it out. Pétain, without consulting Parliament, had taken the awful responsibility of the Armistice; he had to be given the responsibility of executing it to the best possible advantage.

Because the members of Parliament knew the obvious drawbacks of our Constitution of 1875, had suffered from them and, like the French people, wanted them to be corrected, they entrusted "the government of the Republic" to prepare a new Constitution. But obviously this Constitution could not but be that of an improved Republic, as a republican government was in charge of drafting it and the survival of the two Chambers was clearly stipulated. As for a legal guarantee for the maintenance of the Republic, Parliament thought it had a double one: first, it was to remain in function until the election of a new legislative Assembly; second, the Constitution providing for this new Assembly could not come into force until it should be ratified by the whole nation, whose verdict could not be doubted.

The constitutional law of July 10 conferred upon Pétain the power to *prepare* a Constitution, *and nothing more.* He had the right to prepare that Constitution for final submission to the approval of the nation, but he did not have the right to promulgate laws. In his function *as the executive authority,* Pétain, therefore, was provided with the same emergency powers which had been accorded his predecessors, Daladier and Reynaud.

But what happened? In spite of all his talk about a
"New Order," about a "National Revolution," Pétain
never drafted a new Constitution. He limited his effort
to organizing — if one may say so! — the executive, and
organizing it to his own profit.

He clearly and brazenly went beyond legality when
he published on the eleventh of July, 1940, his "Constitutional Act Number I," conceived as follows: "The Chief
of the French State *has the plenitude of governmental
power.* He exercises the legislative power in ministerial
council."

That was the *coup d'état,* the flagrant betrayal of the
text voted by the National Assembly. It was the swindle.

A little later, the *Journal Officiel* published four more
so-called "constitutional acts": —

Act II. Pétain made Laval his successor in the event of his
death; the former revolutionary socialist became the *Kronprinz.*

Act III. After the *coup d'état* of December 13, 1940, Pétain
dismissed Laval and made Darlan the new *Kronprinz.*

Act IV. After the landing of the Americans in North
Africa he dismissed Darlan; the post of the hereditary prince
was left vacant.

Act V. On November 17, 1942, he gave Laval full powers,
remaining himself only as nominal Chief of State.

The communiqué announcing this last decision appeared in the official French press over the joint signatures of Pétain and Laval. It ought to have discouraged
any who, at that time, were still trying to exonerate the
old Marshal.

Anyone with the slightest knowledge of law can testify that a constitution cannot have any value unless it is complete, and unless it provides for three powers: executive, legislative, and judiciary. The constitutional acts of Pétain, pretending to organize the executive only, are a mere mockery, and are obviously void. The Constitution of 1875 remains the only legal basis of government in France; and Parliament, which is the legislative body provided by the Constitution, remains in possession of its legal rights even though it is prevented from exercising them. For it is a universal constitutional rule that, in a democratic regime, there can be no interruption in the representation of the people. This principle means that elected officials automatically remain in possession of their mandates until successors have been elected to replace them — even if, for one reason or another, elections are postponed beyond their normal date. This principle was applied during the first World War in France, Belgium, and Great Britain; it is being applied in Great Britain at the present time.*

The National Assembly had clearly voted for the maintenance of the Republic. The greatest political swindle of all times came to pass. The National Assembly had trusted the promise given by Laval, in the name of the Man of Verdun, for the release of the prisoners; in saving the 1,500,000 prisoners it tried to save the very flesh and blood of France. A few weeks later Laval, covered by Pétain, gave up Alsace and Lorraine, and abandoned the prisoners in Germany. They sold the flesh and tried to kill the soul.

But the soul lives on.

* It should be noted that the regular nine-year term of the French Senators (one third of the total) elected just before the war has not yet expired.

CHAPTER XIII

Herriot

ON THE DAY after the fateful séance of the tenth of July, the parliamentarians scattered. Several of the ninety-seven who had signed the declaration of collaboration were still hovering around Vichy waiting for the ministerial portfolios with which Pétain and Laval were to reward them for their declaration of allegiance to the new regime. They formed a sort of court of the new sovereign. Most of the others had gone back to their electoral districts, where many of them, shortly afterward, were to receive an imperative "notice" from M. Marquet, the new Minister of the Interior, not to travel.

The Senate and the Chamber of Deputies, adjourned *sine die,* were no longer represented at Vichy except by their "bureaus." These bureaus really amount to executive committees. Each is made up of a president, four vice presidents, and eight secretaries, elected by their colleagues. They transact all business for the two Houses between sessions of Parliament — maintain their relations with the government and all public services, see to their representation in ceremonies, and perform miscellaneous secretarial duties.

The bureaus of the Senate and the Chamber had installed their services and their personnel in two modest hotels in Vichy, and, for a time, they continued to receive evidence of at least outward respect from the government.

Meanwhile the leaders of the Senate and Chamber —
Presidents, as they are called in France — preserved an
attitude of cold and distant dignity with regard to the
Pétain government. Jules Jeanneney, President of the
Senate, continued to live at Vichy. Edouard Herriot, President of the Chamber, lost no time in locking himself up
in his lonely house of Brotel, in the Valley of the Ambie.

In fact, at the beginning of 1941, a decree of Vichy
informed him that he had been replaced by a Vichy
officeholder as Mayor of Lyons, an office which he had
held for thirty years. Herriot was profoundly grieved. By
autumn of the same year, I had sent him word through a
friend that I should like to see him.

"Brotel is at the end of the world; you'll have a time
finding me," he had replied. But I answered that I would
find him all right, and having secured — by the rarest
good fortune, and after many difficulties — a car, gasoline, and a trustworthy driver, I set out for Brotel,
which is in the country near the tiny hamlet of Hyères-
sur-Ambie. After traversing the wide suburbs of Lyon
and rolling along through a flat, monotonous country-
side, I had gone about forty kilometers into the Department of the Isère when suddenly the scenery changed and
hills appeared — then a sort of little mountain. A pointed
rock overhung the valley.

"This is the Valley of the Ambie," my driver said, "and
the President is up there."

It was a very fine day. The ridges showed up sharp and
clear against the blue sky. Nestling on the edge of the
promontory, which seemed to be sliding down into the
valley, stood a little tower. I couldn't tell, from that
distance, whether it was a ruin or a dwelling. Then we
left the highway and entered a rough little road; we
passed over the little Ambie River by a rustic bridge; and

the donjonlike building loomed before us. Soon we stopped before a simple wooden gate fastened only by a latch, and there stood Herriot.

He was wearing a sweater, a cap, and large boots. He came forward slowly, rather heavily; then, as he recognized me, his face lighted up with a benevolent smile. He took my shoulder affectionately and we walked along side by side through the little courtyard in silence. The President was moved but did not want to show it.

As for me, I could not help thinking of Herriot at the time when he represented the power of a France still free. My mind was taking me back to the Palais-Bourbon in Paris, at three o'clock of a certain afternoon. I saw the Republican Guards, evenly aligned on the tiled floors of the *Salle des Pas Perdus,* standing at attention. I heard the command barked, "Present . . . arms!" The drums beat. And between the double hedge of bayonets President Herriot — in dress suit and white cravat, top hat in his hand — advanced slowly. He stopped in front of the officer in command of the detail and bowed. The officer saluted with his sword. *Cedant arma togae* — the army paid homage to the representative of the nation. What a downfall since then!

On the righthand side of the courtyard there was a little one-story building with two windows.

"See," Herriot said, "my guardhouse." His face lighted up maliciously. With his habitual gesture he took hold of my shoulder to make me stop while we went on talking: "I call this little building the Pavilion of Ingratitude. Just listen to this, my friend. After the National Assembly, I spent a little time at Lyon; then I came here one fine September morning to stay in complete solitude. But a visitor was announced. A creature presented himself, very ill at ease. From twenty feet away he smelled of the

police. He was embarrassed as he explained that he had
come from Vichy . . . he was a police commissioner . . .
he had been ordered to billet himself with two policemen
in my house.

"'Then,' I said to him, 'I am your prisoner?'

"'No, but—'

"'Then I am free?'

"'Certainly, but—'

"'I understand. Like Rostand's *L'Aiglon,* I am "not
a prisoner but . . ."'

"The creature knew his literature—and was good
enough to smile.

"'Listen,' I said to him, 'I can't lodge you in my house.
But I have a little two-room cottage which is no longer
in use and which would be comfortable for you. I will
have it cleaned. As for your policemen, I have two servants' rooms. That will be all right for them, eh?'"

Herriot pulled his legendary pipe out of his pocket and
ran his hand up and down it but did not fill it.

"In short, *mon cher,* this spy lived here for three months.
I call him 'this spy' and you will see why. The next morning I started out as usual for my walk. I went into the
little grove and suddenly I had the feeling that someone
was walking behind me. I turned around—there was my
commissioner. I stopped. He stopped. I went on again
. . . twenty yards behind me he started on again.

"That kept up for ten days. My shadow never left me.
One morning I was so exasperated that I couldn't stand
it any longer and went up to him.

"'Listen, Monsieur,' I said to him, 'since we are fated
to walk every morning at the same time and at the same
spot, why not walk together? Come with me . . .'

"And I took him by the arm. My commissioner was
my prisoner. The blackguard, I have already told you,

knew a little about literature. He loved Lamartine. We recited the verses of the poet together. On the other hand, there were gaps in his classical learning. I helped him fill them. He hadn't anything to read. I allowed him to use my library.

"One day when we had taken a little longer walk than usual — and a pleasant enough walk — and were passing this little pavilion on our return, I stopped him.

" 'My dear Commissioner,' I said, 'you have been taking your meals alone for a whole month. That can't be lively for you. Won't you give me the pleasure of lunching with me?'

"He accepted without shame . . . and that went on for three months. He ate at my table, drank my last wine, smoked my last cigarettes, made himself at home in my library. Then the day came when it was decided (Flandin had just replaced Laval) to discontinue this supervision of my person, and my commissioner took his departure. He thanked me warmly.

"A month later I learned — because I still have good friends and hear everything — that he had turned in to Vichy a filthy report about me. All the time I was treating him as a guest, the dirty scoundrel had been taking notes on my most important visitors, my slightest remarks, my gestures, spying on me even in the bathroom, emptying my wastepaper basket. Now, wasn't that dishonorable?"

"It wasn't dishonorable, my dear President. It was Vichy."

Herriot snorted, pulled at his cap, and raising his pipe-stem to point out the path, said, "Come on. Let's go to lunch!"

We went through a low door and came to a narrow terrace. On three sides we looked down a precipice steep enough to make one dizzy. Only the courtyard through which we had come attached us to solid earth.

"I haven't touched the outside of the building," Herriot said. "I have even left the loophole windows, inconvenient as they are. I just furnished the interior."

The refurnishing had been conceived with both simplicity and taste. Everything inside was of quasi-monastic severity. A long wooden table, set on trestles; some rustic chairs; the tall stone chimney — that was all I could see of the dining room, for the walls were almost hidden by war maps.

The only luxury of this unpretentious house was the library — or more exactly, the two libraries. On the ground floor, next to the dining room, was the President's office with a large working collection of volumes on history, geography, politics, and philosophy. On the second floor, to which we climbed by a spiral staircase with decayed treads, was his holy of holies; the shelves were of plain wood, but on these shelves what treasures! Here was the collection of which the President was proudest — a collection of original editions of the Romantic period.

In this library I had an opportunity to interview the President that day. I had not seen him since the last session of the Chamber of Deputies in April 1940, eighteen months before. I thought he was much thinner, and pale. He did not say a word, but just opened his arms, and we two — who had opposed each other many times in the political arena — shamelessly hugged each other.

My son had at one time been preparing his doctor's thesis on one of the strangest personages of the Restoration — Prosper de Barante — a rival of Benjamin Constant, one of the intimates of Mme. de Staël, who was herself an intimate of Mme. Récamier — of whom Herriot had written a valuable biography. The President had re-

ceived my son with paternal kindness, had offered to
help him in his work, and had put his own books at his
disposal, and this incident had made a bond of affection
between us. But now there was a further bond. In the
past we had been courteous but resolute adversaries; now,
united by our concern for our country, we were still
more resolute allies.

After lunch — which was prepared by the President's
faithful old servant, the legendary Césarine, who would
manage to make anyone enjoy even rutabagas — I let him
pour me a few drops from a bottle of old brandy which
was, alas, nearly empty; and, smiling philosophically, he
measured his own share parsimoniously. It was a souvenir
of the happy France we both recalled so well, and it
mustn't be wasted. Then we began to talk about our
country.

All at once, interrupting the conversation, the President
pulled out his big gold watch from his pocket and said: —

"Heavens! We nearly forgot Sottens. It's 2:15, and we
don't let anything in the world keep us from getting the
latest news from the Swiss radio."

But on that day the military situation was stagnant.
Herriot switched off the radio, took his famous pipe out
of his pocket, lit it slowly, and said: —

"Tell me about our colleagues. Have you seen So-and-
so . . . and So-and-so? . . . And So-and-so?"

When I told him of the magnificent behavior of some
of them Herriot's face beamed. But all at once his eyes
filled with tears. He put his hand on my arm, and, lean-
ing toward me, said in a different tone: —

"Do you know they have guillotined Catelas?"

Jean Catelas had been one of our Communist colleagues,
a Deputy from Amiens. He was a veteran of the Great
War, several times cited for conspicuous gallantry, and the

father of five children. I could see in my mind his thickset figure, his genial round face. I remembered him as a fine man. I had learned of his death, but was not aware of the horrible manner of it.

"Yes," Herriot went on, "guillotined, you understand, guillotined — for a political offense — and by Frenchmen."

How could one fail to put the responsibility on the Vichy government? And so it happened that Darlan's name came naturally to the tongue.

"Listen to me, my dear Fernand-Laurent," the President said. "I want to tell you something about Darlan. One can't know what the future may bring. I may disappear. . . . You are younger than I, so I am telling you this, not as a secret, but as a historical fact which I charge you to make known.

"Here it is: On the afternoon of Saturday, June 15, 1940, I was in Bordeaux. Senators and Deputies kept arriving in the city, already overcrowded. Jeanneney and I didn't know where to put them. Then I had an idea: There were warships in the harbor at Le Verdon. Why not use these temporarily to house the members of Parliament? I called our colleague Campinchi, Minister of the Navy. Campinchi said that unfortunately he was too busy to come to see me but that he would send his chief of staff, Admiral Darlan. Half an hour later Darlan arrived and said to me these very words: —

" 'Mr. President, your request is a perfectly natural one, and in any other circumstance I should be most happy to accede to it. But I need all my ships. They are getting up steam, to be ready to sail. With an undefeated fleet, I want to fight. I am not like those two miserable creatures [Pétain and Weygand]; I shall not recognize any armistice.'

"Darlan, very much excited, went on to explain vehemently that Toulon could, and should, be defended. I thanked and congratulated him."

President Herriot went on: "That, you remember, was on Saturday, June 15. The next day, Sunday, June 16, I was in President Lebrun's office with Paul Reynaud, who had come to offer his resignation. Marshal Pétain was announced. He had come to present to the President of the Republic the new government which he had just formed — the government which was to sign the Armistice. And whom did I see at Pétain's side? Darlan, who had accepted the post of Minister, along with those two 'miserable creatures' — *only twenty-four hours after he had made that declaration to me.*"

The next time I saw President Herriot he was no longer a country squire in the solitude of the Isère mountains; he was a townsman wearing a correct black suit in the dull little town of Chatel-Guyon, where the season at the spa was at its height. That was in August, in 1942. I had planned to stay a month at Chatel-Guyon, on the pretext of poor health, but really in order to be at the center of political activity at a time which I expected would be critical. I was right.

Just opposite the mineral baths, the Hotel Richelieu had been requisitioned to lodge what was left of the once august Chamber of Deputies. The presence of the last representatives of the Chamber at Vichy was for the archtraitor Laval a kind of defiance. He had exiled them to the twenty-five-mile-distant spa of Chatel-Guyon.

This dull and dirty third-class hotel was now the rendezvous for all the politicians who still stood apart from

Vichy, and who tried to keep contact with what remained of constitutional France.

At the two ends of the street which ran along the edge
of the park, two unpretentious villas lodged the President of the Senate and the President of the Chamber.
M. Jeanneney's house was directly opposite the headquarters of the Vichy Youth Movement, so that, ironically,
the President of the Senate was awakened each morning
by the ritual chant: *"Maréchal, nous voilà!"*

When I arrived at the beginning of August, to get in
touch with my colleagues and comrades — whose names
elementary prudence forbids me to mention — Laval had
crossed his Rubicon. He was no longer only a collaborator
with the Reich; he had become simply the servant of
Hitler, the executor of his vile works. The *"relève"* was
just beginning — the disgraceful practice of trading
French prisoners in Germany for French workers who
were to be rounded up and sent like slaves to the work
camps of the enemy.

All of us felt that this was the beginning of a terrible
crisis. We knew that the French people would inevitably
resist. Those of our group who still had access to Vichy
tried to say this and came back discouraged. They had
not been able to get to the Marshal; and Laval, fearing
their scorn, had refused to receive them.

On the morning of the twentieth of August, as
M. Herriot and I were discussing these developments
in his little villa, our conversation finally turned to
America.

My own situation was becoming more and more critical.
My son had once again been denounced to the courts as
a patriot. He was certain to be condemned. Should I wait
for him? Or had the time come to try to join Fighting

France? I consulted the President. His reply was positive: —

"There is no question," he said slowly. "Your duty, the
duty of all of us, is to stay in France till the last possible
moment. . . . But evidently you have almost reached this
limit. If by chance you do reach the United States some
day, tell them that I have received all their appeals to go
there myself. Tell them that I am touched to the bottom
of my heart by the friendship of the people of the United
States. But tell them also why, without any qualm of
conscience, sure of my duty, I have decided not to accept.
Under the terms of the vote of the National Assembly of
July 10, 1940, the Parliament is still functioning. It is
around us that sooner or later the legal representation
of the country must inevitably group itself. Our duty is
to stay at our posts to defend the rights of Parliament,
which are the rights of the people, and this is a role I
shall never step out of."

It was on August 25 that I learned of Laval's brutal
and blundering decision to dissolve the "bureaus" of the
Senate and the Chamber of Deputies — an arbitrary act
designed to destroy their last chance of functioning as
official bodies. MM. Jeanneney and Herriot sent Marshal
Pétain their letter of protest, calm, noble, indignant. This
letter appeared in the American press, but I might mention here one detail which perhaps was not noticed: it
did not begin or end with any kind of salutation. I mentioned this to President Herriot.

"That was intentional," he told me. "You know that
M. Jeanneney and I have always paid the greatest attention to courtesy — even with the Vichy people. But this
time! The order for the dissolution bore the signature of
the Marshal. Yet Pétain, who, before, when writing to me,
had always signed himself as 'most faithfully yours,'

didn't have the courage to inform us directly of his decision. Our first news of it was from the press. That is why, when we addressed our letter of protest to him, we, for our part, would not use any salutation."

*   *   *

On August 30, a little before noon, in the drab, commonplace little salon on the ground floor of the Hotel Richelieu, President Herriot said farewell to the personnel of the Chamber of Deputies — to the General Secretary; to the faithful secretaries who, refusing to go back to Paris, had followed him into exile; to the humblest of his employees. The scene was immeasurably moving. The President had for each one a word from the heart. All eyes were moist. . . . And I, who had so often fought under the President's rule at the tribune of the Chamber, stood there in a corner completely overwhelmed.

"God knows when we shall see each other again."

"Before long . . . in free Paris!"

Since I have been in this country, Herriot's death in captivity has been rumored several times. I profoundly hope these rumors are false. There is no other man in France whose presence would be so reassuring to friends of the Republic he so valiantly strove to defend.

CHAPTER XIV

Weygand

IF WE CONFINE OURSELVES — as we should — to strictly authentic documents, to indisputably proved facts, then according to the best information we have today General Weygand is still an enigmatic figure. I make no pretense of solving the enigma. But I do have one piece of first-hand evidence which may add something to our picture of him.

After his retirement in 1936 General Weygand habitually showed a bitter and discontented attitude and never missed an opportunity to express the severest criticism of Pétain. He spent a good deal of his leisure time in writing works on military history — among others, a life of Turenne, of which certain passages have a special interest for us. One of them reads: "Then Turenne revealed his thoughts and his hope in this sentence, which will remain true as long as France exists: 'Mark my words, no military man in France can afford to rest as long as there is a single German on this side of the Rhine in Alsace.'" The author reminds us that this sentence was inscribed on Turenne's statue in the Invalides, and he adds: "Since the war [the first World War] the inscription has disappeared. It was doubtless judged to have become useless."

"It was doubtless judged . . ."! The words contain all the bitterness, all the scorn which Weygand feels toward the government and the leaders of the country.

Weygand was a convinced and declared partisan of a military alliance with Soviet Russia. On this point there is plenty of evidence. One day he asked Colonel des Isnards, my colleague in the House Military Committee, to go to see him; he knew that des Isnards opposed such an alliance, and wanted to bring him around to his own point of view. Weygand presented his argument so well that des Isnards was finally convinced. Another of my colleagues, André Daher, a Deputy from Marseilles, had expressed anti-Soviet opinions in the Chamber; the General asked him, too, to call on him, and attempted, in the higher interests of national defense, to get him to change his opinions.

As a member of the *Fédération Républicaine,* Weygand consented to be a member of the party's committee on national defense, where he met a number of his comrades from the first World War. On several occasions during 1939 I had presented to this committee reports on the state of our military preparations; and the General, who had followed these reports with the greatest attention, had been particularly impressed by the deficiencies they revealed. Nevertheless he made — at Lille in July 1939, less than two months before hostilities began — the speech I have already cited in which he declared: "The French Army is stronger than ever. France does not want war. But if she were called to win a new victory I can assure you that she would win it."

We have seen how quickly this war that Weygand had promised to make victorious was lost by the General Staff; how Weygand, appointed generalissimo on May 19, had suggested a separate armistice as early as May 29. We have seen how during the following weeks he fought with Mandel over the question, and finally won out — his only victory in this war. It is only fair to add that, once the Armistice had been signed, he assumed an attitude of dignified sorrow: he understood and shared the country's mourning; he accepted the defeat; but unlike so many others he did not rejoice in it. It was he who said to Laval: "Monsieur, you wallow in defeat as you would in dung"; it was also he who a little later called Darlan a liar in the middle of a Cabinet meeting. At this time he was firmly convinced that the defeat of Britain was very near at hand.

I met General Weygand in Vichy in August 1940. In the course of a brief conversation he described to me in concise and uncomplimentary terms all his colleagues in the government, sparing not a single one except the venerable and inoffensive M. Caziot, Minister of Agriculture.

Weygand lost his post as Minister of National Defense in the ministerial shakeup in September of 1940. He was then made High Commissioner for North Africa. This change, from the point of view of the government, was no more or less than a disgrace; and it was certainly made on the urgent insistence of the Nazis, and as a result of Weygand's protest before the Cabinet against the German annexation of Alsace and Lorraine.

In November and December 1940, Weygand openly opposed the policy of Pierre Laval; there is no doubt that his opinions contributed much to persuade the Marshal to dismiss Laval on December 13. Finally it may be considered as certain that in the spring of 1941 it was Weygand's personal action which prevented French North and West Africa from participating in the Syrian campaign on the side of the Axis.

I was going over these things in my mind as, on the afternoon of February 1, 1942, I climbed the hill toward Grasse. Weygand had shut himself up in solitude in a little hotel there; in order to get his permission to visit him I had had to frame my request in very urgent terms. "My duty," I had written him, "is to insist on seeing you, and yours, without a doubt, is to hear what I have to say." I found Weygand in a banal hotel drawing room whose walls were almost completely covered with maps. His personal flag was hanging in the central panel. The atmosphere was like that of a General Staff headquarters.

Our conversation began immediately. Weygand was in a very bad humor and it was less a dialogue than a fencing match.

"You know that I don't want to see anyone. You insisted; you spoke of duty. That is the only reason I am receiving you."

"Those Frenchmen who have had confidence in you and whose leader you have been, General, certainly have the right, under present circumstances, to know your attitude, your opinion; and I feel it my duty to ask you what it is."

"My opinion about what? In what capacity? I am nothing at all any more. My country no longer wants my services. I cannot serve my country against her will."

"Obviously that depends on what you mean by 'country.' Am I to understand that for you Vichy is still the country? Not for us."

"Whom do you mean by 'us'?"

"You know perfectly well, General, that there are but two classes of Frenchmen: those who refuse to bow before the enemy and those who fall on their knees before him."

"You don't think I am one of those! I fall on my knees only to pray to God."

"The French who refuse to bow are — as you know — the immense majority of the country. They have a right to know what leaders they can count on."

"What do they expect from me? I have lost my post. What did they want me to do?"

"To keep it."

"Incite North Africa to rebel against Pétain? Never! We made the Armistice together. It was I who wanted the Armistice, you understand. I admit it. I take the full responsibility for it."

"You will soon be called to Riom as a witness, General."

"So it appears. Why do you mention that?"

"I, too, am a witness. I believe that we are to go before the court in about ten days."

"I am ready."

"You realize, of course, that your speech at Lille will be brought up?"

"Well, what did I say? That if we had to win a victory we would win it. Should I have told the Germans that we weren't ready?"

"It is also certain that they will bring up the German White Paper, which contains your declaration before the last meeting of the War Council. Did you not say, then, that France had been wrong to go to war without sufficient armament and without a military doctrine?"

The General was annoyed almost beyond words. He got up, walked away with quick nervous steps, then suddenly turned around and exclaimed furiously:—

"Well, what then? They can shoot me if they want to!"

I was silent, stupefied by this outburst, and horribly embarrassed.

Weygand seemed to understand that he had gone too far, and said, with an obvious effort to soften his tone:—

"Well, never mind that. . . . Let's see, today is Sunday: there are no newspapers, and I have no radio here. Could you give me the latest news?"

"The very latest, General, the news that came in over the London station at 2:15."

"Well then, come here. . . ."

Weygand went over and stood in front of an immense map of Russia on which red and black pins indicated the German and Russian lines. I analyzed the latest communiqués while the General moved the pins. The first Russian counteroffensive was just reaching its height; that morning the Soviet troops had made another advance toward Smolensk.

The General had completely recovered his calm and spoke in his usual commanding tone.

"Then according to the latest news I could put a marker for the Russians here? Or maybe nearer here?"

He held out one pin, then another. With the third he hesitated. I showed him how to correct its position.

"According to the latest bulletins, General, you may even move it forward to here."

Weygand drove in his last pin and then turned around: —

"But that changes everything!"

And crossing the room with a brisk step, he motioned me to come over and look at a map of Africa.

There, too, the news was good. Red pins marked the latest advance — a very considerable one — of the British troops.

This interlude eased the situation. We sat down again. Stubbornly I continued my interrogation.

"When we see this map of Libya, General, and think of our Africa . . ."

The General was touched.

"Come, come, the French know perfectly well that I did all my duty in Africa. And you know how I was thanked for it. What a dirty trick!"

We were both silent for a moment.

"I did my duty too well, I suppose. Didn't I get rid of all the Germans they sent me just as soon as they arrived?"

"Then, General, as far as the immediate future is concerned, can't I take the same message from you . . ."

"No, no, I've told you already. They took away my job. Now I am retired. I want to be left alone."

The General thought for a moment, then added: —

"And then, you see, whatever happens I have definitely decided now that I will never again serve anyone who does not entirely share my political and religious opinions."

This declaration was so unexpected, so far from the subject, that I was unable to answer. I murmured some sort of polite good-by and got up to leave.

The General saw how troubled I was and said as we reached the doorstep: —

"I was seventy-five years old today. Maybe it's time to find someone younger."

I saw Weygand for the last time Monday morning, November 9, 1942, at the very moment when the Germans and Italians were getting ready to invade the zone that was still unoccupied. He was shopping in Cannes with his wife. When he went back to have lunch at his house on the Croisette he found a summons from the government. Pétain had sent one of his private automobiles to take him immediately to Vichy. He left during the evening — and never came back.

Weygand stayed only a day or two in Vichy. Pétain wanted to consult him on African affairs. No one has ever been able to find out what definite offer Pétain made Weygand on that occasion, but one thing is certain: Weygand refused, purely and simply, to consider any suggestions. He had been dismissed from his post in North Africa; why should he go back? He was in retirement and wanted to stay there.

He left Vichy early in the afternoon of November 11, in the Marshal's car; his son, Captain Weygand, and his daughter-in-law were with him; they wanted to get back to Cannes sometime during the night. But they were only about fifteen miles from Vichy when two German military cars, forcing them to give way, passed them at full speed. In the first of these two gray cars were a colonel and another German officer. In the second, an escort armed with sub-machine guns. On the front seat of each car, beside the chauffeur, was a helmeted German with a machine gun. The more powerful of the two cars stopped some five hundred yards in front of the one in which Weygand was riding; then, with a quick jerk of the wheel, the chauffeur turned it across the road. Weygand's driver had barely time to put on the brakes. The German Colonel jumped out of the car, ran to Weygand, saluted and said: "General, I have been ordered to arrest you. Captain and Madame Weygand may stay in this car, which is going back to Vichy; they will soon hear from you. As for you, General, kindly follow me into my car."

Weygand hastily said good-by to his children; then, without a word, climbed into the car. The next moment he was on his way to Germany.

CHAPTER XV

Pétain

PÉTAIN AND WEYGAND, closely united in their mutual desire for an armistice, had based all their calculations — their entire policy — on the certainty that Great Britain would not resist the onslaught, and that the total victory of Germany was only a question of a few weeks.

As the months passed and the war went on, what must have been the secret state of mind of these two men in the face of the glaring fact that belied their judgment?

It so happened that I was able to converse privately with Pétain after the Armistice, and his remarks on this occasion seem to me of such importance that I feel it my duty to all to record them for future historians.

I saw Pétain for the first time since the Armistice at the beginning of January 1941, in his office in the all too famous Hotel du Parc in Vichy, about three weeks after the discharge of Laval. I was then publishing my paper — in Marseille, wishing to stay as far away as possible from the rest of the government — and I went to Vichy, where the atmosphere seemed to me unbreathable, only when my professional obligations forced me to do so. On the occasion of which we speak I had told my Vichy correspondent beforehand that I wanted to see the Marshal. He had held out little hope of my being able to get an appointment. The Chief of State was deluged with requests for interviews; it was necessary to apply at least a week in advance, and even then . . . Nevertheless I was able to see Pétain late in the afternoon of the day I arrived in Vichy. His physician, Dr. Ménétrel (who has recently resigned) made him rest every day for two hours after lunch, so that he did not see people again until four o'clock; and at six he had to leave his office again for another rest before dinner.

"*Monsieur le Maréchal,* you told me in Bordeaux that you had been wrong not to see me again. In my turn, I must tell you that I should be doing wrong in the sight of my conscience if I did not come to you of my own accord to speak to you more candidly than your associates, doubtless, feel free to do."

"As a matter of fact, you have always spoken to me with a frankness which I have not found displeasing."

"*Monsieur le Maréchal,* for twenty-two years, as a representative of the people, I have had to keep in close touch with public opinion; and it is the people's deepest feelings that I want to tell you about today."

"Do you think I don't know what they are?"

"I hope you do, *Monsieur le Maréchal,* and in that case we shall soon reach an agreement. You know that just after the meeting of the National Assembly, just after the defeat, you had three quarters of the country behind you. The French, in their despair, clung to you (I hope the word doesn't shock you; it's the only exact one) in the belief that you would free their prisoners, save them from famine and disorder."

"I know it."

"And you know that when you went to meet Hitler, and because you went to meet Hitler, you lost the best part of your popularity?"

"I know it. The French didn't understand. I can't blame them for it."

"But you also know that the day you discharged Laval you gained back all the ground you had lost?"

"I know it. Do you know M. Laval?"

And before I could even answer he flushed purple and added, hammering out each word as if he wanted to drive a blow home: "*He is a wretched creature.*"

"*Monsieur le Maréchal,* to say I know Laval is not enough. I am certainly one of the three or four men in France who know him best and have known him for the longest time."

And we began to speak of the career of this man, who is today the *Gauleiter* of France.

Laval, as everyone knows, began his career as an anarchist who ranted against French imperialism. By 1914 his name was in the files of the Intelligence Service among those to be arrested in case of mobilization. He took no part in the first World War. In 1919 he presented himself as a Socialist candidate in the suburb of Billancourt, in a district inhabited chiefly by workers in the Renault and Farman factories, and was badly beaten. For five years after that he remained without a political position and without a job. Then in 1924 he was among the members of Parliament elected on the ticket of the coalition known as the Cartel des Gauches, and immediately began his cynical and rapid evolution. Now as chance would have it, in 1932 I stood for election to Parliament in this same district of Billancourt and won the vote of the majority of these same workmen. The coincidence and the contrast made a great impression on Laval.

I had seen him for the last time at the beginning of September 1940, and on that occasion had expressed my certainty of an ultimate German defeat. Nothing could have pained him more than such a statement coming from me. He had answered it with an explosion of reptilelike

Anglophobia. "At Chateldon," he had cried, "I sleep on English bones that have been there since the Hundred Years' War."

I repeated this remark to the Marshal.

"He told me the same thing," said the Marshal. "He hates them."

"He hates them because they forced him to abandon power in 1935. He is making France pay for his personal grudges."

"He wanted to govern over my head. I had him arrested. The Germans insisted that he be freed."

"*Monsieur le Maréchal,* I came here to tell you about the fears of the public. The people certainly have no doubt of your good intentions, but your meeting with Hitler at Montoire shocked them to the core. They know your associates; they know how powerful the Boches are. The Germans caused Laval to be set free; mightn't they make you take him back tomorrow?"

The Marshal seemed to hesitate, then said emphatically: —

"*I had the courage to get rid of him; I'll certainly have the courage not to take him back.*"

Alas! Fifteen months later Laval was again in power, France was becoming more and more Nazified, racial persecutions were increasing, and the Gestapo ruled supreme.

Eighteen months later Laval said over the radio: "*I hope for a German victory.*" And Pétain, a few days later, proclaimed: "*I walk hand in hand with Monsieur Laval.*" His fate was thenceforth sealed.

But before this I was to have one more interview with Pétain — the longest, the most dramatic, and the most memorable — in Vichy on February 3, 1942.

I had gone to show the Marshal a copy of a letter I had

written to the late M. Pucheu (then Minister of the Interior and since executed in Algiers), which read as follows: —

Vichy, January 31, 1942

Monsieur le Ministre,

I wish to call your attention to the fact that my son, Lieutenant Fernand-Laurent, a wounded war veteran, 75% incapacitated, holder of the *Croix de guerre* with a Palm, Knight of the Legion of Honor, having been convicted of patriotism, is now being held in the prison of Clermont-Ferrand; I want you to know that he shares a disgustingly filthy cell with ten other prisoners, among whom are six common criminals, swindlers or thieves. I want you to know this: obliged to receive medical treatment every day, this wounded man is taken from the prison to the hospital on foot, with his stiff leg, between two policemen and handcuffed.

Such a situation causes me the deepest sorrow.

FERNAND-LAURENT

"*Monsieur le Maréchal,*" I asked when I saw Pétain, "do you want to read this letter or would you rather I read it to you?"

"Read it to me."

As I read, the Marshal, resting his hands on the arms of his chair, leaned further and further toward me and, as soon as I had finished, asked in an angry voice: —

"What does that mean?"

"Exactly what it says. That is the way your Minister of the Interior treats the best of our soldiers."

"Let's see . . . I don't understand. Your son has been arrested? Why?"

"You heard; he has been convicted of patriotism."

"What do you mean by that?"

"We call 'patriots' those who refuse to accept the defeat and the German occupation. My son was called to the colors and severely wounded in order to protect French territory from the enemy. He considers that his task has not changed, that it continues. His position, as you know quite well, is that of the majority of the French."

"But, more specifically, what is he charged with?"

"With being one of the directors of the newspaper *Combat*."

"I never heard of that paper."

"I should be indeed surprised if anyone put it on your table. *Combat* is a patriotic newspaper which tries to tell the truth and for that reason does not please your Minister of the Interior. . . ."

"Have you delivered your letter to M. Pucheu?"

"This very morning."

"Did you see him?"

"Yes."

"What did he tell you?"

"*Monsieur le Maréchal,* in order not to waste your time, I'll tell you the gist of our conversation. You said in one of your messages: 'To succeed, a revolution must have the people with it.' I told M. Pucheu that his government was so far from having the people with it that in a free election it wouldn't get five per cent of the votes."

"What did he answer?"

"That he knew it perfectly well, but that it didn't matter. He said the French were imbeciles who must be led without being consulted."

In reality Pucheu had used a much shorter and more brutal word. I purposely repeated it aloud in the Marshal's office, where it doubtless echoed for the first time.

Pétain gasped.

"What? He dared . . . He told you . . . ?"

"That the French were —— ? Yes, *Monsieur le Maré-chal*."

"How horrible! What did you say?"

"That as far as abstract ideas were concerned, he was probably right, since he was much more intelligent than the average Frenchman, but that the Franco–German problem was much more a matter of feeling than a matter of ideas. And the feelings of the French people about this problem are quite definite. In their hearts they hate all forms of collaboration. And you cannot force the hearts of the French; they are given or refused; you can't win them over through a ministerial decision."

The Marshal looked at me sadly.

"You know I didn't select M. Pucheu. But Admiral Darlan went to Berlin; he came back with a government ready-made; I could do nothing but accept it or break. . . . Do you know M. Pucheu well?"

"I knew him as secretary general of Monsieur Germain-Martin's committee. . . ."

"What committee?"

Before the war there were two big employers' organizations: the *Confédération Générale du Patronat Français,* directed by Monsieur Gignoux, which handled matters of general policy, and the *Comité de Prévoyance et d'Action Sociale,* at the head of which was Monsieur Germain-Martin, a former Minister of Finance. *That one took care of propaganda and electoral campaigns. Monsieur Pucheu was its secretary general.*

Pétain's face lighted up.

"Ah! Yes," he said. "Synarchy."

He had just received a voluminous report on "synarchy" and had been much impressed by it. Slowly, gravely, he explained its main points to me. In reality, synarchy is nothing but a new and fanciful name to describe the permanent understanding among a certain number of inspectors of finance and graduates of the Ecole de Polytechnique by which they assure themselves the control of all the great industrial enterprises of the country.

None of this was new to me.

"You know," said the Marshal, "that I have taken a definite stand against the trusts."

"And that your government is under the control of the representatives of the great trusts — alas, yes, *Monsieur le Maréchal.*"

At this moment a characteristic incident occurred. The Marshal's usher came into the office.

"*Monsieur le Maréchal,* Monsieur Xavier Vallat, who has an appointment, has been waiting for a long time already."

Monsieur Xavier Vallat, a former colleague of mine at the Chamber of Deputies, was then Commissioner General for Jewish Affairs.

Pétain, without even turning around, said over his shoulder, "Let him wait."

He turned to me: —

"And Monsieur Barthélemy [then Minister of Justice]? Did you see him?"

"Yes, *Monsieur le Maréchal.*"

"Well?"

"In a very long conversation, he made this one strikingly ridiculous remark. 'Yes,' he said, 'our prisons are too small. Just now I have 80,000 people in them. As for your son, I saw to his case myself. Obviously there are vermin, a great many vermin, in his prison. But what can be done about it? The head jailer said he would destroy them with the blowtorch. But there's no gasoline for the blowtorch.' "

"What squalor!"

At this point the usher, probably urged on by the impatient visitor, opened the door again.

"Monsieur Xavier Vallat."

"Let him wait!"

And, raising both arms above his head in a gesture of exasperation, Pétain exclaimed: —

"That man!"

"That man, *Monsieur le Maréchal,* has only implemented, by order of your government, the anti-Semitic decrees that you yourself signed."

Pétain turned sharply to me.

"Come, you know perfectly well that I am a Christian like yourself, that my opinion on that subject is exactly the same as yours. *Give me time and I'll fix all that.*"

Then he added, to change the subject: —

"Come, tell me about the general situation. What's your opinion?"

I told the Marshal my reasons for being optimistic. The Russian offensive was developing; the Russians were pushing a threatening spearhead in the direction of Smolensk.

"Yes, yes, of course," said Pétain. "But they must beat the Germans this winter, without giving them a chance to recover, otherwise they will never beat them."

"But America is in the war now. Her industrial strength will be the deciding factor."

This time, Pétain's face lighted up.

"You are right. *I count a great deal on the Americans.*"

Then he added, suddenly: —

"You are really well informed."

"*Monsieur le Maréchal,* it's my duty as a politician. And then, too — don't tell your Ministers — I listen to the news broadcasts from everywhere."

"I'm afraid they don't tell me about all of them. . . ."

For ten minutes more the conversation continued, touching various subjects. I mentioned the presumptuousness of the German and Italian Armistice commissions, their daily encroachments on French sovereignty, their demands, the flagrant violations of the Armistice. Pétain interrupted me in an angry tone: —

"The Armistice! It's been violated a hundred times!"

Suddenly, in the middle of a sentence, the name of Doriot dropped like a bomb. I reminded the Marshal of Doriot's famous speech in the Chamber of Deputies, when he was a Communist boasting that he was the ally of Abd-el-Krim's rebels against French imperialism, against France.

"Don't talk to me about him!" interrupted Pétain. "About that time I went to Africa on the same boat as Doriot, without knowing it. *I discovered it too late, half an hour after we landed. I would have had him shot.*"

I had been in the Marshal's office for more than an hour. I rose to leave. Moved in spite of myself by the spectacle of this confused old man, I tried to think of something sympathetic to say. And all I could think of was: —

"*Monsieur le Maréchal,* those who love you pity you."

The Marshal accompanied me to the door of his office, then into the little hallway that leads to the entrance of the Hotel du Parc, and there, offering me his hand, said: —

"Pity me indeed, for I have got myself into a sorry mess!" ("*Plaignez-moi, en effet, car je me suis mis dans une drôle d'histoire!*")

That was February 3, 1942. Three months later, Doriot was in Vichy, and Pétain was shaking hands with him and inviting him to dinner.

*　　*　　*

Yes, Philippe Pétain had gotten himself into a sorry mess; not only himself and his reputation, but — what is infinitely more serious — his country. A dozen times the occasion had been offered him to get out of it, and he had not had the energy to want to do it. He had not possessed the noblest sort of courage of all: the courage to admit his mistake. His whole regime had been based on the defeat of France. He could not bear to condemn himself by condemning that defeat.

CHAPTER XVI

Bloody but Unbowed

IF I HAD TO DESCRIBE in a few words the evolution of public opinion in France since the Armistice, to name the four stations of my country's road to Calvary, I should say: —

1940: Stupor.
1941: Uncertainty, and the beginnings of resistance.
1942: Complete disillusionment and revolt.
1943: The rising of a people.

In the months that immediately followed the Armistice the French people idolized Pétain. Most idolatry is the result of ignorance — in this case it was the result of despair. The French were still stunned by misfortune. Their faith in Pétain was increased when Washington promptly and unconditionally recognized his government. (The United States acted so quickly that the French people, believing that Washington must be fully informed as to Pétain's plans, were strengthened in their belief that it was hopeless to continue the struggle.) The period which immediately followed the Armistice and this recognition — from June to October, 1940 — was the darkest time for my country. Those were the days when all Vichy repeated the words of General Weygand: "In three months England will have its neck wrung like a chicken." In those days Vichy sought to gain the favor of the victor, while the people of France waited in silence, bitterness, and despair, unconscious still that in transferring their loyalty to Vichy they were being made the victims of a gigantic piece of political trickery.

The interview between Hitler and Pétain at Montoire, on October 25, 1940, was the first shock which roused the French people from the mortal torpor into which they had been plunged by the defeat and its treasonable exploitation by those most responsible for it. By the beginning of November, the climate of opinion had begun to change. England had not been invaded; the bombardments had shaken London but not the English people. The men of Vichy, who had been sure of the immediate defeat of Great Britain, began to realize that the war might be a long one, and as a result there were internal struggles in the Pétain government. For Laval and Brinon and their henchmen, a German victory was an absolute necessity; they were to do everything they could to facilitate and hasten it. Some of Pétain's Ministers, having had time to remember that they were Frenchmen after all, began to realize their tremendous responsibility and were terrified by it. Others were playing both ends against the middle in the vain hope that some day Germany and Britain, exhausted, would ask France to arbitrate between them.

On the thirteenth of December, 1940, a sudden wave of hope swept the country. Laval had been arrested. The Marshal, then, had not played traitor. He was only seeking to gain time. . . . There were reports that he was going to leave for Africa with the fleet and join the Allies.

In February 1941, however, this premature hope was swept away. Flandin came into power, then Darlan. Once again the French people were plunged into uncertainty. Many of them kept their confidence in the Marshal, in the "Old Fox" who would outwit the Germans. All were becoming accustomed to their misfortune; they were getting into contact with one another across the line of demarcation; they were learning to adjust themselves to want, cold, privation of every sort.

On March 27 the *coup d'état* of young King Peter, and Yugoslavia's entrance into the war, caused delirious enthusiasm in France. But soon the occupation of Belgrade and the Allied setbacks in Libya marked the beginning of another period of lassitude. The strain was beginning to tell; the weak were falling into despair.

But on June 22, the news of the German invasion of Russia burst like a bombshell. And as, during the months that followed, the Soviet troops resisted, the French began to understand that Germany was no longer a sure winner. The hope of the patriots was inflamed by the example of General de Gaulle, who, for most people, became the symbol of the salvation of the country. The spirit of resistance was reborn. At first it was timid, cautious. Fervent patriots began to organize quasi-military committees. In the streets, passers-by began to exchange secret smiles expressing the common hope.

In the humblest dwelling, from this time on, people would gather at 9:15 in the evening to listen in silence to the Free French broadcast from London. The radio offered their only means of getting real news, since the press, controlled by Berlin and Vichy and in the pay of Vichy, published only the D.N.B. communiqués. But the radio was enough; for there was hardly a family which did not possess a set and did not listen religiously to the evening broadcast, despite the fact that listening was punishable by death, and many owners of radios were already in prison. By 1942 the unity of France was being reforged.

It was being reforged in the fire of common suffering.

Immediately after the Armistice the Germans had begun systematically and pitilessly to pillage France.

The first thing they did was to demand an enormous sum for "occupation costs" — 500,000,000 francs a day — a yearly tribute equal to three times the amount of our heaviest peacetime budgets.

At the time of the Armistice this sum was supposed to pay the expenses of an army of occupation of 4,000,000 men; later this army dwindled to a mere skeleton, but the tribute has never been reduced.

The Germans arbitrarily fixed the rate of currency exchange at twenty francs to the mark, thus enabling themselves to buy without regard to price whatever was left to sell — and to enrich the few thousands of wretched collaborationists who acted as agents and fences for them.

They cut down our forests — beginning with some of the finest trees of Boulogne, Vincennes and Fontainebleau. They exhausted our soil by forcing us to convert our fields to the most intensive production possible, for food crops, whatever had been their previous use. Nine tenths of our livestock were prematurely slaughtered. They got their hands on our banks, mines, and industrial enterprises, through a methodical series of operations facilitated by the reorganization of corporations by decrees from Vichy. The Germans today are majority stockholders, holding fifty-one per cent of the shares, in almost every large national enterprise — electricity, chemical products, mines — and the banks.

Translated into terms of individual lives this sort of pillaging meant that it was soon impossible for French people to buy, at any price whatsoever, such common objects of daily use as a toothbrush, a hairpin, a ball of string. What purchases could be made were no longer wrapped — there was no paper. Soap completely disappeared. More and more shop windows stood empty; sometimes the proprietors, with a bitter attempt at humor, filled them with jars and crates of imitation preserves and foodstuffs.

For as the Germans made more and more requisitions on French agricultural produce, food became scarcer and scarcer. Soon the situation reached the edge of famine — and, for many, passed beyond it.

The health of the population suffered almost as much from cold as from hunger. Winter became, for the French, a terrible season. Diabolically the Germans added to its horrors by putting the country on Berlin time, which is two hours ahead of sun time, so that in winter it is still dark in Paris at nine o'clock in the morning and people must scurry shivering to work without benefit even of the little warmth afforded by the pale winter sunshine. Since it is impossible to buy cloth of any sort, much less wool, most of them wear the strangest possible assortment of threadbare garments. There are no buses, of course, and they must go to work on the Paris subway — which, crowded as it is, has the advantage of providing a certain amount of collective warmth. For the same reason, they go to the movies as often as possible, since there is no way of being comfortable at home. The houses are glacial. The whole family lives in a single room, which there is no longer any means of heating. There has been no coal for a long time, and hardly any wood. During the winter of 1940–1941 electric or gas heaters could still be used, but since then rationing has been so severe that it is practically impossible to run them.

But it was not physical suffering alone that was drawing the French together.

Perhaps more potent still as a unifying force was the moral indignation they soon began to feel at the behavior of the Vichy government. With a complete dis-

dain for the national psychology, this government perpetrated three wrongs which the French people found it
impossible to forgive. These were the abandonment of
Alsace-Lorraine, the persecutions of the Jews, and the
excesses of the Vichy-created *"Légion,"* which eventually
became a kind of French equivalent of Hitler's S.S. guards.

When King Francis I, having lost at the battle of Pavia
"everything but honor," was in prison at Madrid, he was
visited by certain envoys — the Lavals and Brinons of
their time — who coolly proposed to him that he recover
his liberty in return for handing over to Charles V the
two provinces of Gascony and Guyenne. King Francis
looked them up and down and said simply: "I am not
worth that." Less modest, the men of Vichy thought that
they were worth Alsace-Lorraine and our two Departments of the Nord and the Pas-de-Calais. In order to keep
themselves in power, they handed over French soil to
the enemy — without a scruple, without a regret.

Laval himself, during a press conference in his office
in the Hotel du Parc in Vichy at the end of September
1940, likened Alsace and Lorraine to "children of divorce,
eternally torn between their parents, going constantly
from one to the other," and added, rapidly and brutally,
"That is their fate; we can do nothing about it." He said
that the Nord and the Pas-de-Calais would probably have
to be given up too, and that the Germans might demand
still others. "If I succeed in saving one or two of those
that they demand, that won't be so bad," he said. "That
is what I am working for."

Beginning with the next month his censorship forbade
the printing of the words "Alsace" and "Lorraine." In
their haste to abdicate, the men of Vichy abandoned them,
cut them off from the community of France, even before they were seized by the enemy.

Knowing that the only way in which the military can prevent themselves from being held responsible for the defeat of France is to present what has happened as a divine punishment, the men of Vichy have been industriously preaching to the French people during these years — moralizing to them through all manner of supposedly edifying spectacles, tableaus, reconstructions of historic scenes, and children's fancy-dress parades — degrading *tartuferies* which insult the national intelligence. One of these shows was held one spring day at the municipal stadium of Vichy. It was called a *fête des provinces françaises* — though one might well ask what particular reason there was to rejoice at this time and what could possibly be feted. But no matter. All the government authorities were there; and if the audience was rather small, there were plenty of *Gardes Mobiles* with drums and trumpets. Arlesians, Perigourdins, Savoyards, and of course Auvergnats, and also refugee Bretons and Normans, had been invited to take part in this symbolic demonstration in their regional costumes. But when a quarter of an hour before the beginning of the *fête* six young girls, refugees from Strasbourg, naïvely appeared at the main gate of the stadium in their great black Alsatian coifs with the tricolor *cocardes,* they were refused admittance and sent away — the great wings of their headdresses drooping — weeping with chagrin for themselves and with shame for their country. For Vichy wanted no mention of Alsace and Lorraine in its Sunday-school stories.

Nothing is more worthy of respect than the spirit of the veterans of the first World War. But we have seen how the veterans had been exploited by the appeasers, before the war of 1939, and what part some of their leaders had played in the plot that brought Pétain to power. Vichy hastened to exploit them even more completely for the vilest ends.

In the years before the present war, the veterans' associations had been torn by politics. When it was proposed, after the Armistice, that they should all be combined in a single fraternal society, completely divorced from politics, the idea met with such favor that great numbers of veterans joined the new group spontaneously and in good faith. But they soon saw that they had been deceived.

The nominal chief of this new "Legion of Veterans" was Marshal Pétain, but its real moving spirit, its leader — its Fuehrer, in a word — was Joseph Darnand. Before the war Darnand had been in the transportation business in Nice, and his affairs (which now are prosperous) had been in sorry plight. In 1939, he had been arrested by the Daladier government as one of the principal instigators of the fascist *Cagoulard* plot. But immediately after the Armistice, he became one of the great men of the new regime. He made Nice into one of the two big centers of German propaganda in the unoccupied zone; the other center was Marseilles, where for a long time there had been numerous followers of Doriot working under the direction of the notorious gangsters Sabiani, Carbone, and Spirito. Great numbers of *légionnaires* were recruited in these two towns; few elsewhere. The official mouthpiece of the Legion was the *Eclaireur de Nice,* which was at the same time the most fanatically pro-German newspaper in France.

Under the influence of Darnand, the Legion lost no time in broadening its field of activity. As "The Legion of Veterans and Volunteers of the National Revolution," it opened its membership to all — men, women, and young people — who intended to support Vichy; it became, in effect, a pro-Hitler falange: an attempt to form a single party, on the German model, upon which the dictatorship could count for support.

Thereupon the real veterans left it. Its badge, which at first had been much sought after, lost all prestige; aside from a few fanatics like Darnand, the only people who continued to wear it were wretches who hoped it would help them get a government job, or merchants and *bistro* proprietors who hoped thus to get into the good graces of the officials and the police, or such creatures as the ragged porters at the Marseilles railway station who wore it in the hope of attracting customers' attention.

But this did not stop Darnand. He wove into the *Légion* a wide web of espionage. *Légionnaires* became informers, even went so far as to send for the police and instigate arrests. Nothing is more contrary to the French character than spying and informing; and now, by means of *Légion* delegates and committees in every village and factory, spying and informing had become a system of government. It is hardly surprising, therefore, that the membership of the *Légion* began to melt away rapidly under the pressure of public scorn — scorn which was soon to turn into real hatred.

To combat this tendency Darnand persuaded the government to grant to the *Légionnaires* special material advantages and scandalous favors. The finest quarters were requisitioned for *Légion* offices and propaganda centers. While France was virtually in a state of famine, restaurants exclusively reserved for *Légionnaires* were opened in every town; wearers of the badge could find in them better food than anywhere else, and at very moderate prices. They also received special facilities for travel, extra ration coupons for food and clothing, and other privileges.

Protected by the influence of their leader, the *Légionnaires* thought they could get away with any kind of conduct they chose.

But by the time Laval came into power in April 1942, the *Légion,* utterly renounced by the great mass of the population, was in its death throes. With the help of Darnand — the two understood each other very well — Laval planned a new move. He would replace quantity with quality. From the remaining members of the *Légion,* the most unscrupulous were selected — a group of tough-fisted desperadoes who would stop at nothing. These became Laval's personal gangsters. Their organization was known as "the S.O.L." (*Service d'Ordre Légionnaire*) and was copied exactly, as to recruiting, discipline, uniforms, and equipment, after Hitler's S.S. Darnand, in an inflamed and grotesque proclamation, called them "The knights of modern times"!

"Knights" — these henchmen of Laval who, daring to call themselves war veterans, accepted a slacker as their chief! Knights, these ruffians who dishonored their country by making spying a system of government! "Modern" — these Nazi apprentices whose idea of progress was a return to the worst forms of German barbarism!

But the *Légion* was to go through still another transformation. By the beginning of 1943, dropping all pretense, Darnand had built out of the S.O.L. the "Legion of French Volunteers," dedicated to defending the Fuehrer's policy in France and to fighting beside the Germans in Russia. Not more than three thousand men at the outside went to Russia, though the pay for this service was very high; and they did not stay long. (There are now no Vichy troops on the Russian front.) But they were much publicized because of their propaganda value to the Germans. With a great deal of fanfare, Doriot enlisted with these Volunteers, had his picture taken in the uniform of the *Reichswehr,* and set out for Russia — on what appear to have been some three short visits, none of them lasting over a fortnight.

It was at the beginning of March 1942 that the oath of allegiance was administered to the first members of the S.O.L.

The ceremony took place in the arena of Cimiez, at Nice, with all the spectacular pomp the Vichy government likes to display on such occasions. No more dramatic site could have been chosen than these Roman ruins, under a Mediterranean sky, near a famous old monastery and only a little way from the former residence of Queen Victoria, the Hotel Regina. The Queen is still there, sitting majestically in her marble armchair in the garden — but daubed with paint, covered with filthy inscriptions, and headless, for the blind Anglophobia of the *Légion* is prone to take such stupid ways of expressing itself. The statue of Edward VII in Cannes has been smashed; and — most ironically of all — *Légionnaires* have knocked from its pedestal even the statue of Lord Brougham, who made Cannes into a successful resort and to whom the town owes all the prosperity it has since enjoyed.

The ceremony itself was copied from the traditional one that marks the graduation exercises at St-Cyr — but with what a difference! Standing on a platform, wearing high boots and a revolver in his belt, Darnand pronounced the formula of the oath; and at the end of each sentence the *Légionnaires,* kneeling, arms stretched upward in the Hitler salute, answered in a single voice: "I swear it."

One of the questions was: "You swear to fight the Jewish leprosy?"

"I swear it," answered the *Légionnaires*.

This was the time when the persecutions of the Jews reached their height.

One day more than five thousand Jewish men, women, and children were rounded up and held in the Stade Buffalo in Paris for twenty-four hours, covered by machine guns, guarded by *Gardes Mobiles* and German *Schuppos,* with strict orders not to leave the benches where they were sitting — unable to sleep or to wash themselves, forced to eat where they sat in this shameful promiscuity, with all the odious details that it implies. On another day a whole trainload of Jewish children, boys and girls, were locked into railway carriages — without anyone to look after them — and sent off to a destination which to this day is unknown. Jewish property was being seized, and a strict census of the Jews was being taken — which caused the writer Tristan Bernard, himself a Jew, to remark with bitter wit, "Strange times — they are blocking accounts and counting Blochs." In those days no Jew in Paris dared to sleep in his own house because Jews were being rounded up by the thousands for deportation to Germany.

The torch of liberty, which France in the past had raised to the stars, had been lowered by the men of Vichy to light the faggots of this new Inquisition.

One final blow drove the whole French people to desperate indignation and transformed its increasing but latent resistance into open, irresistible rebellion. This final blow — Vichy's last crime — was the arrangement I have already described, which Laval had the insolence to call "*la Relève.*"

"*La Relève*"! The word is sacred to the soldiers of Verdun, for "*la Relève*" was the arrival on the firing line of fresh troops which came to relieve their exhausted comrades who for days and nights had held fast in the mud of the trenches under merciless fire and were now able to go back to a hot meal and sleep. The shamelessness of Laval's daring to use this word shocked the French people beyond measure; and he will certainly have cause to regret it to the end of his days.

The Relief — the so-called exchange of one war prisoner for two volunteers for work in Germany — didn't bring back our prisoners, but it did mark the beginning of a sinister man hunt. From the very start, the enlistments for work in Germany were so rare that to save its face the government had to hire people to act the part of volunteers. In Nice, Darnand rounded up a gang of unemployed whom he paid to do nothing but this special kind of work. Every time a trainload of "volunteers" left Nice — after a great deal of advance publicity in the press — these wretches were collected in the station, put in special cars on which were scrawled in chalk "*Vive Laval! Vive la Collaboration!*" and sent as far as a way station just beyond Toulon, where they got out of the train and went back to Nice to play the scene over again when the next train left.

But in October 1942 and more especially after the occupation of the whole country by the enemy, the man hunt became serious — and tragic. There was no longer any question of volunteers. All men under thirty were systematically trapped by the administration and the police and, through the use of threats, blackmail, and often physical force, made to leave for Germany. It was a real slave hunt. Many preferred to run every conceivable risk rather than go. Leaving their homes and families, they took to the woods and joined the bands of guerillas — whose number, in all the occupied countries, the roundup of slave labor for Germany has done so much to increase.

It would be impossible to betray a people more completely than Laval has done. But it would likewise be impossible for any traitor to defeat his own ends more completely. For the French people, goaded beyond endurance and realizing that they had nothing more to lose, turned against him like one individual and found in the depths of their despair the strength to continue the struggle, and the unity of purpose to assure its ultimate success.

As these lines are written, the tragedy is reaching its climax. Two opposing forces are hurtling toward a bloody conflict, which only the liberation of the country can arrest. Laval and Darnand can no more stop in their career of treason and crime than the patriots can stop in their campaign of insurrection.

The harried Germans can no longer afford to worry over such questions of policy as "appeasement" versus persecution of their victims. They do not even take the trouble to keep up appearances. Pétain has become nothing more than a senile prisoner whose opinion is not even asked for; and Laval himself has been assigned a robust guardian who is ordered to make him walk the straight and narrow path. This guardian is none other than Darnand himself, the "strong man" of the *Légion*.

His career thus reaches its bloody apogee. On December 30, 1943, he was given the job of "Secretary General for the Maintenance of Order" — which means in plain language that he has now become the Himmler of France, the chief of the butchers — for he can carry out his functions only through murder. His special police, the "militia," has already gone to work: patriots are pursued relentlessly, arrests and executions are increasing. For Darnand, the great hunt is on; for the patriots, the battle is beginning — the battle which soon, let us hope, will become the battle of liberation. Isolated incidents have become guerilla warfare, and guerilla warfare is easy to change into organized combat. From the moment these soldiers without uniform receive the necessary minimum of arms, the United Nations may count on French resistance as a factor in their general strategy.

CHAPTER XVII

Back on the Firing Line

DEFEAT OBLITERATED and honor retrieved — that is the miracle which France owes to General de Gaulle, who, hardly twenty-four hours after the fatal order issued by Pétain to surrender arms, flung forth to his despairing countrymen a challenge and a hope. At that moment General de Gaulle became more than a military leader; he became a symbol — the symbol of uncompromising patriotism and total resistance to the enemy. He will remain that symbol forever, no matter what the future may hold, because at the climax of the tragedy of France two voices clashed in the torn soul of her people — Pétain's voice, that of resigned abdication, saying: "Frenchmen, I tell you in sorrow that we must lay down our arms"; and the voice of de Gaulle, which said: "France has lost a battle, but she has not lost the war. The struggle continues."

In the same broadcast, de Gaulle went on to remind his countrymen of what the defeatists had never clearly seen or had stubbornly wished to ignore: —

"Nothing is lost for France. She has a vast Empire. She can form a bloc with the British Empire and make with it unlimited use of the enormous industry of the United States. . . . There are in the universe all the necessary means to crush our enemy. Overwhelmed today by a mechanical force, we can conquer in the future by a superior mechanical force. There lies the future of the world."

Because, with a clear vision of the future, he thus defied

the Armistice and declared that France remained in the war, General de Gaulle became at once the symbol of resistance toward the enemy and the founder of the movement which bears his name.

All those who have known and shared the life of enslaved France, as I have done, will agree with me in the following definition of "Gaullism": Gaullism is the embodiment of the almost unanimous wave of resistance of the French people toward the occupying forces; this resistance was symbolized by General de Gaulle, and voiced in the daily French broadcasts directed to France from London.

It is impossible to overestimate the part played by these broadcasts in the lives of the French people. They provided the daily shot in the arm which gave them the strength to hold on, the provision of courage without which they could not continue. The speakers on the London radio began to be for each and every Frenchman so many personal friends without whose daily messages it would have been almost impossible to carry on. What more natural than that Gaullism should have thus become the rallying point for all resistance?

It is almost impossible to explain to those who do not know by experience just what an enslaved people endures. The facts are presented, statistics are cited, the misery is depicted. You have been listened to — with obvious sympathy. You feel that at last a bridge of understanding has been thrown from one people to the other. And suddenly you perceive that you have not said everything, that you have not even been able to say the essential things, because slavery is a form of suffering which is not communicable. We know that, in a sense, for a nation to lose its liberty and to be submitted to the law of the foreigner is to die. But what is impossible to conjure up in the imagination is how, in spite of everything, a nation continues to live after that death; and with what loathing, what shame, what revulsion, it drags out the false and soulless existence which the master is wont to accord the slave. Only one thing remains to give life any meaning, and that is the hope of escape.

And so it has come about that in France an entire nation resists naturally, and at times unconsciously, as it breathes. Resistance is the mother who, feigning a headache, deprives herself of nourishment in order to give her meager ration to her children. It is the ten-year-old who draws himself up like a little man to show the Germans that hunger and cold have no terrors for him. It is the railroad employee who changes the directions on the German convoy, and dispatches trains to Blois which should have gone to Lille; it is his friend the switchman who risks death to turn the switch which wrecks the munition train a few minutes later; it is the children of Paris who, when they get out of the subway, cut their tickets in a V, throw them under the nose of a German officer and decamp with a sneer; it is yesterday's frivolous Parisian woman who today hides a British agent in her apartment; it is the resolute patriots who, from relay to relay, conduct that agent to the frontier; it is the young men — students, workmen, priests, Communists, all fraternally united — who have held out for so long in the mountains of the Haute Savoie; it is the officers who, rather than let themselves be disarmed after the total occupation of France, have become the instructors and the leaders of the patriots; it is the men and women who risk their lives to bring them the arms smuggled in by the Allies.

*   *   *

To keep up their almost superhuman effort, these people must have hope. And in the midst of so much moral and material suffering, hope will die if it is not constantly renewed. Almost from the start, the heroic deeds of the Fighting French forces have been the strongest single factor in sustaining, along with their hope for an Allied victory, their self-respect as a nation. The Armistice had discredited some of their most respected military chiefs, and there had been times when they had been tempted to doubt whether even the army itself was equal to its predecessors. The French officers and soldiers who joined de Gaulle reassured them magnificently.

Before the end of 1940 — a matter of weeks after Pétain's and Hitler's handclasp at Montoire had opened the eyes of the French at home to the extent of their betrayal — Free French troops were already being congratulated by the King of England for their record in the Libyan campaign. In succeeding weeks and months, the *résistants* at home were to acquire an enormous debt of gratitude to thousands more of these volunteers: to Catroux and Larminat and their men; to General Legentilhomme; to General Monclar; to Lieutenant Colonel d'Ornano (heir to a line of Marshals of France) who fell before Mourzouck in Libya, and to all his comrades who are inscribed on the roll of those killed in action on the field of honor; to Koenig, besieged at Bir Hacheim by crushing forces, refusing Rommel's ultimatum three times, replying to all summonses to surrender by fresh prodigies of valor, holding out against every probability, holding out for sixteen days of hell, in what was to become an African Verdun. "My orders are to hold Bir Hacheim," he said, "I will hold Bir Hacheim." General Koenig is an Alsatian; one may guess his frame of mind when he met again, on African soil, the eternal tormentor of his native land.

Among those who fought with Koenig at Bir Hacheim was Father Savet, a Dominican monk, in command of a battalion of marines. He had fought in the first Libyan campaign in an advanced unit. During the Eritrean campaign he was the first to enter Massawa, where he hauled down the Italian flag with his own hands. He had declared that in fighting the Axis he was fighting for Christ against the Devil.

As for Leclerc — made a general at an age when most military men are still captains — he terminated a series of brilliant expeditions from the Chad when he set forth late in 1942 with a handful of men and, pressing northward through the desert, arming his troops with booty captured from the Italians, fell upon the rear guard of the enemy, brushed them aside, marched through their ranks, and finally joined our main army in Tunisia. Future generations of French children will thrill to read this story, which takes its place among the most marvelous of all tales of adventure. The climax came for the *méharistes* of Leclerc when, on that memorable day, in January 1943, they met the *goumiers* of Giraud in the desert southwest of Gafsa. From that day on the old and the new French Armies were fighting side by side.

Since then the new French Army, rejuvenated and henceforth unified — the army of vengeance and liberation — has played an important and sometimes decisive part in all the Allied operations in the North African and Italian theaters. When Rommel went into Tunisia, General Giraud's army of 75,000 men were at first the only ones available to send against him. Making up in daring what they lacked in modern equipment, they checked the

German advance and gave the Americans and British time to organize.

In Corsica, where they fought without assistance from any of the Allied armies, Giraud's troops had the immense satisfaction of delivering a part of the territory of France from German domination. But if they were the only Allied army sent into the island, they were not the only one that fought there; they were met by another army: that of the Corsican patriots who had awaited only this chance. The effectiveness of its help gives an interesting indication of what may be expected on the territory of France itself.

But our gratitude to the French forces who have taken such a great part in the campaigns in Africa and Italy should not lead us to forget other French fighting men who, less in the limelight, are doing their share for the common cause: the fliers of the Normandy squadron who have won such praise from the Russians on the Eastern Front, or the thousands of young French paratroopers now training in England for the day of invasion.

It is easy to imagine the sense of consolation and of pride that we French felt when we read General Mark Clark's communiqué on the French forces in Italy: "General Juin and his troops are daily adding a new page of history to the highest traditions of French combatants, and I am proud to count them as members of the Fifth Army."

It is a citation of which they have a right to be proud. But the new page of history that is most in their minds as they work their way up the Italian peninsula is the liberation of their homeland — and the citation they are most anxious to win is that of the French people.

CHAPTER XVIII

The Government of Postwar France

ALMOST AS SOON as they had caught their breath after the defeat of France in 1940, sympathizers with the Allied cause abroad began to speculate on what her political future would be after she was freed from German bondage. The American landings in North Africa caused a new flare-up of discussion, and the political activities of the French Committee of National Liberation in Algiers have kept the subject in the public eye.

It is interesting to note that the question of the government of postwar France, so hotly discussed beyond the borders of the country, apparently preoccupied the people inside France itself very little indeed up to the time when the formation of the Committee of Liberation brought it forcibly to their attention. Never once, from the time of the Armistice until I left France at the end of 1942, did I hear the man in the street allude to such a thing.

But I am sure that if he were questioned on the subject, the average Frenchman would be very decided about what he did *not* want, and that is a military dictatorship. On this point, the French people — I mean those who have the foremost right to speak in the name of their country, the people of occupied France — are practically unanimous. The Pétain government, which has otherwise been so harmful to France and to the cause of the United Nations, at least has done one outstanding service to the French themselves: it has thoroughly disgusted them with

the rule of the soldier. Napoleon, MacMahon, Pétain —
three military men, three experiences in a little over
a century, have cured the French of that sort of disease
for a long time to come.

Pétain in one of his speeches referred to "the country
of which I am the incarnation." The phrase was an af-
front, a sacrilege. No one man can boast of being the
physical embodiment of the French nation. Nor will
there be any place, in the France of tomorrow, for a
"leader" who, under any pretext, tries to impose upon the
French people an authoritarian regime. The French people do not need to be led; they are quite capable of leading themselves — and they fully intend to do so.

France's nearest approach to a government at the present time (for it is an insult to the country to dignify
Vichy by that name) is the Committee of Liberation in
Algiers headed by General de Gaulle, who from a purely
military man has become a political figure.

General de Gaulle began in 1940 as the magnificent
symbol of French resistance, and no one can ever dispute
that title. He also began as a soldier, and it was in this
capacity that he was recognized, in August 1940, by the
British government. In those days not one Frenchman
in a hundred could have imagined him as a politician.
Soon, however, listeners to the Free French broadcasts in
London began to sense the fact that he was undergoing a
metamorphosis, and some of them began to worry about
its possible consequences. When I saw Edouard Herriot
for the last time, in August 1942, Herriot, who knew that
I might soon be forced to escape from the country, said
to me: "Let de Gaulle keep to three slogans: 'I fight for
the liberation of French territory; I fight for the punishment of the traitors; I fight to restore to the French people

their political liberties.' The moment he adds anything at all with regard to the political situation, he commits a grave mistake."

The gravest mistake General de Gaulle could possibly commit would be to let any misunderstanding come between him and the French people. Yet the union between him and his compatriots at home has, lately, been seriously threatened by a combination of such factors as references to the founding of a Fourth Republic, references to the general himself as "President de Gaulle" rather than "General de Gaulle" in the Consultative Assembly at Algiers, and announcements by the Committee on the future policy to be followed in regard to the French Empire — as if the Committee, a provisory body, had any right to decide.

The underground newspaper *Combat,* one of the principal organs of French resistance, published in December of last year its fiftieth issue. This special number contained an editorial whose principal passages, as reproduced on December 7, in the *Courrier de Genève,* ran as follows: —

Thus, our newspaper is that of French resistance, and not that of what Vichy calls Gaullism. It is not a man whom we glorify. We know too well by the experience of Germany (Bismarck, Wilhelm II, Hitler), of Italy, of Spain, and of our own country (Napoleon I, Napoleon III, Pétain) what it costs a nation to deliver itself up to an individual. We exalt de Gaulle because he was able to see clearly the reasons for hope even when Germany seemed invincible; because France, the champion of liberty, saw in him a general worthy of those of 1793. We exalt de Gaulle because he represents to the highest degree the common ideal of ninety-eight per cent of the French people.

Our movement is not in the service of a single man, there-

fore of a new fascism, like the French militia. It is in the
service of the France which that man is defending. De Gaulle
knows that we will rise against him, as against all dictators,
if it should happen that he would, in his turn, install his personal government.

The same general theme was echoed a few weeks later
in a meeting of the Consultative Assembly at Algiers by
Pierre Cot, Minister of Aviation in Léon Blum's Cabinet.

"We do not want," said Mr. Cot, "any part of a presidential form of government which opens the door to
dictatorship. We do not want anything that, put in one
form or another, under one pretext or another, could repeat the adventure of Napoleon III, Prince-President.

"Nor do we want representatives of the French people
to delegate their powers to one man; the experience we
have had with Pétain has been sufficient for us.

"The Government of France on the morrow of its
liberation applies the formula of Robespierre: 'The magistrates derive their powers from the people, the people
derive their powers from the law, the law derives from
reason.'"

For the political errors of General de Gaulle (of which
not the least is the curbing of the liberty of the press)
we must hold chiefly responsible certain of his advisers.

Through force of circumstances, he was compelled to
choose his collaborators practically at random, and such
choice is not always the best. He accepted offers of assistance almost indiscriminately, for the simple reason
that those who made them were on the spot. The moment Free French headquarters was set up in London, it
became of course the rallying-point of all patriots who
escaped from France or who had happened to be out of

the country at the time of the Armistice. But — human
nature being what it is — it also attracted opportunists
who saw in the movement primarily a chance for personal advancement, embittered politicians or would-be
politicians hoping for a chance to recoup their previous
failures, and party men seeking to further the interests
of their own particular groups. Such people brought with
them their own shabby jealousies, their disappointments,
their prejudices, their rancor, and their personal ambition. These factors have contributed a great deal to
give the Fighting French movement a political character, and at the same time served as so many internal
strains to hamper its action. Unhappily, their influence has
appeared plainly in some of the more recent — and in
my opinion the most regrettable — actions of the Algiers
Committee. One of the most serious of these, I believe, is
to have suggested the founding of a "Fourth Republic."

In the first place, it is wondrously illogical. It is illogical to reproach the French Parliament for having
confided to Pétain the task of preparing a new Constitution, and to announce at the same time that they themselves want to give the country an entirely new Constitution — that of the Fourth Republic.

It is illogical to accuse Pétain of having wanted to substitute his dictatorship for the Third Republic, and at
the same time to condemn implicitly that Third Republic by insisting that it must be replaced by a Fourth.

In the second place — and this is far more important
— the suggestion of a Fourth Republic is a serious psychological mistake.

Outsiders may wonder why the French lay such stress
on the difference between a "Third" and a "Fourth" Republic — as if there were so much importance in a number! But, as is so often the case with political questions

in France, historical precedents have more to do with the matter than cold reason.

We have seen how the issue of revision of the Constitution, because it had been brought up for the first time by the reactionary Boulanger, remained associated in the minds of the French with attempts to install an authoritarian regime. A similar association surrounds the question of a Fourth Republic, which had been raised in France long before it was mentioned in Algiers. It was the slogan of a reactionary movement started shortly after the first World War by Pierre Cathala, who was subsequently to become Laval's righthand man. At that time, Cathala, young and ambitious, wanted to organize a personal political machine, and he could think of no better program for the group he hoped to found than the convenient, purely negative one of abolishing the "rotten" Third Republic in a general housecleaning. Like the issue of revision, the issue of a Fourth Republic has always been looked at askance by democratic forces in France, who were conditioned by experience to see in any attempt to change the fundamental laws of the land the shadow of a reactionary *coup d'état*. This mentality is obviously reflected in the declaration of the underground paper *Combat* which I have already cited.

From a practical point of view, one may wonder why it is necessary to take so much trouble to prepare a Fourth Republic when the Third still exists.

When the bureaus of Parliament were suppressed in August 1942, MM. Jeanneney and Herriot, presidents of the Senate and Chamber of Deputies, wrote an energetic letter of protest to Pétain, reminding him of the exact nature of the authority given him by Parliament on July 10, 1940. "The National Assembly at Vichy gave you your full powers," they wrote. "Furthermore, it specified that the [new] Constitution [you were authorized to prepare] be ratified by the nation and applied by the assemblies it created. Whether you like it or not, the National Assembly gave its mandate to the government of the Republic. The mandate is violated when you try to eliminate the essential institution of the Republic."

At that time Pétain had done nothing more toward preparing a new Constitution than to promulgate by decree a series of "constitutional acts"; Herriot and Jeanneney took the position that the Parliament of 1940 retained its authority, since it had not been replaced.

Over a year later Pétain, wishing to clear his conscience, endorsed this point of view. On November 13, 1943, the old Marshal was to have delivered an important speech over the Vichy radio. At the last moment the Germans prevented him from doing so. The text of this speech, and that of a decree which was to accompany it, were transmitted by neutral channels, and appeared in the Swiss press. The text of the decree, signed by Pétain on November 13, 1943, ran as follows: —

We, Marshal of France, Chief of State, decree in virtue of the constitutional law of July 10, 1940: If we die before having been able to obtain ratification by the nation of a new Constitution of the French State, of which the promulgation by one or several laws had been foreseen in the terms of the constitutional law of July, 1940, the constituent power mentioned in Article Eight of the Constitutional Law of February 25, 1875, will return to the Senate and the Chamber of Deputies, sitting jointly as the National Assembly.

The present decree abrogates all the measures taken since July 10, 1940, to reduce the authority of the National Assembly and the exercise of its rights.

Pétain thus made honorable amends to the people whose sovereignty he has usurped, and recognized the full authority of the Parliament which is the expression of this sovereignty. (It was, incidentally, his last attempt at direct contact with the people in France: the alarmed Germans saw to it that he was kept quiet thereafter.)

Thus the Third Republic is not only the sole legal basis of government in France today; it is recognized as such by the man who three years ago tried to destroy it.

"But," say the partisans of a Fourth Republic, "the Third Republic had grave faults." Granted. The important question is whether or not its virtues outweighed them. I believe they did. Within the space of seventy years, it raised France from the disaster of 1870, strengthened her within and rebuilt her colonial Empire, instituted social security laws, encouraged industry and art, and raised both the level of literacy and the standards of living of her citizens higher than they had ever been before. Finally it created a France strong enough to sustain almost alone the assault of 1914, and to win, with her allies, the victory of 1918.

Its faults were costly. They should have been corrected long ago. But they can be corrected, and the job of correcting them will be both simpler and less dangerous than replacing the whole Constitution, because the virtues of the present one have been tested and tried by experience.

The most serious of its faults by far was the instability of our government. I wonder how many foreigners would have been able to tell on any given day the name of the Prime Minister of France? He had hardly appeared on the stage, you had hardly had time to get a look at him, before he was gone. One Ministry followed another like marionettes on a toy merry-go-round. The same faces appeared again and again — the same men carrying different portfolios. Some were simply run-of-the-mill politicians who, because of their rank in their parties, kept bobbing up in Cabinet after Cabinet. Others were men who had held positions of leadership and lost them under more or less trying circumstances; even these would often stage surprising comebacks.

Take an example familiar to Americans.

On the eventful day of February 7, 1934, Daladier was compelled to resign his premiership while buses burned on the Place de la Concorde and *Gardes Mobiles* fired on the mob which was trying to get across the bridge to the Chamber of Deputies. Everyone thought that "with this blood on his hands" Daladier was a doomed man, would never be in office again, and would have to give up politics altogether. And yet on June 5, 1936, he was Minister of War, and less than two years later he was again Prime Minister — a position which he kept until Reynaud succeeded him on March 20, 1940.

Adrien Hébrard, the wise old editor of *Le Temps,* would doubtless have explained such phenomena by repeating his favorite aphorism: "It is not the Seine that flows through Paris, it is the Lethe." The real reason was of course that with ministerial changes as frequent as they were, there was bound to be a great deal of repetition. Consequently premiers did not always take parliamentary defeat as a disastrous blow; in fact, for an expert chief of government, falling had come to be quite an art: some fell lightly, almost elegantly; others heavily, clumsily. But, at the delicate moment when the votes were counted and the defeated premier silently picked up his briefcase and walked out of the Chamber, there was likely to be more speculation about his personal future than about the issue that had brought about his downfall.

Often that was not the issue on which the vote had just been taken. In practice, the Deputies and Senators very seldom challenged the government on matters of foreign policy in a debate which might involve international consequences; they preferred to bring about a fight on some secondary domestic question. One of our governments, at a time when the international situation was particularly tense, had to give up power because its minister of finance, M. Chéron, had stubbornly opposed the Senate, asked for a vote of confidence, and finally been beaten by a slight majority at the conclusion of a debate regarding the right of a married woman to dispose of her salary!

Such occurrences as this in legislative halls lent a final touch of ridicule to a situation that was really too tragic to be laughed at. Having to defend itself every day on minor issues of home policy, to be always ready for debates in both Houses, when could the government find time to devote itself to the problems which really bore on the life of the country? And with such frequent changes of government, how could any policy be followed consistently?

The instability of French Cabinets was due to the fact that whereas Parliament could overthrow any Cabinet at will, the Cabinet had no means of appealing Parliament's decisions. There was no real system of checks and balances. The Cabinet was under the constant necessity of keeping parliamentary approval of its policy, while the Parliament had to answer for its deeds to the electors only once a term. Holding the executive (the Cabinet) thus at its mercy, the Parliament had itself become the executive, in violation of the principle of the separation of powers which is the essential basis of a healthy republic.

The simplest remedy to such a situation is to be found in English parliamentary usage. Members of the House of Commons are elected for six years but, in fact, rarely reach the end of their term, for the government has the right to dissolve the Parliament at any time. On the other hand, the British Parliament cannot command government policy as closely as the French Parliament; its only right is to approve or disapprove it. As Prime Minister, Mr. Churchill is a very strong executive, but he must submit major policies to Parliament. If it rejects a major policy, the Prime Minister may resign, but he is not bound to do so; he may also dissolve Parliament and force it to go before the country for a new election to decide whether the people themselves support the policy of the parliamentary majority or the policy of the Prime Minister.

Since we knew the drawback, since we knew the remedy, why did we not, years ago, apply the remedy to the disease? Again the reason is historical rather than logical: the French had got the habit of regarding all proposals to revise the Constitution as ruses for destroying republican institutions. Boulanger had suggested revision on the pretense of wanting to make a more perfect republic; what he actually planned to do was to set up reactionary authoritarianism. Once bitten, twice shy.

In the years since Boulanger's downfall the question of revision has been brought up more than once, and the old rule held good right up through 1934, when Gaston Doumergue was called in as Prime Minister after the riots of the sixth of February. He made up his mind to take the leap, summon the National Assembly (as Parliament is called when it meets in joint session, as it is required to do for such a purpose) and propose an amendment to the Constitution such that, in the future, neither the Senate nor the Chamber could overthrow the government by a vote of no confidence without having to go before the electors and ask them what they thought about it. The risk of having to undergo a new election would have been for the Parliament the best incentive to wisdom, the best guarantee of ministerial stability.

But just as soon as Doumergue announced his intention to summon the Assembly (it was in a broadcast, and the first time that a French statesman had used this modern means of communicating with the people) opposition to such a project showed itself in all its classical strength. Herriot, who had entered Doumergue's Coalition Cabinet as the chief representative of the Left, resigned. Doumergue had to give up and return to his peaceful retreat at Tournefeuille.

The ghost of the past, the fear of reaction, thus prevented us from sending for the doctor and applying the medicine which could so easily have cured our sick republican institutions. It was only in the summer of 1940, when the patient was *in extremis,* that the doctor was called in. He promised to send a prescription, but actually he never did. Returning shamefaced over three years later, he confirms what we already knew ourselves: that the patient's heart is still beating. There is still a chance to save her; we know the means: I am convinced that the French people, when the time comes for them to decide upon their political future, will recognize the Republic's accomplishments and confine their efforts to correcting its faults. I am convinced that, in justice, they will not separate the cause of the Third Republic from that of France herself.

As it was quite correctly termed in the Quebec declaration, the Committee is a "trustee." More precisely it is, as we say in French, a *gérant d'affaires* (*negotiorum gestor*), or self-appointed trustee. French lawbooks define *negotiorum gestor* as one "who agrees to take charge of an affair or concern for another person, in the latter's absence, but for his interest." American lawbooks define a trustee as one "in whom a power is vested upon an expressed or implied agreement to administer or exercise it for the benefit or to the use of another."

The Committee of National Liberation answers point by point the terms of the first definition. It has undertaken, on its own initiative, the direction of French affairs in the absence of forty million Frenchmen who are under the heel of the enemy; it administers these affairs in the capacity of a trustee, of a temporary custodian, on behalf of the French people, who alone remain sovereign. Once the trusteeship is over, it is to the French people that the trustee, the administrator, must give an account.

According to both law and common sense, a trustee should confine himself to looking after the property of which he has taken charge, and in the absence of the legitimate proprietor abstain from making any change, whether superficial or fundamental. He should only attempt to conserve; he should not innovate.

This being true, the National Committee of Algiers has incontestably overstepped the bounds of its authority in pronouncing the independence of Lebanon, in giving the natives of North Africa the right to vote, in promising a greater degree of autonomy to Indo-China, in planning, at the Brazzaville Conference of 1944, a new status for the French colonial Empire, in granting women the right to vote, in announcing a French New Deal and, in particular, the nationalization of the banks. The advisability of such measures in themselves does not enter into the question; the point is that the French people alone have the right to make such grave decisions. A scrupulous agent left in charge of the house in his employer's absence should, if asked to make an important decision, answer, "I can't; the boss is away." That is the only reply the Algiers Committee ought to make, if asked to make decisions affecting the political future of France: the "boss" is the French people. Boundlessly grateful as they will be to General de Gaulle for his courageous stand in 1940, they will nevertheless hold him to an impartial account for everything he has done since.

I do not believe a single true democrat can be found who would contradict this point. Did not de Gaulle himself, some time before any of these decisions were made, express himself clearly on the matter? In his memorandum to General Giraud from London on March 13, 1943, he wrote: —

As long as the enemy occupies part of the territory and more than one million Frenchmen are prisoners, the pursuit of political aims, and notably the change of the fundamental institutions and laws of France as they existed on June 16, 1940, constitutes an attack against the union of citizens and the war effort of the nation. In consequence the transformation of the Republic into a "French State" and the so-called legislative measures inspired by Nazi or Fascist ideology and imposed on the people by usurpatory power must be considered null and void. Republican legality must be re-established. Local republican institutions must be restored. Changes, which no doubt will have to be made in our political institutions, can be so made only by the French people in full and free exercise of its sovereignty.

No doubt should remain as to the determination of any French authority to help in assuring, immediately after liberation, the free expression of popular will by the election, with universal suffrage, of a national representation that in turn will alone be empowered to establish a constitution of France, to designate her government and to judge finally the acts accomplished by any organization that would have assumed the provisional management of national interests.

But there is another text that is still more definitely binding. It is the text of the Algiers communiqué of June 3, 1943, announcing the formation of the French Committee of National Liberation. It says: —

The Committee will turn over its power to the temporary government, which will be constituted *in conformity with the laws of the Third Republic,* as soon as the liberation of the metropolitan territory permits it. . . . The Committee solemnly commits itself to re-establish all the French liberties, *the laws of the Republic and the republican regime.* [Italics mine.]

Because I have for de Gaulle, the soldier and founder of resistance, a profound and warm-hearted gratitude such as the entire French nation entertains for the man who raised the torn banner of France in 1940, I earnestly hope, in the interests of my country and for the glory of Charles de Gaulle, that he will keep that clear and solemn promise: *"Republican legality must be re-established; local republican institutions must be restored."*

But what, under the circumstances, are the means of re-establishing republican legality?

The most obvious means are suggested by the Tréveneuc Law, which was designed to provide for contingencies such as the one in which France now finds herself. Tréveneuc was a member of the French National Assembly which prepared the Constitution of the Third French Republic. His name until recently has been completely unknown, and four years ago not one Frenchman in a thousand knew the law of which he was the author. It was inspired by the events of the Franco-Prussian War of 1870-1871. Part of the national territory had been invaded. Tréveneuc wanted to devise a means of safeguarding the legal representation of the people in case of another invasion. The Tréveneuc Law provides: —

If the National Assembly has been illegally dissolved or prevented from meeting, the General Councils [of the Departments] meet immediately and automatically. . . . An assembly composed of two delegates elected by each General Council convenes with the members of the legal government and the deputies who have been able to escape violence. . . . This assembly is instructed to take for all of France urgent measures to maintain order. . . . It provides provisionally for the general administration of the country. . . . [It] is validly constituted if at least half of the departments are represented in it.

In recent months there has been a great deal of discussion in the Committee of National Liberation and in the Consultative Assembly of various projects which resemble the Tréveneuc Law in greater or less degree. Even if the special circumstances of the liberation of France prevent the exact application of the Tréveneuc Law, it will remain, because it is based on democratic principles, a yardstick by which the sincerity of the Committee's republican intentions may be judged. General de Gaulle himself was the first to cite it, after the Armistice — in the "Organic Declaration" which he made in the first number of his *Journal Officiel de la France Libre,* dated from Brazzaville (French Equatorial Africa), November 16, 1940. This declaration, made "in the name of the French people and the French Empire," is at once a justification of what de Gaulle calls his "assumption of power" and a bill of indictment against the Vichy government. Its very first sentence is a reference to the Tréveneuc Law as the means provided by the Constitution for assuring Republican government "under exceptional circumstances"; and the document concludes with a statement that "We, Charles de Gaulle . . . declare that we will accomplish this mission [the liberation of the country] within the framework of the institutions of France and that we will give an accounting of all our acts to the representatives of the French nation as soon as it is able to designate them freely and normally."

General de Gaulle thus foresaw in the beginning the provisional status of the Committee of National Liberation. Whatever measures it may adopt, it must remember that everything that is done in Algiers can only have the character of expediency — for it is impossible for Algiers to be anything more than an incident; only what is done in metropolitan France can be definitive.

The Consultative Assembly of Algiers, whose role and influence must be considered an important factor in the situation, shares this temporary-provisory character; it must be temporary and provisory by reason of its composition. The majority of its members are not elected, but appointed by the same Committee whose decisions they are supposed to review. At the present writing, 14 of a total of more than 90 seats are occupied by members of Parliament, but this minority cannot be taken as representative of the Republican Parliament as a whole: no member of that body who voted full powers to Pétain in 1940 is allowed to sit in the Assembly unless special measures are taken for his "reinstatement" — and more than two thirds of the Parliament did vote for Pétain.

*   *   *

As to the value that should be attached to the Assembly, we may ask the General's own spokesman. *La Marseillaise* is his official journal in London and in Algiers; its editor-in-chief is M. F. Quilici. The Consultative Assembly having shown itself somewhat restive, M. Quilici, in his editorial for the first of January, 1944, makes it a New Year's present of a round scolding.

"This Assembly is only consultative," he says. "It cannot be anything else. It does not hold the legislative power. It cannot hold it. It possesses no part of the popular sovereignty. It cannot possess it. For it did not issue from an election." As to the "delegates of the Resistance" who (including a score of representatives of resistance groups in New York, Montreal, Buenos Aires, Cairo, Martinique, Madagascar) form a majority of the Assembly, M. Quilici states that they were "selected by representative elements of the organizations in which they were militant, under the mysterious and often precarious conditions which secrecy imposes." And he concludes: "Not having been elected, the delegates are responsible to nobody. The whole responsibility has never belonged to anyone but, successively, to General de Gaulle, to the National Committee of London, and now to the Committee of National Liberation."

For a long time Washington and London deferred the statement of their position toward the French Committee of National Liberation. A large part of the responsibility for this delay must be laid at the door of those who would lead General de Gaulle into a narrow and chauvinistic policy of xenophobia which might appear to the United Nations both antidemocratic and anti-American. These advisers represented General de Gaulle as being on the worst terms with President Roosevelt and Prime

Minister Churchill, and interpreted this position as showing proof of a meritorious spirit of national independence.

Actually, it would be difficult to estimate the harm
done to France by such a policy. What would we say of a
man who had an important case to plead in court and
who chose as his lawyer a man who boasted of his
unfriendly relations with the presiding judge and the district attorney? It would be folly to deny the necessity
of a close, intimate understanding between France
and the United Nations; it would be folly to rejoice that
the man who represented France and plead her case
before the United Nations was on bad terms with their
leaders.

At long last the position of the government of the
United States was defined in Secretary Hull's declaration
of April 9, 1944. Mr. Hull said that the United States
could not recognize the Committee as the government of
France, but added that he and Mr. Roosevelt were "dis-
posed to see the French Committee of National Liberation
exercise leadership to restore law and order under the
supervision of the Allied Commander in Chief."

The circumstances of Mr. Hull's speech and the favorable reaction to it in London make it safe to assume that
his statement corresponded to the views of the British
government. It was preceded by a *rapprochement* of
de Gaulle and Churchill which was dictated, on the part
of the latter, by the demands of a policy which has always
been essentially realistic. This new *entente cordiale* has
been in the air since the Teheran conference. In the famous
speech which he made shortly before this conference,
Field Marshal Smuts expressed the conviction that after
the war Russia would be supreme in Europe and that Britain's only hope lay in organizing a West-European bloc
as a counterbalance to Soviet power. France, which after

the defeat of Germany will be the strongest single state on the Continent outside of Russia, is indispensable to any such bloc.

Mr. Hull's long-awaited declaration came in the middle of a crisis in Algiers — one of the many which are bound to occur in such a situation, but one which was particularly grave. On April 3, General de Gaulle had called to sit on the Committee of Liberation two members of the Communist Party, one of whom, Fernand Grenier, was given the very important post of Commissioner for Air. Communist representation on the Committee was a question that had been warmly discussed ever since the Committee's foundation. The appointment of the two Communist members came at a time when Russia, which alone among the United Nations had granted the Committee limited recognition, was showing marked coolness toward it. Within a week after their appointment, they led a protest (and even publicly threatened to resign) because of the release of a decree of the Committee abolishing Giraud's post of Commander in Chief of the French Army and vesting supreme military power in de Gaulle.

The decree was announced on April 6. It had not been communicated to General Giraud beforehand. He refused to accept it, backing his refusal with a reference to an earlier statement of General de Gaulle himself. This statement was part of a memorandum written from London in April, 1943, during the course of the negotiations which preceded the formation of the Committee of National Liberation in Algiers. It read: —

4. Furthermore, the actual commander in chief or the actual commanders in chief of the armies must be subordinated to the central authority and should not participate in it. To add the functions of commander in chief to those of member

of the central authority would be contrary to the Constitution and to the 1938 law concerning the organization of the nation in wartime, as well as to the secular tradition of the French State — with the sole exception of the period of the Consulate and of the Napoleonic Empire. Such a regime would certainly be disavowed by the French people after the experience that they have just had with the personal power, both civilian and military, imposed by Vichy.

This disagreement between the two generals raised an important question of principle — that of the separation of military and civil power — and an urgent practical problem — that of the relations between the Allied High Command and the French Army in the coming invasion — which cannot fail to be acutely painful to the people of France, for whom the invasion is not simply the next move in a global war but deliverance from misery and humiliation.

This does not mean, however, that the French are indifferent to the problems of the longer future. The supremacy of civil over military authority is — as I have tried to show throughout the course of this book — one of those issues on which they will never compromise. Charles Beard, in *The Republic,* defines the American political regime, as it results from the Constitution of the United States, as "the civilian way of living together in the Republic, the way of preserving our liberties and the decencies of social intercourse against the frenzies of the despotic and violent temper." The French people ask for nothing more — but nothing less. Following this protest, the Committee put General Giraud on the retired list. Yielding with dignity to the *fait accompli,* he took leave of his troops in a last order of the day in which he reminded them of his sacrifices for his country (and they had been very real), expressed his regret at not being able to command them "at the end," and added: "My life has been sufficiently full. Men may come and men may go, but France remains."

The Committee of Liberation can reassure the French people only by taking, now, the steps necessary to ensure the normal functioning of republican institutions until the time when the liberation of all France will permit general elections — not hasty, trumped-up affairs, such as were held in Corsica, but real elections, duly prepared by the restoration of free speech and a free press. For nearly four years, the French people have been denied these rights. Liberation would have no sense whatever if it did not bring about their recovery — and we may depend upon it that the people of France, one way or another, are going to recover them.

CHAPTER XIX

Democracy: Shield of the Peace

THE DESTINATION OF FRANCE is certain: it is democracy. For over a hundred and fifty years now the French have had their Gallic Charter of liberty, equality, fraternity; they seek only to broaden its application. But the road ahead may be straight (though, alas, not smooth) or needlessly tortuous and difficult. Apparently the Allies, realizing that the difficulties could be aggravated by too much outside interference in French affairs, have decided to avoid a course of action which might send the liberators home embittered, disillusioned, and convinced that there was simply no way to get along with these uncomprehending and incomprehensible people. Should such a misfortune occur, the stage would be set for a return to an isolationist mentality on both sides.

And that would spell disaster.

We are all agreed on the absolute necessity for close international co-operation after the war. The task of organizing for peace will be an extremely delicate one at best. Mutual mistrust among the very nations which have just fought together in the same victorious cause would be the best way to sabotage it in advance.

But if there is a grave danger in anything that looks like needless interference by one nation in the internal affairs of another, there is likewise danger in the attitude that a nation's domestic arrangements are strictly its own business so long as it behaves itself as far as the outside world is concerned. If the planners of tomorrow's peace do not recognize this fact, they are sealing their own doom.

Recently Mr. Sumner Welles proposed that "as a condition of adherence" to an international organization for the preservation of peace, a nation be required "to show that its citizens are guaranteed" freedom of religion, of speech, and of information "by its national Constitution." Why not simply say that tomorrow no land may be admitted to the council of civilized nations if it is not endowed with a democratic Constitution? For if we do not set up such a goal, then what, may I ask, will be the meaning of this war which we are fighting at the price of so many sacrifices?

We are fighting this war to protect ourselves from a present threat and to prevent other wars from breaking out in the future. But there is only one protection against recurrent wars: democracy. And democracy in one part of the world will not suffice; we must have it all over the world.

The French democracy was insufficiently prepared for this war; the other democracies not at all. Why? Because war is not the job of a democracy. Democracy naturally abhors war. It can only live and thrive in peace. Democratic institutions cannot function freely in a state of war, because by their nature they work slowly and in the full light of public opinion — whereas the conduct of war exacts decisions that are both rapid and secret. The necessity for secret and rapid action leads forcibly (at least for the duration of military operations) to one-man rule, to dictatorship.

For dictatorship, on the other hand, war is at once a necessity, a profession, and an objective. In a world where Jules Verne's hero would be considered a leisurely traveler, dictatorship anywhere is a threat to democracy everywhere. It is therefore an act of legitimate defense for democracies to suppress dictatorships wherever they may be found. In future we cannot afford to allow any country, anywhere, to adopt an authoritarian regime on the pretext that its people are "not ready for democracy." Democracy can exist only in peace, and peace can be assured only by universal democracy.

Universal democracy, and real democracy — democracy in fact as well as in name. There are times when the temptation to compromise democracy in the interests of national security, of order or efficiency, or even of a special group within the country, is very strong. Concern for "order" prevented France and England from interfering in the Spanish Civil War. Concern for national security led them to sign the Munich pact, on the theory that Hitler would content himself with aggression in the East. When they saw belatedly how false the thesis was, they changed their tactics and went to war — under the worst possible circumstances. But the errors of political judgment that had put them in such a position were not weaknesses inherent in the democratic regime as such; the trouble was not that England and France had been too democratic, but that they had not been democratic enough. Calling themselves democratic at home, they had nevertheless tried to compromise with dictatorship abroad.

In the battle that followed, France was the first to fall. She has lived for almost four years in slavery. Great as her sufferings have been, they have had one compensation. What time alone could not effect, what the victory of 1918 could not permanently seal, has been achieved by common hardship and humiliation. The mass of the French people — now — are united as they have never been before in modern history. To a great extent economic interests have been swept away; ideologies have tottered under the impact of an incredibly harsh reality; prejudices have disappeared in the light of mutual understanding.

This tremendous wealth in human assets must not be lost again. What we must have in France tomorrow is a generous democracy recognizing the modern technological revolution as an accomplished fact, and admitting, not only in words but in practice, that the immense possibilities for human well-being which have resulted from it must be realized, as equity demands, for the benefit of all those employed in its mechanism and not, as in the past, for the exclusive profit of a small number of privileged individuals. But we must also have a democracy of wisdom, a democracy of the middle road, for it cannot be repeated too often that inasmuch as a democracy can live only in a world of peace, it can likewise live only in a world of freely consented discipline; after dictatorship, its worst enemy is demagogy: one cannot make the weak stronger simply by weakening the strong, or promote human brotherhood by inciting class hatred.

In the realization of our hopes for the future, what can be, and what should be, the part played by the Allies? They have already promised us the finest gift that can be given — that of freedom. Let them be as good as their word. More precisely, as soon as France is freed from the invader, let them do all they can to assure that an independent press may prepare free elections as soon as the prisoners of war are returned, and the French themselves will do the rest.

If the United States, for its part, will assume this attitude, at once generous and full of wisdom, it will deserve France's undying gratitude; it will weld together more strongly than ever that Franco–American friendship which is today, more than ever, a necessity. If the voice of

France can make itself freely heard, no one can doubt the nation's future.

Toward the end of the first World War, I arrived in the Somme with the British troops, in a village that had been bombarded and pillaged, only a few days after its evacuation by the Germans. An old peasant was standing at the door of what had been his house, his head bowed in sorrow. But as he saw us coming he straightened himself proudly, looked us straight in the eye, and said, "*Allons!* The walls are still good. I can rebuild it."

In the house of France — devastated, pillaged, enslaved though it is — the walls are still good. We will rebuild it.